POLISHED

Polished

COLLEGE, CLASS, AND THE
BURDENS OF SOCIAL MOBILITY

Melissa Osborne

The University of Chicago Press   CHICAGO AND LONDON

The University of Chicago Press, Chicago 60637
The University of Chicago Press, Ltd., London
© 2024 by The University of Chicago
Published 2024

33 32 31 30 29 28 27 26 25 24   2 3 4 5

ISBN-13: 978-0-226-83302-6 (cloth)
ISBN-13: 978-0-226-83304-0 (paper)
ISBN-13: 978-0-226-83303-3 (e-book)
DOI: https://doi.org/10.7208/chicago/9780226833033.001.0001

Library of Congress Cataloging-in-Publication Data
Names: Osborne, Melissa, author.
Title: Polished : college, class, and the burdens of social
mobility / Melissa Osborne.
Description: Chicago : The University of Chicago, 2024. |
Includes bibliographical references and index.
Identifiers: LCCN 2023037501 | ISBN 9780226833026 (cloth) |
ISBN 9780226833040 (paperback) | ISBN 9780226833033 (ebook)
Subjects: LCSH: College students—United States—Social conditions. |
Educational sociology—United States. | Social mobility—
United States. | Elite (Social sciences)—United States.
Classification: LCC LC205 .O74 2024 |
DDC 378.1/980973—dc23/eng/20230814
LC record available at https://lccn.loc.gov/2023037501

FOR OSBORNIA

Contents

Introduction

I first met Morgan, an outgoing young woman, in the spring of 2017, when she was a first-year student at East College. A first-generation student from a working-class family, Morgan was attending East on a full scholarship that was part of a financial aid program that the College launched in 2012 for students from low-income families. Morgan had grown up in Southern California in a multiracial household. Her father was a mechanic by trade and a first-generation American who had emigrated from Mexico in his teenage years. Her mother worked part-time at the local elementary school and raised Morgan and her three younger brothers while taking night classes in office management at the local community college. In our first interview, Morgan was struggling with being nearly 3,000 miles away from home for the first time and missed her family a great deal—a common experience I came to see in most of the students I interviewed. She wished she had been able to see her family during winter break, but her stipend from East was barely enough to cover the essentials, let alone the $500 it would cost to fly home.

When we talked, Morgan spent a lot of time describing that she felt out of place as a first-generation student at East, but repeatedly emphasized that she was grateful for the opportunities afforded by attending such a prestigious school. She detailed her coursework and how she was faring in her major, and then laid out her 10-year plan that detailed her path from East to medical school to opening a children's clinic in the low-income neighborhood she grew up in—a dream she shared with her parents. As Morgan explained it, for her and her family, East was more than a school. It was an opportunity at mobility and a chance to change her life and the lives of her family and surrounding community.

A year later, I waited for Morgan outside a library at East on a warm spring day. The area was bustling with activity. There were food trucks parked nearby with lines so long they intersected the main walkway. Hurried students dodged and zigzagged through the lines in order to enter the library. There was a small stage set up in the middle of the courtyard, and the voices of two young women reading a collaborative poem punctuated the low buzz of conversations as people enjoyed their lunches in the spring sunshine. After scanning the crowd for a few minutes, I noticed Morgan come rushing through the iron gateway that separated one of East's residential quads and the courtyard space near the library. She was wearing a T-shirt emblazoned with her school's name, and when she reached me, she gave me an unexpected hug and said, "It is so great to see you!" I smiled at her and asked her how she was doing. We started to walk across campus and she let out a heavy sigh, telling me that she was stressing about her finals and that some drama at home was getting in the way of really focusing on her work. As we wound our way across the beautifully manicured campus full of old shade trees and stately historical buildings, she went into detail about how her uncle had borrowed money from her parents to pay for her grandmother's diabetes equipment but had blown it on a weekend out with his friends instead. Her little brother had called her in a panic over a particularly bad argument between her dad and uncle, and now her aunt was asking her for money to cover the loss.

It was a beautiful day, so we decided to walk the mile down a major artery of the city to a coffee shop. As we walked, Morgan continued laying out the events that had transpired in her family over the last few weeks. I interjected comments or questions here and there but mostly listened intently as our scenery slowly began to change from the dignified architecture and high-end eateries that immediately surrounded East's campus to the more worn buildings that housed fast food restaurants, resale shops, and check-cashing stations down the road between East and another college campus nearby. A man on the street asked us for change as we were waiting for the stoplight, and he offered us a snack from the bag hanging off his shoulder, bulging with convenience-store sandwich triangles. Morgan chuckled as we walked away and wistfully said that this was her favorite area in the city. When asked why, she took a moment to pensively look into the sky and said, "I think it's because this is where East begins to blur into reality. When I walk down this way, I start to feel more like myself for a minute." She went on to explain that that area reminded her of the working-class area she had grown up in in Southern California. Coming to this part of town in her first year had helped with her feelings of homesickness, but now in her second year, she found that her relationship with the space had become more complicated. She said, "At some point this year I realized that maybe I [her emphasis] feel more at home here, but the people here see me as an outsider, as someone that belongs at East. And East is all, 'You belong! We will help you belong!' but that doesn't really cut it for me. It's harder than I realized."

For Morgan, the stark stratification between East College and its surrounding low-income neighborhoods became a way for her to talk through her ideas and feelings around the transformations in identity that she was experiencing as a socially mobile first-generation college student. The way she described her discomfort with both spaces aligned with many of the students I talked to in my research—and resonated with my own experience as a first-generation student from a working-class background who had attended undergraduate and graduate school at selective colleges. Now, as a researcher, I had walked this route a number of times, going between interviews with students at the two campuses that bookend this strip of road. And, while I now had the educational credentials and social and cultural capital to fit in at East College, I remained uncomfortable within its ivied gates. Like Morgan, I too preferred the space between— even as my cultivated university habitus pushed me further away from corner stores and discount shops.

As I will detail in the chapters of this book, this sense of being stuck between two worlds is what it feels like to be a first-generation student on a selective college campus for many students. A precarious in-betweenness surrounds much of the first-generation experience. From the moment they arrive on campus, these students feel like outsiders in the elite spaces of the university that often are drastically different from their home communities. As they try to find a place to belong on campus, they can feel pressures to change in ways that produce tensions and ruptures within their families and home communities. And, while many colleges try to mainstream first-generation students by offering resources to combat "deficits" in skills and capital, such programs that are designed to "level the playing field" often miss the mark of providing the intensive support needed to navigate the unexpected facets of social mobility. Instead of thriving on these campuses that offer the most aid, resources, and support,[1] many first-generation students struggle to navigate the process of becoming socially mobile as a first-generation student—a process that I will show is designed to fundamentally change them in the pursuit of economic mobility.

CONSIDERING HIGHER EDUCATION'S ORIENTATION TOWARD FIRST-GENERATION STUDENTS

First-generation and low-income student enrollment at four-year colleges and universities in the United States has steadily increased over the last two decades.[2] This demographic shift comes, in some part, from institutional initiatives that seek to reduce structural barriers to college access, such as targeted admissions recruitment, eliminating SAT/ACT requirements, and offering grant-based scholarships instead of loans. Such initiatives draw from a large body of academic research that positions social mobility through higher education as the most promising pathway toward achieving more for families with less.[3] In this framework, high-achieving students from resource-deprived high schools are diamonds in the rough who—with enough polish from an elite institution—have the potential to become the bright and brilliant leaders of tomorrow. They are excavated out of their home communities by admissions officers and scholarship organizations who deposit them at the gates of higher education with the hope and promise of not just an education, but also a different life. Selective colleges and universities have made particularly large commitments toward increasing access to these pathways of mobility via education as a means for securing a share of high-achieving first-generation applicants. A population that now makes up a diversity category perhaps as coveted as the one students of color became in the late 1990s and early 2000s.[4]

A number of recent authors have critiqued efforts that focus primarily on getting students into college without investing significant resources into adequately supporting students once they arrive on campus.[5] These critiques leverage the well-documented and meaningful disparities in experience and outcomes that have been identified between low-income and first-generation students and their more affluent counterparts across academic, social, cultural, and economic aspects of their education. For instance, regardless of high school training, most first-generation and low-income students report feeling underprepared academically[6] and socially.[7] This feeling can give rise to substantial internal conflicts for socially mobile students and have dramatic negative impacts on their pathways through college as well as on the likelihood of degree completion.[8] Students' ability to adjust and conform to the social contexts of higher education have a direct impact on their ability to achieve academic and social success.[9] At many campuses, the institutional expectations and practices reflect the White middle- and upper-middle-class normative order, and students from racial minorities and low-SES (socioeconomic status) backgrounds face a distinct disadvantage in these environments.[10] In addition, personal and family obligations can heighten the precarity of low-income and first-generation students and compromise degree completion.[11]

Low-income and first-generation students often describe a feeling of mismatch between the working-class cultural capital they come to college with and the upper-class capital that is normative and expected in higher education environments.[12] This mismatch leads some students to manage their identities through suppressing their working-class backgrounds and habitus while others construct morally based narratives that justify and exalt their class position relative to their more affluent peers. These students produce symbolic boundaries between themselves and higher-SES students, and many develop identity ambivalence toward their experiences.[13] Low-SES students not only gain academic knowledge and skills during college, they develop cultural and social capital[14] and their classed behaviors and presentation of self, or habitus, often begin to transform during college.[15] Although there are surely some students who flourish in these circumstances, research points to this as a time of struggle and tension. For many, the dramatic changes in class position that social mobility via higher education produces result in a crisis of identity that often leads to familial tension, the erasure of working-class identities, and increased prevalence of attrition.[16]

Many selective colleges and universities have invested in programming and resources designed to improve the experiences and outcomes of first-generation students. These programs generally emphasize the critical value of transmitting economic, social, and cultural capital to first-generation students as a way to ensure success in college and beyond.[17] And campus initiatives are designed to bring low-income and first-generation students up to speed with their more affluent peers by offering economic, academic, and social resources. These programs seek to reduce the well-documented[18] disparities between these students and their more affluent continuing-generation peers, with the long-term goal of stimulating individual upward mobility under the logic that, with enough first-generation students in these academic pipelines, the negative impacts of intergenerational poverty in marginalized communities will decrease in the long run.

Colleges have tried to close the gap in economic capital that many low-SES students face by increasing grants and scholarships, establishing no-barrier funding structures, instituting food pantries, and developing stipend programs that specifically target low-income and first-generation students.[19] Many schools have worked to reduce barriers around accessing valuable social capital by developing mentoring programs, fostering connections in alumni networks, and providing internships at elite employers across industries.[20] Finally, many universities have invested substantial resources in developing programming around the accumulation of cultural capital and now provide a robust array of workshops on topics like networking, office hours, impostor syndrome, budgeting, and dressing for professional jobs and interviews; as well as opportunities like bridge programs, dedicated academic support staff, guided cultural outings, and specialized orientation programming designed to acclimate first-generation students to college.[21] And, while not all schools offer the same programming and resources, it is generally the case that more selective, or elite, schools offer the most financial aid, have the most valuable networks of alumni, and provide the most programming and resources for students while they are on campus.[22]

These interventions have contributed to significant improvements in low-income and first-generation students' outcomes, experience, and retention. And, for the most part, schools that are able to provide the most in terms of funding, resources, and support boast the highest outcomes and completion rates for their low-income and first-generation students.[23] It is still important to note, however, that even at the schools with the most resources and support, first-generation and low-income students often continue to report lower levels of campus engagement, higher levels of reported stress and anxiety, lower average GPAs, longer degree completion times, and higher rates of attrition than their more affluent continuing-generation peers.[24] This enduring set of inequalities between low-income first-generation students and their peers raises questions around what these programs that focus on capital accumulation might be missing and how gaps between programming and students' unmet needs may be sustaining these inequalities.

This book takes up the question of why, with more resources than ever before, do we still see first-generation and low-income students struggling? To make sense of this gap, this book looks at the experience of being a first-generation student in this new era of significant institutional access, support, and attention—an era that has, in many ways, fundamentally reshaped what it means to be a first-generation college student. These initiatives not only give students access to the valuable knowledge, skills, and experiences they need to navigate college more seamlessly, they transform them into integrated members of their campus communities and, for many students, ultimately produce lasting social mobility. Yet, as I show, these institutional initiatives can have unexpected personal costs for students. Drawing on participant observation and in-depth longitudinal interviews with 150 first-generation and low-income students at 18 selective colleges and universities across the United States, the research outlined in this book reveals the unintended consequences of these institutional strategies for attracting greater numbers of low-income and first-generation college students to selective campuses. I argue that the same institutional support that gives these students what they need to succeed in college also changes them in ways that they, and their families, often cannot anticipate. In order to fully take advantage of the opportunities set before them, they are faced with difficult choices that can put their changing identities and beliefs at odds with the expectations of their peers and families.

The student experiences detailed throughout the chapters of this book demonstrate that the full impact of trying to support and reshape first-generation students into elites is fundamentally misunderstood by selective colleges. Even with a "level playing field," the unexpected challenges associated with jumping the economic ladder can become too much for many students as they try to navigate their precarious positions as socially mobile college students. In many ways, the work that selective colleges and universities do to provide first-generation students with valuable social and cultural capital pushes these students to conform to the normative and elite culture on campus in the name of social mobility. This work aids students in the process of becoming part of their campus communities and provides them with invaluable resources and access to elite networks. This work, however, also fundamentally reshapes how these students understand their identities, beliefs, and positionalities in ways that many of them are not prepared to navigate—especially without the support of a community that has the experience and knowledge to guide them through it. While many selective colleges successfully produce upward mobility for first-generation students, this often comes at an unexpected and major social and psychological cost—a cost that most often goes unnoticed and unaddressed across campuses nationwide. By asserting the importance, and in many ways, the superior quality of the capital these students gain during college, selective universities are also reshaping the ways that first-generation students frame the communities they came to college from, and the capital they bring with them, as undesirable and inferior. And, while students often are excited for the support, they often face unexpected and unintended social and emotional consequences as they go through this "refinement" process.

As I show, undergoing rapid social mobility during college can generate intense periods of emotional distress and self-doubt for students, as well as social isolation from their peers, families, and home communities—all while students are maintaining full course loads and high grade point averages that are a necessary condition for continued institutional support. The majority of low-income first-generation students and their families cannot anticipate the realities of becoming socially mobile during college, and the unexpected changes and effects that arise as part of this process often lead to significant conflicts and crises. The experiences of students contained in the chapters of this book provide a window into how the unexpected consequences of this process impact student outcomes and experiences—and in some cases prompt many students to reconsider their college choices and begin to fundamentally question the nonfinancial costs associated with social mobility and selective educational spaces. The tension between staying in college and staying connected to families affects students' emotional well-being and their academic outcomes at school, leading them to question what are the social and emotional costs of being the target of a social mobility initiative?

This book answers this question, highlighting the often-unanticipated trade-offs students face as they navigate a selective university setting. As high school seniors, first-generation students look forward to growing and developing academically in college. They are grateful for the opportunity to pursue a college degree, and they feel the same excitement and anticipation about starting college as their more affluent peers. Yet, the complexities of navigating college and social mobility as a first-generation college student often create an unintended burden for students—a double bind, or a sense of being stuck between two worlds. From the moment they arrive on campus, many of these students feel like outsiders in the elite spaces of the university that often are drastically different from their home communities. As they search for a place to belong on campus, they can feel pressure to change in ways that produce tensions and ruptures within their families and home communities. Their ability to be a student in these elite settings demonstrates their dedication and commitment to social mobility—often motivated by their desire to be able to give back to their families and lower-resourced communities. Yet, as they progress in college, they must balance the personal and social transformations that college can bring with their histories and ties to home. Unlike their classmates from more privileged backgrounds, these students feel competing pressures to "buy in" to the elite educational context without "selling out" in the eyes of their home communities.

The student experiences throughout this book highlight that many college campuses are missing a key component that can ease such a transformation in other settings, namely the intensive work of supporting individuals through change and stewarding them into their new identities and roles. When students turn to their colleges and universities for direct support and help with contextualizing and navigating their experiences, they are often left empty-handed, referred to inadequate and inaccessible campus mental health services, or directed toward additional programming designed to assist them in developing even further capital. This gap between the support students need to understand and unpack the experience of becoming socially mobile and the programming and support available on selective college campuses produces further challenges, and in many cases lends to increased feelings of alienation and the development of anger and resentment around the first-generation experience. This book shows that in many ways, selective colleges provide all the resources that first-generation students need to build extensive amounts of capital, but they do not provide students the direct support they need to navigate the complicated process of change that they experience as a result. And while some students are able to develop strategies and build informal peer support teams in order to make it through to graduation, others struggle to keep up this extended balancing act. These students are faced with a difficult choice that they should not have to make—college and mobility or community and authenticity.

REIMAGINING AND REFRAMING MOBILITY

A consideration of how social mobility is approached academically and understood more broadly is helpful for examining emergent questions around why inequalities in student experiences and outcomes may continue to persist in the face of robust interventions. Academic research and popular cultural imaginaries most often frame social mobility in almost exclusively economic terms.[25] This is due, at least in some part, to the fact that economists have dominated this area of research with studies on income mobility.[26] Social mobility is most broadly understood as a process in which an individual moves up in socioeconomic status, advancing from one income quartile to another, or from a lower salary to a higher one.[27] And, while aspects such as occupation and social status are important to this process,[28] the goal of economic gain is still often at the core of how upward mobility is conceptually understood. Rooted in this economic understanding of social mobility is the notion that mobility is something to achieve—it is seen as an end goal to be reached and not a process that is experienced. In this framework, economic mobility has finite boundaries that are measured incrementally in terms of income or wealth and divided and grouped into an orderly set of linear categories like quartiles.[29] The points of division between income levels are often interpreted visually as rungs on a ladder, and the metaphor of "climbing the ladder" has become central to the way Americans describe working toward social mobility.[30]

Higher education has long been seen as the primary vehicle for climbing the ladder and achieving the kind of upward mobility that is central to the American Dream.[31] And, while sociologists have demonstrated that this vision of higher education does not accurately reflect the opportunity structure it provides for the majority of students,[32] it persists as the dominant cultural frame for preparing and recruiting K–12 students for a college trajectory.[33] This is particularly true for students from underrepresented backgrounds. Students from these backgrounds, who are often unlikely to have unfettered access to social mobility via higher education,[34] are also the most widely featured in the popular press and media as feel-good examples of how hard work, determination, and intelligence can overcome adversity and lead to extreme mobility.[35]

The stories of the most disadvantaged students in the United States who have made their way from deep poverty to schools like Harvard University have become our modern-day Horatio Alger story. If these students can jump the ladder in such a spectacular fashion, then surely the American Dream must be thriving. What isn't as often discussed in popular media, however, is that the deeply stratified class structure in the United States is what often prevents the poorest students from taking an incremental approach toward climbing the ladder.[36] Barriers around resources, education, and employment abound for the lowest-income students in the country and, although exceptional, the highly publicized path of those that skyrocket to the top of the ladder via excellence is often considered the most feasible path.

Social scientists have produced a robust perspective of how low-income first-generation students experience their time at selective and highly selective colleges and universities.[37] And, while much of this work has highlighted how this experience can produce a sense of division between these students and their more affluent continuing-generation peers, we know far less about what happens as these students become more like their peers and less like the families and communities they are coming to college from.[38] This gap in the larger picture of the first-generation student experience is due at least in some part to the academic and popular framing of social mobility as an economic goal instead of a social process. This dominant perspective of social mobility misses how individuals and their communities frame and experience the process of becoming socially mobile as they embark on and navigate their college careers. By thinking solely in economic terms, the ways that college acts as a transformative process to change individual and community perspectives, beliefs, and behaviors are often overlooked. In doing so, the ways in which the competing demands that arise out of being situated within and between two social spaces reproduce inequality for first-generation students have been underinterpreted. And, while the first-generation and low-income students with experiences that cement them as the poster children for social mobility are exceedingly rare,[39] understanding their experiences as they navigate the murky waters of extreme social mobility is deeply valuable for understanding how social mobility impacts individuals more broadly.

This book's robust qualitative approach richly details these students' experiences and provides the data needed to reexamine the unintended consequences and outcomes of social mobility initiatives on campuses across America. When these students' trajectories through college are evaluated in traditional academic or institutional research, the focus is on graduation outcomes, career placement, and whether or not mobility was achieved. What this static focus on outcomes misses, however, is what happens to individuals and their communities as they navigate the *process* of social mobility. This book highlights how this institutional focus on outcomes is reflected in the messaging that many students receive from their colleges and universities—social mobility and a college degree should be your focus, no matter how painful or alienating the process of getting there may be. For many students, it is the process of pursuing social mobility, not the potential outcome, that defines their college experience.

THE STUDY

This study focuses on the experiences of 150 socially mobile low-income students, the majority of which are the first in their families to attend college. I spent time with and interviewed these students from 2016 to 2021, while they were attending 18 unique selective and highly selective[40] private colleges in Illinois, Massachusetts, Oregon, and Texas. This cohort of colleges includes nine liberal arts colleges and nine research universities, with the largest undergraduate population being approximately 16,000 students and the smallest being approximately 1,300 students. I assigned pseudonyms to the colleges and universities and grouped them by region when referenced directly—producing four composite schools: East College, Midwest College, South College, and West College. I group campuses this way to help protect the privacy of the students in this study. I selected private colleges and universities because, in general, they have the most resources available to support low-income first-generation students in terms of financial aid, academic support, and programmatic support, and yet they still see the similar gaps in performance, outcomes, and experience between their low-income first-generation and non-low-income first-generation students that have been documented at less-selective and public institutions. This paradox, or puzzle, is largely what brought me to this project in the first place, and focusing on these highly selective private institutions seemed like the best way to begin understanding why.

I found participants for this study in three ways: by emailing recipients and applicants of the Jack Kent Cooke College Scholarship, by contacting first-generation student groups and organizations on each of the campuses in the study, and through the social networks of students already participating in the study. All of the students who participated in the study were considered low-income by their colleges and universities—with the majority of students having families with annual adjusted gross incomes of $30,000 or less. Eighty-eight percent of students identified as first-generation—with neither parent completing a bachelor's degree. I decided that including low-income students who were both first-generation and not first-generation was an important part of the story I wanted to tell with this project. There are debates around what it is about a student's parents (such as their economic vs. cultural capital) that matter the most for students' college outcomes and experiences, and I hoped that this project could bring further data to the table. What I found is that a parent's ability to understand, connect, and recognize touchstones of the college experience matters. And that this element, having parents with the ability to anticipate and frame at least some aspects of a child's college experience, becomes a significant advantage that first-generation students most often do not have.

Of the 150 students I spent time with and talked to, I interviewed 100 of them in person once during their college career. The remaining 50, who were nearly all first-year students at the time of our first interview, agreed to participate in a series of longitudinal in-person and virtual interviews. I had the opportunity to reinterview these students at multiple points throughout their college careers and, for some, into their postgrad lives. When I could not talk to students in person because of scheduling or a global pandemic, I conducted interviews online or had students answer long-form qualitative survey questions. I decided to incorporate a longitudinal approach toward my interviews with students because I thought this would be the best way of capturing how students change and experience college over time. The questions I had coming into this project necessitated that I talk to students at different points in their college careers to see how their perspectives were changing, and to understand when and how important elements of social mobility emerge for these students during college.

Because I started this project without knowing for certain that I would be able to recruit a significant number of students to participate in a longitudinal study, I selected students from across class years, with 40% in their first year and then 20% each in their second, third, and fourth years of college. A significant amount of research on college students draws primarily from interviews and surveys from students in their first year. And, while this is valuable information, it speaks to the very beginning of a student's journey and perspective in higher education. I sought to widen this perspective with this project and recruited a student population that spanned years of enrollment. I did not limit my investigation to students from a particular racial or ethnic background—35% identified as White, 14% as African American or Black, 20% as Latinx, 16% as Asian American, and 15% as more than one race. Finally, 48% of the students identified as female, 46% as male, and 6% as gender nonbinary and/or transgender at the time interviews and fieldwork were taking place.

I also spent a significant amount of time hanging out with and following students through their daily lives. I was able to make a visit to each of the campuses where students were attending school, but I spent most of my fieldwork time on 10 of these 18 campuses. From 2016 to 2019, I spent 650 hours with students shadowing their daily lives, accompanying them on and off campus, and working with select student groups around initiatives on their campuses. With the exception of attending classes and spending time in private residence hall rooms, I did nearly everything I could with these students. We drank countless cups of coffee, shared meals in the best college-town dives and worst college dining halls, went on grocery shopping trips, stood in endless lines in college offices across the country, attended social and professional events and activities on and off campus, volunteered on service projects, played video games until all hours, and traversed the campuses, towns, and cities they lived in.

I supplemented interviews and participant observation with follow-up survey data, self-reported income and outcome data, and data from

12 focus groups conducted with incoming first-years and returning students. In addition to collecting student data, I completed in-depth formal interviews with 10 members of the Jack Kent Cooke Foundation Higher Education Division staff—a major source of funding for first-generation students nationwide, including a portion of the students who participated in this study. I also included 30 semiformal interviews with higher education staff and administrators on different campuses included in my study. I sought to include the perspectives of staff at colleges and outside scholarship foundations in this project, as a means for considering the interplay between institutional interventions and individual experiences. This triangulation of data allows me to expand on existing research that overwhelmingly focuses on a single campus context at a particular moment in students' college trajectories.

When thinking about the whys and hows of the students I spent time with, it is critical to note that I was a low-income and first-generation college student myself. This matters in terms of both the ways that I approached my research and the kinds of questions that I brought to this project, but also in terms of how I relate to the students in this study. Being a first-generation student that had gone to selective schools gave me an immediate rapport and shared experience with the majority of the students I spent time with. Even though many aspects of our actual experiences in college were likely significantly different (I was also a nontraditional[41] student with a family while I was pursuing my bachelor's degree), we had a common thread that served as the foundation for each relationship I built with a student. I believe this positionality improved my ability to recruit and build rapport with respondents. However, my position as a researcher (who was an advanced graduate student at the beginning of this project and an assistant professor at the end of it) also located me as an outsider who was removed from the stakes associated with campus communities. This positional duality allowed me to occupy an "in-between" status[42] that I felt minimized bias and produced robust and open dialogue during interviews and fieldwork.

CHAPTER OUTLINE

Throughout the chapters of this book, I consider the ways in which the unintended consequences of university programming and initiatives impact first-generation and low-income students and detail how they navigate the unexpected outcomes of social mobility that accompany attending these selective and highly selective colleges and universities. The chapters of *Polished* are arranged in a way that traces student experiences across time, aspects of college, and stages of mobility and the polishing process—with each chapter building on the next. I begin chapter 1 by detailing how selective colleges and universities frame and market the primary purpose, value, and promise of an elite college education. I outline how low-income and first-generation students and their families interpret these narratives and then select, frame, and prepare for college. I demonstrate that, for the majority of students and their families, attending a selective college is understood as an opportunity to achieve social mobility via a prestigious degree that will lead to a well-paying and meaningful career. Through this, I highlight the ways that families calculate the perceived values of prestige, cost, and distance to inform their decisions around college selection. I demonstrate that while some families frame college and social mobility in relatively uncomplicated and positive ways, a complex framework emerges around social mobility for many first-generation students and their families. For these families, upward mobility can simultaneously be seen as a promise to be pursued and upheld as well as a threat to be safeguarded against. The mixed frameworks that arise out of this dual perspective of what it means to be educated or become socially mobile produce a variety of responses across families. I explore the variations in the ways that mobility and college are framed across families and detail how different perspectives inform student choices around developing identity strategies as they prepare to enter college.

In chapter 2, I explore the hurdles that first-generation students face during their first year of school and demonstrate how unfamiliarity with institutional structure and social expectations impacts their ability to easily navigate bureaucratic, academic, and social demands. I compare experiences across students and show how access to community resources or prior educational experience with selective schooling produces major advantages for a select group of low-income and first-generation students. Through this, I take up previously explored divides in the low-income student population and argue that further variation should be considered. I then explore how some students assign a privileged status to particular backgrounds and how this notion of privilege is being used to make distinctions within first-generation student populations on some campuses. For readers who are acquainted with the literature on first-generation student experiences and outcomes, this chapter covers some familiar ground, expands on existing research, and builds the empirical and theoretical foundations for the innovative data and arguments found in the chapters that follow.

Chapter 3 provides a look at the institutional approach that selective colleges and universities take toward supporting first-generation students on their campuses. I show that the formalization of targeted support and interventions for underrepresented students—what I call the "polishing process"—has come to supplement and enhance more organic means of capital accumulation that have been the historical focus of many studies. I explore how a focus on enhancing students' social and cultural capital undergirds the majority of programs, resources, and opportunities that target first-generation student populations and highlight how this work occurs both within selective colleges and universities as well as through external scholarship and education organizations. I then consider how students perceive and respond to these initiatives and begin to detail the direct impacts they have on students.

In chapter 4, I explore how the rapid changes that often occur as a result of the social mobility brought on via the polishing process and attending a selective college as a first-generation student are often unexpected and how this, combined with existing feelings of alienation on campus, can produce moments of crisis. I then focus on what happens when these students return home from college for the first time. I explore the divide in experiences between first-generation students new to selective schooling and their low-income peers that either attended selective private high schools or had college-educated parents. Through this, I show that being able to draw on prior experience with navigating social mobility—either from their own experience during high school or their parents' experiences during college—shifts the framing of perceived changes from traumatic and unexpected to mundane and part of a known and accepted process. I also demonstrate how narratives around the virtues of particular majors and areas of study help reframe the changes associated with social mobility as a necessary step for "fitting the part" of a desired career outcome rather than "selling out."

Finally, in chapter 5, I consider the institutional support available to first-generation students as they navigate the unexpected changes that emerge as part of going through social mobility at a selective college, the tensions and conflicts that often arise as a result of these changes, and the double bind that comes from trying to meet the conflicting demands and expectations of home and campus communities. I demonstrate that many campuses lack sufficient support, and detail how some first-generation students learn navigation strategies from reliable peer networks and external institutional interventions. I focus on the long-term strategies and outcomes of these students. Drawing on longitudinal interview and survey data, I detail the different pathways that first-generation and low-income students take through higher education. I consider the vital role that community and community building play in student success and detail the often taxing strategies and trade-offs that many students must develop in order to successfully complete their education. Through this, I demonstrate that not all first-generation students find an equilibrium to managing change in the long term. And through this, I argue that even for those who can, the often overlooked costs to pursuing social mobility via higher education have significant social and emotional consequences for students that must be considered. Across these cases, I provide an in-depth account of the excruciating choices—often between pursuing opportunity and preserving community—that students must make to alleviate the often overwhelming pressures of the double bind.

The conclusion of this book draws on findings from this extensive study of first-generation students' experience to put forth recommendations for colleges and universities, scholarship organizations, and education scholars. The central thrust of these recommendations is grounded in the notion that colleges and universities must reframe their understanding of what kind of work goes into fully supporting the trajectories and transformations of their low-income and first-generation students. In many ways, this requires a fundamental acknowledgment that colleges and universities can and should be doing much of the same intensive work that other people-changing organizations—like social services—do. It is critical that colleges and universities move beyond access to skills and capital. They must prioritize the one-on-one work of assisted identity management and begin to build programs that explicitly address the impact of social mobility if they want to ensure the success and well-being of their low-income and first-generation students.

· 1 ·
College Frameworks, Fit, and Function

In the spring of 2018, I shuffled alongside an enthusiastic guide with roughly 15 high school students and their families on a tour of Midwest College. We walked together across campus on well-worn pathways that were flanked every 20 feet or so with light posts holding banners that celebrated the accomplishments of esteemed and diverse alumni next to block lettering that included directives like INNOVATE and EXPLORE. Our tour wound its way into the main quad just as our guide finished regaling us with a story about their personal journey of intellectual discovery and their decision to become a political science major. The quad was filled with activity on this particularly sunny springtime day. Students dotted the grass in small groups enjoying picnic lunches and reveling in the opportunity that warm weather brought for doing homework on the lawn instead of deep within the library. On the far-left end of the quad, a class was being held outside, the professor seated cross-legged on the grass discussing the symbolism of colors in the work of Frantz Fanon. Nearby, a handful of student groups had tables set up and were offering snacks in an attempt to recruit new members to their organizations. On one of the larger stretches of grass, a group had broken out frisbees and were deftly tossing them to one another as they jumped in the air, just barely catching each pass. Framed by the grandeur of old brick buildings and pristine landscaping, our view of bustling student activity and higher learning evoked the essence of the quintessential American college experience.

As the guide began describing the different course requirements for students at Midwest, many of the prospective students and their parents held whispered conversations about their thoughts on the visit thus far. To my left, a man commented to his wife that he had read that Midwest had recently gone down in the rankings—to which she rolled her eyes, saying, "It's not like you even know what that means, George." This got a laugh out of their daughter as she asked the guide about the different student groups on campus, pointing in the direction of the tables at the far end of the quad.

To my right, two separate families had struck up a conversation—one explaining to the other that their older son was currently attending Midwest and that he had "thoroughly enjoyed his time thus far and really started to come into his own as a young man." The mother went on to explain that she thought that while Midwest "certainly offers world-class academics, it is the opportunities for personal growth and discovery that are worth every penny." The mother from the other family echoed her emphasis on this aspect of college, saying, "Oh, that is just so key! Janie will do well academically anywhere, I am sure, but we want a place where she can really explore and find herself, her passions, you know?" Both mothers nodded in approving agreement at this as they continued their conversation about the merits of Midwest.

Meanwhile, the family in front of me was having a tense argument about whether Midwest offered the right majors and resources for a future career in aerospace engineering. Their son, Miguel, had started listing off other schools that offered more in terms of engineering specialties at the same time that his mother was listing off students they knew who had been offered impressive financial aid packages from Midwest. Visibly frustrated that his mom was not on the same page, Miguel sighed heavily as he shoved his arms into his hoodie and muttered to himself. In an attempt to soothe them both, Miguel's dad put his arms around his wife and son and said, "Don't you worry, *mijo*. We will find the college that will get you your dreams and [turning to his wife] the money to go with it. Have patience! We will find the right fit soon enough."

Throughout my fieldwork, I took campus tours with countless families like these, standing next to them as they got their first glimpses of the daily life and resources available at some of America's most selective colleges. Notions of prestige, student life, career prospects, affordability, and "fit" dominated discussions and questions on tours across each college campus I visited. And, like the majority of prospective college students in America, the students I interviewed emphasized how these central themes played a role in shaping how they ultimately selected what college to attend. Wrapped up in the mainstream imaginary of college as a time for self-discovery, a center for gaining skills and knowledge, and an engine for social mobility, many students and their families used these themes to frame how they understood the purpose of college and the impacts they perceived it would have on shaping students' lives.

This chapter considers how the purpose, function, and promise of higher education is framed and understood by prospective college students and their families, our broader cultural imaginary in the United States, and colleges and universities themselves. It explores both how colleges and universities frame what college is for as well as how low-income and first-generation students and their families interpret these frameworks and combine them with media and cultural representations of higher education to build their own frameworks for evaluating, selecting, and preparing for college. Drawing on the experiences of my respondents, this chapter explores how students and their families work through selecting a college that balances student dreams with financial needs and perceptions of risk and reward with desired career outcomes. I highlight how perspectives on the purpose of attending college commingle with beliefs about the value of upward mobility to form a wide range of frameworks across students and families in terms of what it means to be a low-income or first-generation college student. I show how these frameworks come into play at different stages and how they impact the ways that students and families discuss, select, and prepare for college. As I show, for many students, being the first member of their family to attend college produces a complex situation where social mobility is seen simultaneously as a promise to be pursued as well as a threat to safeguard against.

THE COLLEGE'S FRAMING OF COLLEGE

Open up an admissions web page or glossy printed look book for any given four-year college or university in the United States and you will find very similar information. It will include images of a diverse cast of students engaging in classroom discussions and activities, participating in campus clubs and traditions, and living the quintessential "college experience." These images will be juxtaposed with a series of data points that emphasize selectivity and rankings, boast small student-to-faculty ratios and class sizes, highlight course offerings and majors, and provide evidence of postgraduation security via graduate school enrollment and career placement stats. Weaving these visuals and data points together will be well-crafted narratives about the college's long history and current reputation as a place for academic development and challenge, social exploration and growth, and career preparation and development. Each of these pieces come together masterfully to effectively communicate to prospective students and their families that this college will live up to their hopes and expectations about higher education, and that choosing this school will create the perfect "fit" needed to ensure success and happiness.

While it is true that colleges and universities have real differences in terms of resources, outcomes, and cultures, the ways they are marketed to prospective students and their families are in many ways just variations on a theme. This is due in large part to the evolution of American higher education from the historically small collective of private schools meant to educate the country's elite White men to the extensive contemporary landscape of public and private colleges and universities competing for their share of the country's college-going population.[43] At this point, the organizational field of selective higher education operates as a highly competitive field of structurally isomorphic business organizations that provide virtually the same service to a limited supply of customers. While colleges and universities are still a place for academic learning and skills development, they are now run much more like a business than a collective community of higher thinking and learning.[44] Each school is competing for the best and brightest students who are all essentially in the market for three things: academic development, social exploration, and career placement. In the case of selective schools looking to increase their diversity profile, they are essentially in competition with each other for a small pool of high-achieving underrepresented students, including those who are the first in their families to attend college.[45] They must produce marketing and media that promote their image and reputation as a school that has what students, and their families, are after—a place to learn, a place to grow, and a place to thrive.

SELECTING SCHOOLS AND WEIGHING PRIORITIES

The work done by highly selective colleges and universities around creating marketing and media that effectively communicate a school's academic, social, and career offerings perhaps matters the most for low-income and first-generation students who often cannot physically visit campus. Much like their first-generation peers across the United States, the students I spent time with described a college application and selection process that was narrowly informed and often self-directed.[46] Felix, a Latinx second-year attending East College, explained that it was only after starting school at East and meeting students from more affluent and resourced backgrounds that he realized how much his college search was constrained by his limited knowledge and time:

> It's comical really. I didn't really know what I was doing and didn't have a lot of time to figure it out. My parents never went to college and were too busy working to help me. I just applied to the schools that I had heard of, which were basically a couple Ivies, Stanford, and the Cal System . . . When I got here I found out about all these other schools that I had never even considered because I didn't know what they were. Like, until last year, I totally thought liberal arts colleges were basically community colleges [laughs]. Can you believe that?

Felix's experience aligns directly with research that has established a meaningful gap in access to resources and information about searching for, applying to, and selecting colleges between first-generation students and their continuing-generation peers.[47] First-gen students must decipher the complex system of college and scholarship applications often while juggling school, extracurriculars, work, and family responsibilities. In order to meet these competing demands and finish applications within the short time frame allotted during their senior year, most first-generation students target their college applications toward schools that yield the most prestige and financial aid, with the notion of fit only coming into play in negotiations with parents or as a retrospective narrative applied after committing to a school.

During a focus group I ran with a handful of Jack Kent Cooke Scholars during the summer between their senior year of high school and starting their first year of college, I asked how they came to learn about the schools to which they applied. Many of the students described researching schools they had heard of, such as the more well-known Ivies, and using the internet to supply a list of Ivies or *US News and World Report* Top 20 Schools. Lucas, a White student headed to East College, noted: "Other than my state college, I only applied to the Ivies because those are the best, right? Like, I googled Ivies, went to the Wikipedia page, and then entered them into my Common App.[48] That was the extent of my research." Janna, a multiracial student also headed to East College, snapped her fingers in support, saying, "Word. It was, like, Ivies or bust and then, like, on the other end all the state schools as safeties in case I was actually delusional or something." As for the selection of which schools should stand in as safeties, Garrett, an Asian American student headed to East College, added that community reputation and track record helped him select a group of public schools in his state. He noted, "There are something like seven or eight state schools in Oregon, and I didn't want to apply to all of them. I just picked the ones that all my IB[49] friends from the year ahead of me had applied to . . . I figured those were the best ones."

This selection scheme—targeting the most prestigious schools in the nation as well as the schools well known for attracting local, high-achieving students—emerged as the standard approach for most of the students I talked with. Without a lexicon of knowledge about the wide types of colleges available via their high schools or personal networks, these students relied on the internet to find school rankings and filtered those by the schools they either knew they'd get into (that were usually local), perceived as prestigious, or in some cases, had merely heard of. For many students, this approach resulted in applying to the same well-known 5–15 Ivy League Plus schools and a smattering of regional and state colleges.

Differences in Approach

There were, of course, exceptions to this approach. Low-income students who were either not first-generation, were attending a private elite high school, and/or were working directly with a nonprofit or foundation support organization throughout the application process had a more informed selection process. For these students, having access to people and resources that demystified and explained the college application process was key. Parker, a White second-year attending South College, discussed at length how much having an older sister who had already gone through the process had impacted his college search and application process. He recalled that he had initially created a small list populated entirely with famous schools that "everyone in the world knows about." When his sister, a third-year at a private liberal arts college, saw the list, she "literally took it from me and just started adding all these schools I'd never heard of before and telling me I had to check them out . . . [She] didn't want me to go into it blind like she had."

For other students, college readiness and scholarship organizations became a force that helped shape application lists. Janae, a Black first-year at Midwest College, detailed how the staff at a local college readiness program exposed her to new schools and helped shape her college list in a way that she felt "fit me better but still kept schools with high scholarships and lots of prestige in the center." Out of the students I talked to, students with one or more resources available to them were far more likely to apply to and select lesser-known, but still highly selective, colleges and universities. And, while many of them still applied to the Ivy League schools, they described a more informed and nuanced college search process that was more similar to their middle- and upper-income peers.[50]

Chester, a multiracial third-year at East College, ended up applying to a number of liberal arts colleges that many of his low-income first-generation peers had never heard of. He noted that having a mom with a college degree may have played some role in the colleges he ended up applying to, but his elite high school had also been a major influence: "My mom helped me with a lot, but she went to a regional state school and hadn't ever heard of Williams or Middlebury either. I think it was more that my high school is a pretty good school and lots of these liberal arts colleges would come to recruit at fairs and stuff." Chester's comment about the role that admissions visits to his private high school had in exposing him to elite liberal arts schools was echoed by many students who received large national scholarships. A number of major scholarship organizations list the schools that their current and past recipients have attended, or encourage their applicants to apply to a set of top-tier schools that extends beyond the Ivy League. And, in the case of the QuestBridge Scholarship,[51] students are able to select from a list of over 40 college partners that range from Wellesley, an all-women's liberal arts college, to the science-and-technology-focused California Institute of Technology. For students who knew to apply to these scholarships, the range of schools outside of the Ivies that the application process opened up was often cited as a major reason why they considered or selected schools that were virtually unknown in their home communities.

Since most of these scholarships start their relationships with students after they gain admission to college, the work they do is generally not focused on actively enhancing or expanding applicants' college lists. What is interesting, however, is that for many students it is the process of applying for these competitive scholarships that exposes them to expanded information and options around college applications in the first place. This latent function of the competitive scholarship application process is particularly important when considering the notion that the students I interviewed and spent time with are representative of some of the highest-achieving low-income students in the nation. This valuable source of information about college applications that comes from competitive scholarship foundations is not likely to be accessible to the vast majority of low-income and first-generation students, who do not have the academic profiles necessary to meet the minimum application requirements. And, while narrow, this is just another example of the divide in access and experience that arises within the population of low-income first-generation college hopefuls as they navigate the process of applying to and attending college.

SELECTING SCHOOLS: CALCULATING COSTS, BENEFITS, AND RISKS

Going It Alone

Much like their peers at schools across the United States, a number of the students I talked to not only navigated application requirements on their own, they also faced the difficult task of making the final decision on where to attend school on their own. Whether due to language barriers, lack of familiarity with higher education, disinterest, or a limited supply of time, some parents do not or cannot participate meaningfully in the college selection process.[52] While only representative of a selection of the students I talked to, it is important to note that this burden is an added component to an already confusing process for many first-generation students.

Calculating Costs

Every student I talked to—whether selecting a college on their own or with the input of friends and family—listed financial aid and affordability as the first and primary factor that they considered when finally selecting a college. In a focus group of Jack Kent Cooke Scholars headed into their freshman year of college, Kelsey, a White student headed to East College, slapped her hand on the table dramatically when I asked about how she made her final decision and exclaimed, "MONEY!" The rest of the group roared with laughter, and she followed up in a more reserved tone, "No, really though. I picked the school that offered me the most money. Didn't y'all?" Looking around the table, every one of the students was nodding in affirmation as Derrick, a multiracial second-generation college student, spoke up and said, "Word. Money speaks real talk, man. You got small class sizes and fancy lab spaces? Great. But are you gonna give up the cash?" Kelsey laughed in affirmation of Derrick's assessment and added, "For real! It's like all of these schools are basically the same, they are all super fancy, and if I go there, I know I will get a super-fancy job and life out of all of them, but I want to do that without debt. So that's how I picked."

Kelsey and Derrick's narratives of their college choice processes highlight that for high-achieving students with financial need, the notion that a selective school will provide them with opportunities and mobility is an assumed part of the package that these schools offer. In many ways, the nuances of difference between these schools that are marketed to students and their families become meaningless, as selective schools are all seen as essentially the same product with merely different packaging. As prior research[53] has previously established, instead of differences in lab space, classroom size, extracurriculars, or campus culture taking the front seat in decision-making, it is financial aid packages that often matter most for high-achieving low-income students.

What is particularly interesting to consider is that for some high-achieving students with financial need, like Kelsey and Derrick, their college selection process can be characterized by both privilege and constraint. On the one hand, their high achievement in high school produces admission to multiple selective schools offering the opportunities and mobility they desire. On the other hand, when not all financial aid offers are created equally, it is the school that offers the most financial support that ends up on top, regardless of whether they may have shortcomings in other areas of support. This potentially frees them up from some of the stress associated with considering the complexities of each school when weighing their options. Ultimately, some students' exclusive focus on the economic aspects of college decision-making effectively creates blinders that allows them to make a streamlined choice while limiting their awareness of how that choice might actually impact their college trajectories.

Weighing Prestige

For students who found themselves in the enviable situation of having to choose from more than one selective school offering a full scholarship package, prestige became the measure by which many of them made their decisions. Putnam, a Latinx fourth-year attending East College, highlighted the role of prestige and reputation by noting, "I know now that another school might have been a better choice, I'm not very happy here . . . I got into a bunch of schools with a full ride but East is East, you know? I had to go with the top. It wasn't a question." Like Putnam, many of the students I talked to who were attending schools that are among those considered the most prestigious in the nation (or world) noted that reputation and prestige became the deciding factor among the schools that had offered them a full financial aid package. The global name recognition, historically backed prestige, assumed academic excellence, and sense of becoming a part of the elite community of alumni tied to schools like Harvard, Yale, and Princeton, for instance, is a siren's song that is hard to resist as a young high-achieving low-income student.

In fact, a small number of students I talked to were willing to put themselves in tighter financial situations in order to attend a school with this kind of prestige—which aligns with prior findings[54] around the effects that the cultural value of prestige can have on college financial decision-making for students and families. For example, Brittany, a White student in her first year at East College, explained that while her financial aid and scholarship packages covered her tuition, fees, and essentials at East, she still needed to choose between loan debt or work-ing to be able to afford anything beyond the necessities. She noted, "I passed on a handful of offers from other schools that would have given me more room to breathe financially. I knew East had the potential to skyrocket me into a career, into a whole different world. The power and prestige at East is undeniable. I figured it was a good bet because East is the top. It's the best." And, while it is hard to argue against the *potential* that the most elite schools in the nation hold for first-generation student success and mobility, no bet is ever a guaranteed win. In a later interview after a year at East College, Brittany later echoed sentiments that were similar to Putnam's and other students who found that their experiences at highly prestigious schools did not live up to their expecta-tions, stating:

> East is okay overall, I guess. It absolutely offers a lot, but getting ahold of what it offers is hard. And, I don't know, I just haven't had the best year here. The competitive culture here is *a lot* [her emphasis]. It can feel very crushing to be a student at East College [emphasizes grandly with hands]. I think a lot about how I might have been happier at a place that was a little more chill, a little more low-key, you know?

This disconnect between the expectations of a college experience steeped in the prestige of a top university that is deeply entrenched into our cultural imaginary about higher education and the realities of at-tending one of these schools as a first-generation college student pro-duced moments of buyer's remorse for a number of students I talked to. And, while this is an experience that is likely common across all strata of college students, it is important to consider that first-generation stu-dents are less likely to have the support and resources needed to trans-fer. Because of this, they are often stuck in situations that their peers are not.[55]

Parental Perspectives: Prestige versus Proof

For students who had completed most of the college search and appli-cation process on their own, it was during the college selection phase that parental input often became a major consideration. For many of these students, prestige and affordability became the major frameworks through which they explained, and at times argued about, their selected school to their parents. Deondre, a Black first-year attending South College, explained that his working-class parents had been almost entirely hands-off during the college application process. As he moved to the selection process, however, they suddenly had strong opinions: "My parents didn't know how to help me with college apps. But once the offers came rolling in, my mom took charge. She knew about two things—name-brand schools and money. I remember she had all the offer letters and emails printed out and spread on the table. My mom and dad had organized them by amount of aid and what schools they thought were best. Anything that wasn't in the top of both those things got thrown in the trash." Much like the students who I talked to who were making their decisions about which college to select on their own, parents like Deondre's prioritized their ranking of schools first by financial aid offers and then by perceptions of prestige and the value and opportunity they represented.

For students in the position of choosing a college that was well known, highly ranked, and offering major financial aid, negotiations around choice with parents were relatively easy to manage. Hudson, a multiracial third-year at East College, echoed much of Deondre's experience: "I really wanted to go to East, but I thought my parents would say no because it's so far away [from home]. But when I got in with a full ride, they never even blinked before saying yes. I remember my dad was like 'Hudson, of course you have to go. East is the best. It's the best opportunity you'll ever have to make it.'" For Hudson's family, and many families like his, the fact that they knew East College to be prestigious *and* the school had offered a full financial aid package made it the right choice for Hudson, and, by proxy, his family, regardless of how far away it was from home. In many cases, it was the combination of these factors—reputation, prestige, financial aid, and distance—that students felt their parents prioritized when discussing college selection. As in Hudson's case, many parents saw attending a reputable and prestigious college on full financial aid as a good bet for social mobility and career advancement.

For students who were intent on attending lesser-known schools that were albeit still considered arguably quite elite for those familiar with the full landscape of higher education, the selection process was a bit more complicated and often hinged on the ability to provide evidence of a school's caliber as well as having a full-ride offer from the school. Nicki, a multiracial third-year attending East College, described the negotiations she had with her parents over college selection as "long and contentious." She had been accepted to a number of highly selective schools, but not all of them were well known enough to be thought of as a good choice to her family. Like many families of first-generation students, her parents only knew the big names, like the group of schools often referred to as the "Ivy Plus," which include Ivy League schools (Harvard, Yale, Princeton, etc.) and other renowned private schools not in the Ivy League (MIT, University of Chicago, Stanford, etc.). In contrast, they were not aware of highly selective liberal arts schools like Williams or Bryn Mawr College and did not have the experience or capital to know how highly regarded and competitive lesser-known schools like these were.

Nicki described spending hours walking her parents through the website of the selective liberal arts college that she wanted to attend, her financial aid packet, and the glossy look book that she had received in the mail. Even when she was able to demonstrate that the school was well regarded, would be free to attend, and could lead to law school and a well-paying career, her parents were resistant to the point that they were suggesting she stay home for college at the nearby regional school instead. It wasn't until she was able to connect her parents to the alumna that had conducted her interview—who was a successful lawyer in the area—that they began to see the merits of East College and consider it as a legitimate school with the potential to provide the opportunities they wanted for their daughter.

For some parents, the perceived lack of prestige tied to unknown schools translated into a feeling that these locations were less desirable options for their child than attending a closer, public regional college or state university on full financial aid. This was due in large part to the fact that the vast majority of students leaving these communities to attend college were enrolled at flagship and regional state institutions usually located a 2–3-hour car ride away. Seen as success stories, many parents pointed to these students—cousins, friends, neighbors—to make a case that attending a college in-state on scholarship was a better option for their child. Whitney, a White first-year at Midwest College, noted that her parents nearly refused to allow her to attend Midwest, pushing her instead to attend the same state university that her cousin attended:

> My mom was like "No way!" She just kept saying that she hadn't heard of Midwest before and even when I was like "Mom! Look at the rankings. Look at all the famous alumni." She was like "How can we be sure this nobody school is going to do right by you? You should go to Stanford." And I was like "Mom! I didn't get into Stanford!" and she would always just say, "Well, then go to Cal State." Like, Midwest is top 10 for fuck's sake, but since it wasn't Stanford she couldn't conceive of it.

As was the case with Nicki and Whitney, many families across America understand college from a very limited perspective. There are a handful of major universities, usually the oldest and most elite schools in the country, that nearly everyone has heard of. Outside of these schools, the families of students in this study, and perhaps the average working-class American family, are often only familiar with the public flagship schools in their region, like UC Berkeley for California families and UT Austin for Texas families. Further, familiarity with a college often commingles with reputation and prestige in the same way that brand recognition works in terms of consumer goods. An unknown school becomes conflated with a lack of prestige, which then often becomes framed as a less safe choice than a well-known but less prestigious public university with a track record of springboarding high-achieving local students into well-regarded careers. For these families, gaps in knowledge and familiarity with the full expanse of the higher education landscape end up narrowing their selection and often eliminate highly regarded schools that are seen as risky and low quality due to a lack of what is essentially brand recognition. This aligns with and expands on prior findings[56] around how familial perspectives and frameworks around college choice impact student selections. For some families, the uncertainty around whether schools in this unknown category can deliver on the promise of social mobility is enough to rule these schools out as viable options.

Jericho, a multiracial student that I first met during a focus group between his senior year of high school and first year of college, highlighted how these ideas around college prestige, perceived risk, and likelihood of upward mobility impacted his decision to attend the state university within driving distance of his home over a top-ranked liberal arts school on the East Coast. He had received a number of full-ride scholarships from selective private colleges. Much like Whitney's family, however, his parents did not consider any of these schools to be worth attending. In fact, he noted that his parents framed his top choice as risky and argued that he would be better off at the nearby state school that many of his high-achieving peers had selected. He summed this process of negotiation up by saying, "Their top priority was affordability. And I had an external scholarship, so every school would be basically free. Then it was about what school would move me up the ladder. And, well, State was right in my backyard and loads of people we knew had gone there and got good jobs. It was familiar. The safe bet they wanted me to take. So, I was like 'cool, State it is.'"

While financial resources were an important consideration in Jericho's college application and selection process, it was ultimately the perceived guarantee of mobility that the nearby state university offered that had the most impact on his family's decision around where he would go to college. From a comparative perspective, it is arguable that East College could provide the same, if not more, opportunities than State. However, Jericho's family did not have access to the kind of proof they needed—positive outcomes and experiences for friends and family in their community—to trust that East College would guarantee the same for their son. In absence of this kind of evidence, Jericho's family translated their unfamiliarity with this selective college into uncertainty and concerns around risk that ultimately became central to his final decision to attend his state's flagship university.

A year later in a follow-up conversation about this process, I asked Jericho whether he regretted his choice to attend the nearby state university. He shrugged and said that he was happy at State and that he felt like he made the most logical choice. He explained,

Picking a college was like shopping for cereal. There's lots of choices out there. I wanted a fruity cereal, and I had a coupon for it so I ignored all the other cereals. When it came down to it, there was the generic one that everyone I knew had been eating, it had been at the store for ages. And there was this new fancy cereal I'd heard about that looked good but, I don't know. They cost the same, and like, what if that new one was nasty? So, I did what anyone would do and put the generic cereal in my cart and headed to the milk aisle.

Jericho's breakfast cereal analogy highlights an important aspect of how many high-achieving low-income and first-generation students frame and make their choices around college. For the majority of these students, comprehensive financial aid packages ensure that the cost of college takes a back seat once it is time to make a final decision. Schools not offering full financial aid coverage are eliminated at a much earlier stage in the process. In the end, student and family decisions typically come down to whether they believe that a school can make good on the promise of a college degree and the upward mobility that is associated with college completion in the United States. The quality of a school is often based on perceptions about prestige and a proven track record of producing superior career results and social mobility. These families combine information about personal experiences and outcomes from their networks with their knowledge of a school's brand recognition—or the historical data, cultural depictions, and media representations of a school's worth and power—to narrow down and ultimately make decisions about what college to attend.

High-achieving students like Jericho have the potential to fulfill their dreams of becoming surgeons and engineers at whatever school they choose to attend. For most families, the best bet is the one with the best perceived odds of success. For some students, this means choosing a less prestigious but better-known in-state public university that may not skyrocket them into the highest strata, but has a proven track record of producing measurable upward mobility. While this may seem like a bad bet to those focused on the highest mobility returns on investment, these families are ultimately choosing what they see as a state school's proven track record of producing concrete outcomes over the unknown potential of the unproven prestige of a more selective school.

PREPARING FOR COLLEGE: POTENTIAL PROMISES VERSUS PERILOUS PITFALLS

Meanwhile, the majority of students and families I talked to chose to attend selective private schools in hopes of maximizing their access to the networks, resources, and ultimately mobility ascribed to these institutions. For students who ended up selecting an elite college or university, choosing a school was often just the beginning of a much longer set of conversations with their families. When I talked with students on their campuses, they described the shared expectations they and their families had around the potential changes that college might bring. Nearly every student noted that their families saw the promise of a degree and a well-paying career as the central reason students were attending an elite college—believing this was a positive aspect of the kind of upward mobility that can come with a college education. During focus groups with incoming first-years, we discussed what expectations they had about starting college in the fall. Violet, an Asian American rising first-year at East College, talked at length about the anticipation that she shared with her parents and younger siblings. She explained that as the child of a Vietnamese immigrant family, she had spent much of her life listening to a parental lecture about the importance of working hard and going to a good college. "The American Dream was really strong in my house. Work hard, get into a good college, become a doctor, change your life." After she was admitted to East College, family mealtime discussions revolved around preparing for college, how she should approach her time during college, and forming an idea of "the kind of student I should be at East College."

While Violet sometimes found these familial expectations overwhelming, she had witnessed how higher education had changed the lives of other people in her community. She had an aunt who had gone to a prestigious liberal arts college, then attended medical school at a top-ranked program on the West Coast—earning a high salary that afforded her the ability to care for her parents. Violet also had a close friend, Briana, who had started at East College the year prior. She could see almost immediate changes in what sociologists would call Briana's "cultural capital." She noted: "I remember when Briana came back for winter break. It was so exciting. She had only been away for a few months, but she was so much more . . . refined. She really seemed like someone that went to East College." She added that she looked forward to experiencing the same transformation so she could be a good role model for her younger siblings.

Violet's dual focus on the importance of both increased wealth and refinement—or the financial and status benefits of a college education—was a common thread for other students. Chris, a White fourth-year at South College, recalled how he and his dad had spent a significant amount of time during the summer before his first year discussing his future as they worked outside as landscapers. "It was funny, really. We were digging in the dirt and lugging giant bags of fertilizer talking about how someday I would be the guy standing on the deck smoking a cigar while some schmucks took care of my lawn." Rena, a Mexican American second-year at Midwest College, described a similar experience. She had spent her summers picking fruit with her mother to make extra money. One afternoon after work, her mother approached her in the kitchen with a nice skirt and blouse she had made Rena as a present. Her mother told her, "This is for college. From now on, you're the type of woman who makes money wearing nice things, not wearing old jeans and work boots." As she relayed this story, Rena teared up a little bit, saying, "It was beautiful. I think that moment was really important for both of us. It really cemented who I was becoming." Chris and Rena's parents celebrated the upward mobility that higher education could bring for their children; they imagined futures that held opportunities for careers that diverged from their families' physically intensive work. These parents also had an understanding well before the start of college that an important part of becoming upwardly mobile would include changes to their children's appearances that allowed them to align with their desired economic and social status.

It is important to note that, while not exclusive to them, families like Violet's and Rena's who had immigrated to the United States tended to have significantly positive perspectives about the transformative aspects of attending college—in terms of transforming both an individual and their life trajectories. This aligns with prior research on first- and second-generation immigrant families and the emphasis placed on educational opportunity as a springboard for producing social and economic mobility.[57] Many of these families moved to the United States seeking opportunity with an explicit desire for attaining an education, career, and level of financial gain that was perceived as impossible in their countries of origin. For these students, this translated into a narrative growing up where education was emphasized as crucial for attaining social mobility—and that social mobility was a positive force that would transform who you were and the opportunities you had access to.

For other students, the time leading up to leaving for college was filled with concerned conversations with their families and friends about whether attending an elite college would change them fundamentally as people—a change that was imagined as negative. Chloe, a White first-year attending East College, commented that she was still "wary of the ways that college might change me." She had spent much of the summer before college fighting with her parents and older brothers about her decision to attend a highly selective private university on the East Coast over the state college two hours away from her home in Texas. Although the distance was part of the concern for her family, they also worried that she would "forget who she was" and "become a stuck-up, snooty bitch." Like Chloe and her family, a number of students had serious misgivings about attending a highly selective private college. Yet, as I noted previously, these schools typically offered students more financial aid than local public and private colleges. To justify this choice to their parents, students emphasized the financial benefits of an elite college degree—benefits that could lead to a good career and financial security for them and possibly their families.

While students might emphasize the financial benefits of an elite college to their families to ease pre-college tensions, they, too, worried about how becoming upwardly mobile might change what they positioned as their core or authentic selves—an identity that was inherently tied to their home communities. Bryant, a Black first-year at Midwest College, spoke at length about this anxiety during a small-group discussion at a workshop on impostor syndrome. He explained that he was worried that being at Midwest College was going to change him so drastically that he would "forget where I came from and start acting a fool." When another student wrinkled their brow disapprovingly at this comment, Bryant responded, "Look, I am really happy to be here and wouldn't trade it for the world. But I know what a place like this does to people. It changes them. And that ain't a good thing, either." After the workshop, I invited Bryant to join me for coffee and asked him to elaborate on his comments. He explained that when he was accepted to Midwest College, he and his family were elated. Not only was he the first in his family to attend college, he had gotten a full-ride scholarship to one of the top schools in the nation. He was excited about the prospect of earning a degree, starting a career as an engineer, and returning to his poorly resourced community on the east side of Indianapolis to build parks and green spaces. Still, he had witnessed changes in priorities and commitments among the few young men and women who had left his community to attend elite colleges:

> Listen, the name of the game where I am from is working hard and getting out. Everyone wants you to rise up above poverty and gangs and whatever and live the dream of the promising young Black man that gets out and goes to college. The people in my neighborhood want that, everyone wants that. It's a trope in, like, I don't know, 100 movies probably. And that's me. I did that. But the other side of that is that once you make it, all anyone says is "Don't forget where you came from. Now you gotta give back and help the next generation." They say it as a reminder, but also I think out of fear that you're going to leave and never look back. Because let me tell you, most people end up as sellouts; once they leave, they never look back.

For many students like Bryant, the pressure to become socially mobile as a way to give back to a larger home community came with external and internal concerns about failing to make it—in effect falling off the ladder of mobility—or achieving the financial outcomes of an elite degree at the cost of personal transformations that family and old friends viewed as "selling out." Much like prior work[58] around academic opportunity and low-income students has noted, these students' academic opportunities became inherently intertwined with their relationships and responsibilities to their families and communities. While their academic achievements and college acceptances are celebrated, they are framed either explicitly or implicitly as means for gaining the skills and opportunities needed to return back to their communities and enact positive change. This places an added level of pressure on many of these students to succeed academically, but as students like Bryant demonstrate, they also face a strong sense of pressure to maintain their authenticity and sense of self as a member of the community they originate from.

For some students, the pressure to maintain authenticity and community membership was something they had seen play out in the experiences of slightly older members of their communities. Tyson, a White third-year at West College, had initial concerns of not just becoming "someone unrecognizable to my family" after going to college, but also about his ability to maintain relationships and patterns at home while also balancing his hefty academic schedule. His cousin Jerry served as a cautionary tale. Two years earlier, Jerry had been accepted to a private college about two hours from their small rural hometown but had dropped out at the end of his first year. Tyson felt that familial concerns about "selling out" in college had played a large part in Jerry's trajectory. While their family was excited about Jerry's college acceptance, they continually expressed their opinion that people from Jerry's community didn't fit with their image of the average private-college student. Tyson explained, "Jerry took that to heart, probably too much. He spent all of his free time coming back home—hunting and mudding and just fucking around with his buddies. He failed out and now he has a lot of debt. When it was my turn to go to college, they almost didn't let me go." For Tyson's family, college was a great opportunity, but one that came with real financial and social risks that deserved serious consideration.

In contrast, students who diverged from their families' beliefs and perceptions about the value of attending a selective college often described their senior year in high school as full of conflict at home about their decision to attend a selective college. When Violet talked about positive experiences planning for college with her family during a focus group, Ryder, a White rising first-year, responded, "Oh wow, that's so crazy to me. My parents are still pissed that I am going to East College. Even after winning scholarships and stuff. They're convinced it's a bad idea." Gillian, a multiracial rising first-year, looked quizzically at Ryder and asked him why his parents were so mad. Ryder laughed a little and said:

> College isn't really a thing where I am from. My parents wanted me to go to work with my dad and my brother [in construction], but I have bigger plans and they hate that. They can't understand that I want a different life than them, I want to travel, I want to have read things, I want to buy a house someday. It makes them mad, they think I am going to change—which honestly that's the plan—but they think I am going to think I am better than them, which I won't. I respect them and what they've done for me. I just want something different.

Gillian nodded at this comment and responded, "I feel that. My mom is way more worried than I am, but I wouldn't say she's pissed. She just doesn't want me to change, and I keep trying to explain to her that that's the whole reason I'm going to East College. To change." These familial tensions that Gillian and Ryder describe had meaningful consequences for a number of students as they prepared for college.

Students with parents who vocally expressed concerns about change and social mobility described feeling torn between their own excitement for college and managing the anxiety and stress of their parents' opposition. Jake, a multiracial fourth-year at South College, reflected on this period, saying: "It was like one minute, I'm so excited and planning my future life, and then, WHAM!, here comes Dad with a major guilt trip about me going to college and becoming 'city folk.' My life was like an emotional teeter-totter that summer." This idea that a rural working-class student would become "city folk" in college was a common way to talk about the behavioral transformations that are imagined to accompany upward mobility and a change in class position—transformations that might make students forget who they were and where they came from.

While not exclusively the case, the overwhelming majority of families that mirrored Gillian, Jake, and Ryder's were similar to the families that Arlie Hochschild[59] describes in her work on right-wing low-income and working-class communities in the United States. These families had made a living for generations from manual labor, often struggling to live paycheck to paycheck, in communities where the wealthy inhabitants prospered in seemingly easier lives. This juxtaposition of their struggles with the thriving of the American upper class produced deeply held cross-generational ambivalence toward the wealthy, their way of life, and the institutions—like higher education—that they represent. For students like Ryder, Jake, and Gillian, making a break from these ideological frameworks around wealth and education was seen as a slight on their families' way of life and a dangerous recipe for becoming an unwanted outsider.

For some students of color, in contrast, forgetting who they were didn't look like an option, as they were moving into predominantly White institutions. Kendrick, a Black third-year at West College, explained to me in a conversation we had during a visit to his grandmother's house in the summer before his third year of college, "nobody was talking about class that summer [before college]. It was about being a Black man in that kind of White space." As he recounted these discussions with his family, pastor, and neighbors, his grandmother came into the room and added, "For me I figured, well, he is always going to be a Black man no matter where he goes in life. So, I better focus on preparing him for that over anything else." Kendrick smiled up at his grandmother's comment and squeezed her hand as she walked out of the room, saying, "She's right. Being Black in that White space is hard. But let me tell you what, I'll never have stress over becoming White like I stress over becoming a rich asshole." Kendrick went on to explain that he had not come to college prepared to think through his class identity, let alone changes to it, and that he was still struggling to articulate his complex feelings around the intersection of race and class in his college experience.

Like Kendrick, many students of color emphasized the abruptness with which their class identities became salient during college and pointed to the malleability of this status as a major concern. Porter, a Latinx student in their final year at Midwest College, explained that they were caught off guard when it was their class, not their race, that took a front seat as a point of friction and contention during their first year of college. They explained that they had come into Midwest College knowing that it was a predominantly White institution and as prepared as possible to be in the stark minority as part of the Latinx students on campus. Once they arrived on campus, they immediately gravitated toward other students of color on campus in an attempt to find and preserve community. And, while Porter noted that this did give them a sense of community that offset the starkness of being a student of color on a predominantly White campus, they were not prepared for the feelings of alienation they felt within these BIPOC student spaces. They explained,

You may have never heard of this before, but there's a saying "not all skin folk are kin folk" and like, before I came to Midwest I always just interpreted that to be that not all people of color are your homies. Which obviously some people are dicks, even if they are brown. But being here at Midwest gave that saying a whole new meaning. Like, some of these fools are about as different from me as you can get because they were raised with money. Big money. Like, it don't matter that we are both Latinx going to school here with an army of White people. Because we are not the same. They're more like the rest of the rich people on campus. They're not White, though, that's just lazy to call them White. It's more than that. Their money makes them different in so many ways, but their race and experience of that makes them the same in some ways. And like, I didn't expect that at all because you know what, before I came here I had never met a rich Latino. So I didn't even know that was, like, a thing to consider.

Porter's experience as a young low-income Latinx student navigating their first year at Midwest College reinforces the established complexity of being low-income and a student of color on an elite college campus.[60] Their experience also brings to the forefront the need for preparing low-income and first-generation students of color for both the racial and classed aspects of attending a selective college that is both predominantly White *and* predominantly wealthy. Having the language and framework for preparing to attend a predominantly White institution or "PWI" is far more often available to students of color than access to similar language and frameworks around the classed aspects of these campuses. And, while race is perhaps the most salient aspect for incoming students of color to consider when transitioning into college,[61] preparing for being in the classed minority—even within communities of color—may help these students mediate some of the added stresses and alienation expressed here.

MAKING PREPARATIONS AND PLANS

Once a student selects a school, the summer before their first year in college becomes a critical period for preparing to face both the possibilities and the challenges of higher education. Many students had little prior knowledge of what it would feel like to be in college and to experience not just academic growth but also personal growth. As the first person in their family to attend college, students could not always get advice from within their networks on how to prepare for the social aspects of college at home and had to turn to alternative avenues of information. Javier, a Latinx third-year at East College, described spending a lot of time consulting the internet and his school's promotional materials as guides for what to expect:

I remember spending hours on the school website after I got in. Looking at like every page on there and scouring their social media too. Mostly I was worried about academics and wasn't thinking about social or whatever. But everything was like "explore this, explore that, explore yourself." It was everywhere. I remember seeing that when I was applying too, but seeing it after actually getting in was different. It made me really start thinking a lot about college in that way, I think. It wasn't just about academics anymore.

As prior research[62] has demonstrated, many first-generation students do not have opportunities to explore their future campus communities in person via flyouts and overnight visits and must rely heavily on digital sources to guide and inform many aspects of their college application and decision process. I found that for many of the students I talked to, this impact of digital and social media extended into the pre-college preparation phase. For students like Javier, digital sources of information like official school web pages and social media became vitally important resources for building their frameworks of what to expect from, and how to prepare for, their impending college experiences. What is particularly interesting is that, like Javier, many students used digital sources not only to gather information about the schools they would be attending, they also used them to shape their understanding of what they would be doing during college, and also who they might need to become to thrive and fit in on campus.

A number of students recounted drawing on digital resources and the experiences of friends and family to actively plan their potential college selves during the summer after high school graduation. Students who looked to college as an opportunity to transform via the promise of social mobility drew on cues from family members and friends who had gone through college as well as narratives from college websites, social media accounts, and popular media about college to imagine an identity that they felt would successfully fit in at their college. Violet relied heavily on the example of her close friend who had attended East College, saying, "It sounds creepy, I promise it isn't, but I spent a lot of time watching her. The way she was walking, the way she was talking. I took mental notes on her wardrobe and asked her probably a million questions about her experience." Without a close friend in college, in contrast, Ryder described the importance of the internet as a source for information. He explained, "I probably spent a couple hours a day for a while there looking at the school website and YouTube videos and social media accounts to figure out what people were like and who I was going to be." Although they had different experiences at home, Violet and Ryder both pulled on their available resources to inform their understandings of their campus communities and to imagine future selves.

Safeguards and Suspended Identities

For students who framed the potential effects associated with social mobility during college as negative and undesirable—or who had parents who did so—preparing for college presented a double-edged sword of opportunity. While other students spent the summer before their first year of college enthusiastically researching and morphing into new college-ready versions of themselves, these students spent the summer trying to invent a separate identity meant only for college that they could inhabit temporarily in order to be successful in school without an impact to what they saw as their true selves. On the one hand, they saw college as the best path toward "getting out," promising improved economic conditions and a chance at potential intergenerational mobility. On the other hand, going to an elite school represented a risk for "selling out," threatening to change individuals and pull them, as potential future resources, out of low-resourced communities.

A number of students attempted to resolve these tensions by making plans to create a college self, a "suspended identity,"[63] that was separate from their real selves. In planning for how to "be" at college, they imagined using this new college self for campus contexts and preserving their true selves for life outside of and after college. In other words, these students hoped to safeguard their identities from unwanted changes by keeping their "home self" removed from college altogether. Much like K–12 students who end up culturally straddling their home and school communities,[64] these students hoped to bifurcate their identity into two distinct and separate selves in order to stave off unwanted personal change and/or avoid conflict with friends and family who perceived change via college and social mobility as a wholly negative result to be avoided at all costs.

Chloe offers a clear example of the labor that goes into crafting a suspended identity in preparation for starting college. Determined to attend East College because of its reputation for producing graduates with high-earning and desirable careers, she entered college with her family's concerns that she would become a "stuck-up, snooty bitch" in the back of her mind. Toward the end of her first semester of her first year of college, we had a discussion about her friends on campus. She expressed an idea that I would soon hear from many other students: that she was living a split life between college and home. "I met a lot of people during orientation and have been getting along with people alright so far. I mean, I don't really know them yet and they don't know the real me either, but so far so good." When I asked her what she meant by the "real me," she replied: "Well, so I guess there is college me and real me. I think there is a certain kind of person that does really well at East College, and I thought to myself, 'Why not just be that person?' Before I started school, I was really worried about doing well here and about staying true to myself. So, I figured, why not be the person that fits in and does well at East College while I am there and then just be myself at home?" She hoped to be able to quell the concerns of her family by leaving her college life at college and remaining "true to herself" and meeting her family's expectations while at home. She noted, "College is really just four years of my life. After that I'll have a degree and a good job." Once she was finished with school, she envisioned her life being relatively similar to her pre-college existence.

Tyson echoed a number of Chloe's sentiments: "I remember right before I came to West College looking at all of my clothes thinking, 'Okay, what is College Tyson all about?' I was really concerned that in order to do college right, to balance everything, I had to put as much distance between my actual self and the me that I would be in college. It was like I was trying to create this completely different, like temporary, person." The distance that Tyson describes here was a common theme among students who described this strategy of identity management. In many cases, distance applied to both the perceived gap between the two identities as well as the ability to temporarily inhabit one identity while at college without families or friends saying the dreaded words "You've changed."

Bryant used the concept of "gay till graduation," a popular culture term for a student who participates in same-sex relationships in college but then returns to strictly heterosexual relationships after graduation, as an analogy for his suspended identity: "This is kind of awful, but it's the best way I know how to explain it. Have you ever heard the term 'gay till graduation' [laughs]? So, it's kind of like that. I'm here and I'm pretty bougie [*sic*] and that works for me here. But my family back home never needs to know about it. Once I'm gone from here, that will all be put behind me." As he notes here, Bryant had explicit plans to leave this constructed identity behind after graduation, and had confidence that the identity he was inhabiting at college would remain temporary and applicable only in that space.

The confidence that these identity suspension strategies were successful was echoed by a number of students in their first semester or year of college. During her first semester of her first year, Gillian explained, "I am a totally different person here than I was at home. I left that Gillian behind and, like, stepped into 'College Gillian' when I got here. When I go home during winter break, I'll just be 'Old Gillian' again, and that will keep my family happy." Jake expressed a similar feeling of early confidence in his efforts to suspend his pre-college identity as an attempt to assuage his parents' anxieties about college: "I remember being a freshman thinking that I had figured it all out. I was one version of myself at college and would be another version of myself at home. It was perfect. My parents would be happy because I would be the same ol' Jake at home and they'd never know what was happening at school." Like many of their peers who were resistant to change during college (or who had parents who were), Gillian and Jake had constructed a new—but imagined and temporary—identity that they believed would be successful in college. Importantly, these identities were built with the expectation of being able to recoup what they saw as their core identity whenever they were at home in their communities. The imagination that such a suspension was possible gave students like them the confidence they needed to embark on their college experiences and begin "buying in" to the college experience of their dreams in a way that felt safeguarded from becoming the "sellout" of their nightmares.

· 2 ·
Great Expectations, Mismatched Beginnings

In the spring of 2017, I sat with Janna in one of the quads at East College. It was a beautiful day out, the sun was peeking into the late morning sky, flowers were in bloom, and tours of families trying to find a school with the right fit were snaking their way across campus. Janna was finishing up her second semester at East and had agreed to give me a tour of campus before our interview. At this point in my fieldwork, I had taken dozens of participant-led campus tours and had the formula down to a science. We would go through the academic and social buildings they were familiar with, they'd tell me stories about what had happened in those buildings or what they meant to the campus culture or history—and all of this would be interrupted no fewer than a handful of times by stopping to chat or greet the friends, classmates, and roommates we would invariably run into. Of course, the tours I took with upperclassmen were disrupted far more frequently than tours with first-years, who generally knew fewer people on campus. Janna's tour was different, however. In our hour and a half of walking, she never so much as waved at anyone as we walked down the crowded springtime pathways. I was struck by how solitary Janna appeared. She was also far more reserved than she was when I had met her the previous summer. My notes from our first meeting described her as animated, outgoing, and excited—today she was quiet and withdrawn.

As we rounded out the tour and sat down under a large shade tree to start our interview, she gave a heavy sigh. I looked up from the backpack I was unpacking, and as we made eye contact, tears started rolling down her cheeks. As she tried to stop the flow of tears, she looked away toward a crowd of prospective students and parents and said, "It's nothing like I thought it would be. What those tour guides are selling is a joke. I never should have come here. People like us don't belong at East." After a few moments of silence, she wiped away her tears and smoothed her hands out on her jeans before launching into a description of what her first year had been like. She explained that as a first-generation student she had thought that attending a highly selective school was the best path toward the social mobility and career stability she desired. She had taken numerous virtual tours on college websites and had had the opportunity to take a small number of in-person campus tours through a program for high-achieving students in her area. She focused a lot on the idea of "fit" when explaining her process, and noted that this concept became the guide she followed when choosing a school and preparing herself to begin college at East. Like many of the other students I talked to, Janna had an idea in mind when it came to what an East student was—they were smart, outgoing, and driven; they wore certain brands of clothes, had read a certain set of books, and saw the world in a certain kind of way. It was this character sketch of an East College student that Janna used to inform the strategies she employed to shape and manage aspects of her own identity as she prepared for the transition into college.

Janna described feeling confident as she began the first days of orientation. Since that week, however, she felt like being in college was an uphill battle. A wide range of issues had impacted her first year. Her parents had filled out a financial aid form incorrectly, leading to a delay in her funding and repeated trips to administrative offices. She had a difficult time keeping up in her introductory science class, which made her question whether her dreams of becoming an engineer were even plausible. Her roommate was from a very different background, and they didn't get along well or spend any time together. She struggled to find a social group she fit in with—she felt distant from her more affluent classmates. As a multiracial low-income student, she was too White and too poor to feel at home in the Black student union, and her campus didn't have a formal first-generation group that met regularly. She explained that if she had only faced one or two of these challenges, she likely would have felt more at home at East, but instead she had ended up struggling in nearly every aspect of her first-year experience. Summing this up, she said, "It's been too much. Every little thing builds up and reminds you that you don't belong here."

For many first-generation and low-income students like Janna, the transition into college is often tumultuous and rife with conflicts over the mismatch between what they expected college would be like and the realities they were facing every day on campus. These students often struggle to understand institutional expectations and processes, find themselves underprepared academically when compared to their peers, and have a difficult time finding their place and fitting in socially.[65] This can lead to experiences similar to Janna's, with delays in funding, poor academic outcomes, and feelings of isolation and alienation on campus.[66] And, while this is the case for many first-generation students, not all first-generation experiences are created equally, and variations across this population are critically important to consider when developing programmatic interventions.[67]

As detailed in the second half of chapter 1, the period before college is often a time of preparation, where students imagine their college lives, begin building the foundations of their college selves, and develop the frameworks they need for understanding and preparing for their positionality as first-generation students at selective colleges. For many of the students I spent time with, this preparation gave them the confidence they needed to head off into the great unknown of college life. However, what many of them did not realize was that although they had carefully studied and prepared to fit in on their college campuses, this did not give them the kind or depth of information, skills, and experiences that they would need to smoothly transition and adequately meet the demands at their schools. I found, however, that although the majority of students felt prepared and even excited for the challenges that college may bring, a relative unfamiliarity with the bureaucratic processes, academic demands, and social expectations that awaited them at these highly selective schools put them at a major disadvantage when compared to many of their peers.

In this chapter, I explore the hurdles many low-income first-generation students face around administrative, academic, and social aspects of college. Building on prior research that has laid the foundations for understanding the difficulties first-generation students face as they enter college, I compare experiences across students and show

how having prior educational experience with selective schooling and/
or external guidance from an outside organization can produce major
advantages. This comparison draws on, and further develops, Anthony
Abraham Jack's distinctions between first-generation student experiences and the benefits of being a member of the "privileged poor" who
come to college via exclusive high schools. I argue that these advantages
come not only from a familiarity with the culture and structure of elite
education, but also from a deeper understanding of what it means to
be a low-income and first-generation student in these spaces and how
to embody and leverage that positionality to one's advantage. Finally, I
consider how conceptual categories from previous research on the differences across first-generation student experiences have been taken up
within this population of students and the impact this has had on community cohesion.

NAVIGATING COMPLEX
ADMINISTRATIVE STRUCTURES

The first meaningful interactions that many low-income students have
with their colleges and universities center around meeting administrative requirements like filling out housing forms and transferring AP
(Advanced Placement) credits. Unlike their more affluent peers, low-
SES/first-generation students are far more likely to need institutional
support and must often navigate a complex array of bureaucratic demands around issues such as financial aid without the assistance of
their parents or communities.[68] This often produces significant hurdles
that can result in delays in funding and major setbacks. This is due in
part to a lack of familiarity with the organizational structure and processes of higher education,[69] but arguably also because many selective
colleges and universities continue to structure their administrative processes with the assumption that their student body has the knowledge,
experiences, and resources they need to smoothly navigate them. This is
simply not the case for many low-income and first-generation students
and, as I will show, the continued assumption that these students do
not require administrative support and guidance as they navigate these
critical elements of beginning college produces unnecessary inequalities that could easily be avoided.

THE BUREAUCRATIC BURDEN
OF BEING LOW-INCOME

During my time in the field, I found that many low-income and first-generation students arrive at college new to the organizational structure and administrative expectations at highly selective schools and struggle significantly with this aspect of their transition into college. These students had attended a range of schools, including underfunded public schools, charter schools, magnet schools, and well-resourced suburban schools. While these schools vary widely in resources, structure, and academic preparation, all of these students described feeling some level of confusion around how to navigate mandatory administrative requirements and access the resources they needed to succeed. Sean, a Black third-year at Midwest College who had attended a well-resourced suburban high school, discussed the impact this unfamiliarity had on his first year:

> I mean, I went to a pretty good school with a lot of extra things, resources and specialized staff. But it wasn't anything like here—there's no financial aid in public school, so that was way new. There was just too much to learn, and it's so complicated. It was like "Go here, go there, talk to your dean, no not that dean, you have to talk to your dean." It took forever, and I had so many questions. "I have a dean? What is their job? What does that even mean?"

Other students echoed Sean's frustration with navigating the administrative landscape of their colleges. Priya, a multiracial fourth-year at Midwest College who had graduated at the top of her class at her underresourced high school, explained to me, while we waited in line at the registrar's office, that moving from a high school that had a single counselor for the entire student body and a "DIY style of finding resources and support" to a college with a "complicated web of resources and requirements that seemed to be written out in a secret language only some folks could understand" was difficult to manage and took time away from her ability to acclimate to the academic and social aspects of college. Instead of attending discussion sessions during the first two weeks of classes, she spent hours attempting to get her financial aid corrected. She felt that these delays limited her opportunities to participate in off-campus outings with her residence hall. While she was spending time catching up on trying to build this knowledge base that many of her peers either already had or had access to, she was missing out on core elements of what college is for—academic development and social engagement.

While in the field, I spent an extensive amount of time with Priya and other students waiting in financial aid lines and administrative waiting rooms as they tried to iron out the details of their funding or academic standing. I watched as they spent hours filling out forms, tracking down offices, sending emails, and patiently walking their parents through complex tax forms and other bureaucratic requirements over the phone. It is important to note that the majority of this administrative work is designed to be completed via online portals and email protocols before a student even steps foot on campus. And, while many of these systems come with instructions and FAQs, they are complex and confusing, require detailed personal and financial information, and are not necessarily designed to be completed by students without adult input. Incorrect and missing information on forms can create inaccuracies and delays in university systems that result in major problems for students once they arrive on campus. This is exactly what happens for many students whose parents (or other adults in their lives) cannot or will not help with administrative tasks like filling out financial aid forms, housing contracts, and transfer credit approval petitions.

Gray, a multiracial student in their fourth year at East College, talked to me about their work-study job in the student business office and how they had noticed a trend with incoming first-generation student files. They explained that "our system is designed to catch missing information, but it can't always catch incorrect info . . . I noticed that a lot of first-gens would have complete files in the system, but that when they got here there would be big big problems we hadn't caught." When I asked Gray why they thought this was occurring, they laughed and said, "Oh, they're 100% filling them out on their own and they have no idea what they are doing!" They went on to explain that while many incoming students fill out their own forms, it mattered that they usually have knowledgeable parents or other adults involved that can help them throughout the process. They noted, "If you don't have someone on your end checking to make sure it's all good, and there isn't someone on our end checking to make sure it's all good, then shit falls through the cracks. And then there's a big-ass mess that's like 'surprise!' when they [first-gens] get here that is probably going to take forever to figure out on the fly."

As Gray notes, these differences in parental and adult resources available to students have a real impact on their first few days on campus. Delays in completing these tasks, which have to be done in order to stay in good standing with the university, mean that a subset of students is missing out on valuable academic resources, such as study groups and office hours, in the critical early moments of their first year on campus. Wyatt, a White first-year student from an underresourced high school, detailed the strain that he felt between meeting administrative demands at East College and trying to engage in the full range of student activities and communities on his campuses:

> I missed the student activities fair because I was in the registrar's office trying to get my AP credits cleared up. I hadn't done it right or my school had messed up or something. I had to do all of this paperwork and meet with all of these people to get it cleared up. And it was, like, the deadline to take care of it—to meet the requirement to get into this class I wanted to take—it was the same day as all of this freshman info stuff, and I just missed it all. That was big.

Wyatt went on to explain that this was not an isolated event. During his first semester of college, he often found himself missing key residence hall meetings or student events because he was balancing a precarious load of academic and administrative work that had to be prioritized over everything else in his schedule.

At West College, I sat with Dylan, a White first-year student, as he waited to discuss a financial aid refund with an administrator. Dylan had recently graduated with honors from a local underresourced public school and, while he had grown up nearby, he emphasized that his community and high school had little in common with his college. As we sat in the quiet waiting room, we could hear a student on a megaphone directing students to visit a booth for their club in the quad, offering "free donuts and friendship" to anyone who was interested. I laughed and turned to Dylan, saying, "Man, I would kill for a donut, I'm so hungry!" He softly chuckled and said, "Donuts are cool, but I'd rather have some friends," as he trailed off into silence. Perhaps sensing my concern, he broke the silence by laughing and saying, "Damn, that was dark as fuck." I laughed and asked him if he had made friends with his roommate or joined any groups on campus. He shook his head no and told me that he had been struggling to find his place on campus. As he filled out a stack of paperwork, he explained that he had missed a large chunk of the orientation programming and early opportunities to meet people and join clubs because of all the administrative catch-up required during those first days on campus:

> I'm telling you, it was like there were two different orientations going on. One for all the rich kids, where they went to the programs and took the tours and played games in the quad and had pizza and shit. And then another one, where all the poor kids were sitting in the admin buildings and offices trying to meet with our advisors and get our money and paperwork handled while all that other stuff was going on without us.

From the moment Dylan arrived on campus, he was inundated with complex requirements that he needed to complete in order to enroll and receive housing. While he had met the basic requirements for enrollment when he accepted his admission offer, he had missed a number of other requirements and deadlines throughout the summer of which he had been unaware. At orientation, he was given a document that read DELINQUENT FILE: SEE REGISTRAR, FINANCIAL AID, HOUSING in large bold letters across the page. Confused and embarrassed, he spent the day trying to gather all of his delinquent documents, terrified that he would not be permitted to move into his residence hall or enroll in classes. While Dylan was able to meet the administrative requirements that he had missed, it was not an expedient process. Without the experience necessary to navigate the organizational structure and administrative demands efficiently, or someone in his life to guide and prepare him, he lost precious academic and social time to these issues over his first semester.

Jasmine, an Asian American third-year from an underresourced high school, highlighted how delays in her financial aid package at East College had kept her from participating in outings with her campus housing community: "As a low-income student, sure, I have to be on a budget, that's like the story of my life, but when I first got here I literally had no money. Like, I couldn't go on these field trips with my dorm and had to make up stories about why I couldn't eat off campus. I was so embarrassed. By the time I had some spare cash, I felt like an outsider. People had already made friends around me, so I just did my own thing." This difficult situation made Jasmine feel out of place and embarrassed, feelings that prevented her from benefiting from the purpose of these events—beginning to embed in her campus community.

As her residence hall neighbors formed friendships around her, Jasmine spent most of her time alone and struggled significantly with whether or not she belonged in college. She eventually took a leave of absence during her second year. As a low-income student, she felt out of place before even beginning school, and that "even the smallest reminder of my difference was all I needed to confirm my fears that I didn't belong." While she did not consider her initial financial situation to be the only reason for her distance from other students on campus, she felt that it contributed to an already impossible situation and had a lasting impact on her college experience.

Although selective colleges and universities have invested in recruiting high-achieving low-income and first-generation students, they often continue to drop the ball in providing them with the scaffolding and support that they need once they arrive on campus.[70] The first few weeks of the academic calendar at selective colleges are structured with the historically traditional student in mind, and unforeseen setbacks in taken-for-granted administrative requirements and organizational processes end up creating an unrecognized and bifurcated set of experiences within the student body. Without the knowledge or skills needed to smoothly navigate these processes, low-income students like Jasmine and Dylan begin their college careers behind their more educationally advantaged peers—losing time, money, and confidence in the process, never quite catching up to their peers or finding their place in their campus communities.

These experiences align with previous research[71] and highlight a key point—the time that low-income students spend on deciphering the organizational structure and meeting the administrative demands of their institution impacts far more than the number of hours they have available to focus on classwork. The time taken up playing administrative catch-up impacts many students' ability to embed in and form connections to their campus communities—an aspect of college that is critical to student outcomes and success[72] as well as future career trajectories.[73] A lack of a sense of embeddedness can contribute to lower academic performance, produce less positive social experiences, and increase the likelihood of attrition.[74] This adds to already existing feelings of insecurity and impostor status that many first-generation students often bring to college,[75] likely compounds the negative effects of feeling like an outsider to their campus communities,[76] and sets them apart from their peers on campus both figuratively and literally.

The Bureaucratic Bonus of an Elite High School Education

All the low-income and first-generation students I talked to had to meet administrative demands at their colleges. However, students who either attended elite high schools or were directly engaged with an outside organization that provided one-on-one advising and mentoring handled these administrative requirements with an ease that set them notably apart from their low-income and first-generation peers. A comparison between a set of roommates attending Midwest College highlights how familiarity with organizational structure and administrative demands matters for early student experiences at an elite college. Jackson, a White second-year who had attended a well-resourced public school, noted that financial aid delays in his first year at Midwest College created a critical situation for the first six weeks of classes:

> So really, going in, I was just under the impression that it was going to be easy. You know full ride is full ride, you don't pay for anything, you just go. And so, I didn't really think much about it until I first got on campus in the fall. And then all of a sudden I was hit with a wall of paperwork and hoops to jump through. That delayed my money by a long time—I think I didn't have money for probably the first six weeks of classes. I couldn't go anywhere. I couldn't even buy toothpaste—I had to borrow from my roommate.

As Jackson relayed this experience, his roommate, Dakota, interrupted from the next room, teasing, "Oh, man, you didn't know anything. I remember you came back to the dorm freaking out that you owed like $2,000 or something. I had to do everything for you." Jackson laughed at Dakota's comment and said, "It's true. He had everything done before school even started. It was crazy." Unlike Jackson, Dakota had attended a private boarding school and was familiar with the nuanced requirements of financial aid timelines. He had been receiving financial aid throughout high school, and while some of the specifics were different in college, the process mirrored high school enough that he had little trouble with the transition: "I just kind of kept doing what I had been doing forever because I was confident that it worked."

This advantage, or bureaucratic bonus, aligns with prior work[77] on the benefits of attending a private preparatory school prior to entering a selective university, and arguably arises from the "institutional isomorphism,"[78] or the similarities in the structures and processes of two organizations, such as elite high schools and colleges that occupy the same field. Although Dakota and Jackson were both low-income first-generation students, the fact that Dakota had four years during high school to learn the administrative requirements and processes tied to attending an elite school on financial aid mattered for his experience. Students like Dakota carry the knowledge they gain from attending an elite high school and rely on their past experiences to inform how they understand and navigate administrative demands at their colleges. This bureaucratic bonus helped Dakota avoid funding delays, ensuring that he would have the money required to meet his needs during the term. Attending an elite high school that was organizationally similar to an elite college put Dakota at an advantage over his low-income peers—something that even Jackson's competitive and highly resourced suburban high school could not provide.

Dakota's ease with navigating the bureaucratic structure and knowledge around administrative processes and requirements was exemplary of students who had attended elite boarding, day, and preparatory high schools. These students reported that the administrative requirements and organizational structures at their colleges mirrored what they had experienced and learned during high school and recounted feeling skilled and confident in their ability to navigate these demands. Kellen, a Latinx first-year at East College who had attended a private boarding school, pointed out the direct links between his high school and the college he was attending. "My high school was a lot like a college. We had houses, there were deans for different parts of the school, and there was an admissions office and financial aid process. So, when I got to college, there weren't many surprises—it was completely familiar." Having attended a school that mirrored the organizational structure of his college provided Kellen with valuable advance knowledge and experience that aided in his transition to higher education.

Similarly, Mindy, a White first-year at East College who had attended a private day school in Boston, emphasized how the similarities between her high school and college contributed to the ease she felt in navigating her college's organizational landscape and administrative requirements: "When I started college, it was very similar to my high school. I hadn't lived in dorms, but I was familiar with financial aid and had gotten help from special resources and offices for scholarship students and students of color at my high school. This made it so I knew what to do when I got here, I spoke the language and knew who to talk to, this made it way easy to get set up." Like Kellen, she was able to easily translate her experiences in high school to college, carrying her skills and knowledge with her between organizations, producing a straightforward transition. She explained that although she did not like spending time on these kinds of administrative tasks, they were more of "an annoyance than anything else." Having been on financial aid since the beginning of high school, she was able to quickly understand and complete these requirements and felt that by the time she reached college, "things like financial aid had just kind of become second nature for me." Not only was she familiar with the basics of how her elite college was structured, she benefited from the bureaucratic bonus that comes from having been socialized into how to operate in and navigate this kind of organization, producing an ease and comfort that is characteristic of elite training and education.[79]

The Benefits of External Organizational Support

Students who were associated with outside scholarship foundations and education organizations that provided one-on-one advising and mentoring, like LEDA (Leadership Enterprise for a Diverse America), the Jack Kent Cooke Foundation, and Bottom Line, reported administrative experiences that were somewhere in between both of these groups. These students came to college with experts in their corner, in the form of advisors that they could turn to for help deciphering the complex organizational structures and often opaque administrative requirements.

As Sarah, a White student in her second year at East College and a Jack Kent Cooke Scholar, noted, "having Travis [their advisor] to call or email all of my million questions to was a lifesaver. He knew everything about everything, because it's his literal job, you know? He was always like 'don't stress, I've got this,' and you know what, he totally did. Without him, I'd have been lost and everything would have taken ages, I'm sure." For Sarah and the many students like her, having this kind of organizational support is an invaluable resource that separates these students from many of their first-generation peers. They are able to save time and avoid emotional turmoil because of the support and resources available to them as part of these programs. And this, in turn, frees them up from many of the challenges that their first-generation peers who are going it alone must face.

And, while these students do not benefit from the ease that comes from lived experience within elite educational structures, they did note that having an advisor that they could turn to for help navigating these demands, for support when they were struggling, and even as someone they could call on to communicate on their behalf to their college mattered significantly. These students expressed that, in many ways, having this kind of support gave them the confidence they needed to not only navigate required administrative processes but also ask more from their colleges in terms of resources and opportunities throughout their academic careers. Mary, a multiracial student in her third year at East College and a Jack Kent Cooke Scholar, noted,

> Having Trina [their advisor] explain how colleges, and funding, and opportunities and everything works—and then to have her help me go through all of that my first year—made me feel like I could do anything! And so I did. I'm always just like "Is there an application for it? Great, I'll fill that out right now! Oh, no application, cool cool cool, I'll just email the office and ask." [laughs] I'm here emailing everyone all the time like I own the place! . . . I'm a senior now, and I've done so many things that I never would have known to do or felt like I could if it wasn't for Trina's support. Honestly.

For Mary and students like her, having the support of an academic advisor through their scholarship organization not only provided them with concrete information and resources as they started college, it gave them the knowledge and support they needed to feel empowered within these complex organizational structures. For many students, this had a lasting impact on their confidence that became compounded as they progressed in college.

This benefit of organizational support that a number of students like Sarah and Mary reported aligns closely with the feelings of confidence and empowerment to navigate administrative processes that some of the students who had gone to private prep schools expressed. Katherine, a fourth-year who attended a private boarding school and was active in a number of student groups at West College, described having a relatively easy time managing the administrative demands of starting college. "It really was a breeze for me when I got here. Everything was set up in a way that I totally understood, so I just kept applying for things and they kept saying yes. I took that as a good sign and kept asking for bigger things. Now I have a budget with thousands of dollars to spend on first-gen students." For Katherine, early successes with the administrative side of college translated into feeling empowered to access additional resources, to form a student group, and to apply for substantial funding to support her campus's first-generation community. In many ways, the bureaucratic bonus she entered college with expanded over time through continued positive reinforcement, producing a sense of agency and power within the organizational field at her college.

Katherine's experiences highlight that what is at stake for many low-income students often extends well beyond time lost to filling out additional paperwork. From the moment that students arrive on campus, they are able to draw on their pre-college experiences with elite education or the support of experts with this knowledge to meet and maintain administrative demands with ease, avoiding the hurdles that other low-income students face. This provides these students with major advantages—freeing up their time and money in a way that allows them to effectively get a head start on engaging and finding student communities. This ease, in turn, often becomes compounded as students report gaining further confidence, feeling empowered to access extended resources and engage in organizational change-making processes while their peers grapple with feelings of inadequacy and isolation—struggling through administrative processes that they experience as complicated and confusing.

ACADEMIC EXPECTATIONS VERSUS EXPERIENCES

The first-generation student population at the most selective colleges and universities in the nation is made up, for the most part, from the highest-achieving high school student applicants across the United States.[80] These students enter college often having near perfect high school GPAs, boasting test scores in the top percentiles in the nation, having accumulated AP credits and International Baccalaureate (IB) designations, and possessing resumes with extensive extracurricular and volunteer accomplishments. And, while nearly all students at the most selective schools come in with similarly impressive credentials, there is often a wide variation in the quality or rigor of the instruction they received during high school.[81] This is true even in the case of seemingly standardized courses like AP classes, as standardized directives in curriculum do not necessarily equal standardized learning experiences, quality of instruction, or depth and breadth of material covered.[82] Disparities in coursework, instruction, and resources that are assumed by many to be equal across high schools can create unexpected and critical disparities in students' college outcomes and trajectories.

Many first-generation students come to college with the assumption that having taken the most difficult classes available in their high schools prepared them adequately for the rigors of any college to which they were admitted. And, having gained admission to selective colleges and universities often serves as further evidence that they have met academic benchmarks for success and thus do not need further preparation. Yet, many students who I spent time with experienced a sense of shock when they began their college coursework. While these students often chose schools based on reputations of academic rigor and expected their classes to cover difficult and unfamiliar topics, they did not anticipate the depth of prior knowledge that many of their introductory first-year courses required or assumed of students.

For instance, Priya had taken (and gotten A's in) every mathematics and science AP course offered during high school and was placed into the upper range of first-year math courses at Midwest College. She recalled feeling pleased with her placement and was prepared (as well as excited) to be challenged in the course. When the course began, however, she felt lost in the material and was unable to keep up even in the introductory lecture. She explained, "I went to the professor and asked if I was in the right course. And he, well, he was a total dick. He asked me a bunch of questions and then simply said, 'No. You need remediation. See your advisor.' It was mortifying." She explained that her advisor then informed her that since she had not taken theoretical calculus in high school she would need to start math in a different course sequence. When relaying this story, she became visibly angry, stopping midsentence to say, "Can you fucking believe that? Theoretical calculus. In high school! Who the fuck takes theoretical calculus in high school?"

Priya's anger around the gap between her academic preparation and the unrealistic expectations of introductory first-year courses was a common theme for many students I talked to. When Dylan arrived on campus at West College, he was excited for the challenge that his college classes would bring. He had been particularly drawn to West College because of the introductory humanities sequence that everyone at West participates in during their first year. Designed as an introduction to the West College philosophy of learning, this course is a survey of classical literature that includes large lecture and small conference components as well as a built-in writing instruction mechanism. He was particularly drawn to the shared aspect of the course, saying, "I was really into the idea that we would all be reading and thinking about the same things. Everyone, regardless of who they are and where they come from, would literally be on the same page." And, while it was the case that the 350 or so first-years in Dylan's entering class were reading the same books each week, he was surprised to find that some of his classmates had already read what he saw as esoteric texts. This realization produced a divide within the classroom that fragmented discussion and made Dylan feel unprepared and out of step with his classmates:

> I know everyone hasn't read the same stuff, but man, I couldn't believe what some people had read. Thucydides, Sophocles, Euripides? Yep. Totally read it already. And they had really read it, they weren't posing. Because they would have these higher-order conversations with the professor about the texts and the rest of us would just sit there waiting for the discussion to come back down to earth. It was horrible. I felt like a total idiot.

For students like Dylan and Priya, the gap between how prepared they believed they were leaving high school, how prepared the college presumed they were when they were admitted, and comparatively how prepared some of their peers were for introductory first-year courses produced feelings of inadequacy and anger at not having a level playing field to learn on alongside their peers. Importantly, this is not an indication that students like Dylan and Priya were academically unqualified for the selective colleges they had gotten into. To the contrary, the majority of the students I talked to had scored in the top quartile on standardized tests (with a significant number having earned perfect SAT/ACT scores), were graduating at the top of their classes, and had taken a slew of honors and AP courses. They were highly qualified and had earned their spots in college, they just could not compete with the exceptional academic preparation of some of their more affluent peers.

Unfortunately, these early and unexpected academic hurdles had a deep impact on a number of students, as this was often the first time they were confronted with the feeling that they may not be capable or well suited for this kind of high-level academic endeavor. Often at the top of their class throughout K–12, they had excelled where their elementary and secondary school peers struggled—and benefited from the attention that comes from being considered the smartest student in the class, school, or town. Annie, an Asian American student at Midwest College, explained that during her first year she went through an intensive period of self-doubt around her academic ability:

> I was taking all the normal first-year classes, and I was doing horrible. I had a D in my math class. I'd barely ever gotten a B on anything before, let alone a D. I never thought it was even possible. And when it started happening—I, I just started to think maybe I was dumb this whole time and that I had gone to school with not very smart people, so that's why everyone thought I was smart . . . I stopped going to class because I was embarrassed. I was really, really depressed. I'd always been the smart one, and now I wasn't, and I didn't know who I was anymore. It was dark A.F. [as fuck].

And, while this is likely a common experience for high-achieving students from many backgrounds,[83] for students like Annie these experiences created stress and anxiety over their self-worth as students, their ability to keep up with peers and succeed, and concerns about maintaining scholarships and enrollment. This not only made them question their decisions about whether they had chosen the right academic "fit" in school, it also had the potential to significantly impact their academic outcomes, social development, and mental health, adding further challenges that many of their more well-prepared peers were able to avoid.

The early academic experiences of first-generation students who had attended selective private boarding schools for high school stood out when compared to their low-income and first-generation peers. Reinforcing prior research,[84] the high schools these students attended offered a range of courses that matched or exceeded the offerings at many colleges and universities across the country in regard to breadth of topic and rigor of instruction and put them at a major advantage when compared to their first-generation peers. Will, a Black third-year at Midwest College who was majoring in computer science (CS) and economics, noted that his private day school offered CS instruction that rivaled the course offerings available at Midwest. As a result, he was well ahead of the curve during his first year, noting: "A lot of people want to major in CS, but most don't make the cut—they weed you out. I came in having done CS all through high school and was fast-tracked, whereas a lot of my friends dropped because even the basic courses here are really high level."

Will was among the group of first-generation students who had taken theoretical calculus and read Thucydides's *History of the Peloponnesian War* in high school. This put him at a significant advantage when it came to pursuing majors that use introductory courses to "weed out" a percentage of prospective majors. More importantly, however, this allowed him the opportunity to maintain a sense of self as a high-achieving and legitimate student during college. Similarly, Aiden, a multiracial second-year at East College, contrasted the relative ease of his first-year experiences with those of his roommate Tobias, a first-generation student from a midlevel public high school district in Florida. He explained, "Tobias and I come from the same background, but I went to boarding school—I was way, way ahead academically. I had done a lot of stuff that he hadn't, and he really struggled in a way I never did. He really questioned his place here—and I just kept pushing ahead." Aiden was able to maintain a sense of legitimacy throughout his first year at East College in a way that his roommate was not. This uninterrupted academic self-image went a long way toward reconfirming that he belonged on campus, that he could achieve his academic and career goals, and that he had made the right decision when choosing East College—allowing him to avoid many of the complications and challenges his peers faced.

Following Jack's work on the "privileged poor" versus the "doubly disadvantaged":[85] if you were to try to place the early academic experiences of these low-income and first-generation students on a spectrum, you could place the ones that attended private boarding and day schools (the privileged poor) on one end—with both their preparation and perceptions being closely matched to course expectations. Along the other end you would place students who attended underfunded public schools (the doubly disadvantaged) as well as students that had attended a variety of other types of schools—including underfunded private schools, charter schools, and well-funded public schools. And, although these different types of schools gave them varying levels of preparation, the vast majority still came to college with pronounced mismatches in their perceptions about their preparation. Somewhere in the middle of this field of student preparation and perception are the students who benefited from the advance mentoring and guidance provided by outside scholarship and education organizations. These students reported that part of the programming and resources provided to them before starting college included dedicated conversations about what to expect academically at their new schools, which gave them what they categorized as a "more realistic perspective" and "an insider understanding" of what their first-year classes might be like.

For these students, this programming went well beyond the standard college-prep advice of staying on top of deadlines and attending a tutoring center when needed. Diamond, a multiracial student at East College, was selected in her final year of high school as a Jack Kent Cooke College Scholar and attended a multiday event that the Foundation refers to as "Scholars Weekend" in the summer before her first year of college. She explained that in addition to community-building events and informational sessions on topics like navigating financial aid, the event included a number of panels that focused on different aspects of what to expect in your first year of college. This included a panel that featured returning Scholars and alumni discussing their academic experiences, strategies, and challenges during their first year of college. She noted that she found the panelists' focus on detailing the gap between what they thought was going to happen and the stark academic reality of being a first-gen student eye-opening. Speaking from midway through her first year in college, she looked back on that panel and explained,

> That panel was so much more useful than the "preparing for college" class I took in my senior year. Like, that was what I needed more than like, how to take notes or whatever. I needed someone to be real with me and tell me what it's going to be like. And, whoa, they were real. Those were people that had already made it, and hearing that they struggled, that they weren't as prepared as they thought, that they had to catch up on the fly, that they felt stupid in their classes, that was mega . . . I'm not saying I had this magical moment where I was like 100% buying in, because I was for sure half saying [clicks tongue] "I'll be alright" in my head during the panel and half legit taking notes on what to expect. And I'm so serious that on the first day of classes things started to get wild, just like they said, and I just went back to that panel and thought about everything they said, and that helped me a lot. I knew I wasn't alone and, like, that this was normal. That was so mega.

In many ways, having access to the experiences of students and alumni that had already attended selective schools as first-generation students—a peer group that many first-generation students do not have—gave Diamond the information and perspective she needed to better align her perceptions about her academic preparedness and her expectations about coursework and classroom culture with the realities she was about to face. And, while this experience could not bridge the gap in Diamond's academic preparation, it normalized it and gave her the insight she needed to better understand and navigate the academic challenges she faced once she arrived at East College. This, in turn, helped mitigate many of the added stressors that her peers, who did not have access to this kind of advance information sharing and preparation, had to wrestle with during their first months on campus.

The variation in academic preparation, expectation, and experiences across these first-generation students is representative of a larger trend in higher education.[86] The disparities that arise out of some students experiencing a critical gap between expectations and experience push us to consider what selective colleges and universities can do to alleviate it. As with organizational structure and administrative demands, these schools are academically structured in a way that anticipates that all incoming students are equipped with a very high level of academic preparation. And, while that might have been the case historically when these schools did not readily admit students from diverse academic backgrounds, the modern student body at selective colleges and universities comes into the first day of school with a variety of experiences, strengths, and needs. A number of authors have pointed to the potential gains that could be reaped from providing extended academic support at selective schools, noting the successes that public four-year and community colleges have had in supporting the academic needs of first-generation students with these kinds of courses and programming.[87] However, this kind of structural intervention is unlikely to be adopted at the most selective schools because in many ways it is counter to their identity as institutions founded on academic rigor and elitism. In contrast, others have noted that adding these kinds of support to already bloated administrative structures does little to actually serve student academic needs and fails to provide tangible returns on investment.[88]

Perhaps another way to approach this is to consider what kinds of conversations colleges and even faculty can be having with students once they arrive on campus that will prepare them for the realities of academic expectations and classroom culture on these campuses. Providing students with exposure to the lived experiences of their peers seems to work well for those with access to this before starting college, but not everyone has these kinds of resources available to them. Adding panels and programming to new student orientation that address these issues, as some schools have already started doing, is a low-barrier intervention that might make a significant impact. And, in fact, there is evidence that when faculty do this work by simply preparing students for the possibility that their classmates may have different pre-college educational experiences and that a shared canon in the classroom is unlikely, it may go a long way toward helping students frame these disparities in a way that is normalized, as opposed to being tied to personal failings and inadequacies.[89]

ARRIVING ON AND DECIPHERING
THE SOCIAL SCENE

The final major landscape that first-generation and low-income students must navigate when they arrive at their selective colleges and universities is the social one. From the moment they arrive on campus, students are thrust into social interactions, relationship forming, and community building that can be overwhelming for everyone involved. In general, students from elite private high schools arrive on their college campuses knowing how to navigate and identify their position within the broader social field of their college and often have an ease with which they interact and communicate in these spaces.[90] This is due in some part to the knowledge, skills, and experiences—or cultural capital—that they gain at these schools,[91] but also due to their ability to leverage that capital to fully understand the expectations and demands of their role as a low-income and/or first-generation student on a selective college campus. Knowing how to fit the part or role of a first-generation student in highly selective educational spaces, or having what I term a "socially mobile habitus," expands options for engaging and navigating campus social spaces as low-income students. Aiden reflected on this ability to embrace being upwardly mobile on campus:

> From the first afternoon of orientation, I felt pretty comfortable in college. I remember going to the activities fair and thinking "okay—this looks just like high school. Those hipsters look like the art kids I know, the guys in that fraternity look like the super-elite kids, but the guys in that fraternity aren't, and those investment kids are totally the gunners." And I could already see what groups I had a chance with and which ones I might have problems with.

While the actors and relationships differed slightly, Aiden was able to connect the roles and relationships that he had learned in high school to his new context in college. Jenny, a second-generation Asian American first-year who attended a private day school, had a similar experience, crediting her high school for her knowledge of the social layout of her college. She likened her experience in high school to a "road map of the peeps and the beefs" that she would encounter in college, and that being aware of not only the people and groups (the peeps), but also the potential relationships, conflicts, and power dynamics between them (the beefs), helped her navigate her college's social landscape and find a place where she fit comfortably. Jenny's explanation here demonstrates that she understands not only the social landscape of selective higher education, but also her specific place in it as a first-generation student.

Students like Aiden and Jenny drew on their knowledge about the social landscape of their campuses, their positionality within these landscapes, and expectations around low-income student identity and behavior to inform their strategies for engaging different social spheres on campus. Many of these students drew directly on the experiences, socialization, and capital they gained during high school to integrate into and feel at ease in their campus communities at large as well as in more elite spaces or groups on campus. Will, a Black third-year from a private day school, applied for and joined his college's prestigious investment group within his first few weeks on campus. He described finding the club during an activities fair and approaching the student leaders, "chatting them up about finance, politics, and sports," and "dropping a subtle hint about my scholarship status, because that would get me diversity points." He had experience with a similar group in high school and felt confident that he would make it through the application and interview process. Will gained entrance into this group and was firmly in the leadership track of the organization by his third year in college.

When asked about his success in joining and embedding in this student group, Will emphasized that knowing how to interact in ways that aligned with the campus community culture was key to gaining at least partial entry into social spaces that required a high degree of cultural capital:

> The thing is that when you are a low-income student at an elite school, you have to figure out what that means. In high school, I learned that I had to act in a way that was expected by my school, my teachers, my classmates. I had to be refined enough to fit their expectations—but I also couldn't be a poser. I had to know my place and act like a scholarship kid acts, like I'm grateful and want what they have. Like you're told to color within the lines they set forth, but you have to use a slightly different shade than the students who are born into this world.

Will's experiences with engaging in the investment club highlight how students from elite schools successfully employ integration strategies by drawing on past experiences and knowledge to embody their low-income status in a way that is well received and legitimated in interaction.

Because Will came to college with a well-developed set of strategies around the embodiment and performance of his low-income status in elite spaces—that were based on four years of experience, successes, and failures—he was able to effectively assert a socially mobile habitus once he arrived on his elite college campus and, in turn, experienced ease when attempting to integrate into elite spaces. Will's experience highlights how Shamus Khan's concept of "ease"[92] translates into higher education spaces. Students like Will feel and act in ways that demonstrate their comfort, or belongingness, in elite higher education spaces. What is important to note, however, is that students like Will are not simply mimicking their more affluent peers in an attempt to don the identity of a student from an elite background. Instead, they are performing the very specific role that sits at the intersections of their identities as a student at a selective college, who comes from a low-income background, and is actively becoming socially mobile. This role, like any other, has expectations.[93] Students are required to demonstrate their legitimacy as part of the elite via their cultural capital, while still acknowledging their outsider status as a low-income student via disclosing their scholarship status or personal background. They must do this in a way that proves they are grateful for the opportunity to become elite while also acknowledging that they will never become a full-fledged member. And they must do this in the most subtle and socially acceptable ways. Students like Will have the advantage of having honed their performance of this role during high school and come to college with a far more developed socially mobile habitus than the majority of their first-generation peers.

Without this socially mobile habitus, many first-generation students struggled to identify and navigate their positions within the broader social landscape of their colleges. Faced with demands to learn the nuances of an unfamiliar social context, many of these students expressed a feeling of being campus outsiders. While this feeling did not exclude students from attempting to find their place on campus, it often limited their engagement strategies. Without the information needed to identify the specific positionality of being low-income in elite educational spaces, these students could not successfully embody a socially mobile habitus. For many of these students, not having command over a socially mobile habitus likely mitigated some aspects of their mobility during college. By existing outside of the more elite social groups on campus, these students had less access to the social capital considered to be one of the most beneficial aspects of attending an elite college or university, such as influential networks.

Angel, a Latinx first-year at East College who had graduated at the top of his class and captained the quiz bowl team at his well-resourced public school, noted how the differences between his high school and college made him feel ignorant. "I had never seen kids like that before—they all had yachts, and it was like they somehow all knew each other from summer programs or whatever. I felt like I was missing a beat. I was clueless to the like hierarchy or whatever—I couldn't see it because where I'm from, we are all in the same lot." Similarly, Lexi, a Black fourth-year at East College who had excelled academically and socially at her underresourced high school, had a difficult time when confronted with attempting to piece together how the different groups she encountered fit together in the social field. She drew on a popular movie trope to describe her process:

> You know that classic scene from just about every teen movie? Where the new kid is being shown around campus and someone is pointing out all the different social groups? The jocks, the goths, the popular kids—it's kind of like that except it's the trust funds, the consultants, and the legacies—oh, and no one tells you. You have to figure that out on your own, and you have to figure out how everyone fits together or doesn't. And no one tells you how it is that you're different and how that is going to matter.

The conceptual road map of peers Lexi developed during high school could not help her make sense of the social fabric of her college campus or where she might fit into it. And while she pieced together her own partial road map of the social field over time, it was an extended process. She noted that it wasn't until her third year in college that she felt like she had figured out the who's who of campus and how they were connected together. As it was, she still felt that in her final semester of college she had a limited understanding of this part of college, and that the details about the form, function, and differences between more characteristically affluent groups, like elite clubs and Greek life, would remain a mystery. Although Lexi had done her homework to the best of her ability on what college life would be like at East College, her resources were limited to online and media depictions that did not quite match up with the reality she found on campus.

Without the knowledge, experience, or cultural capital that comes with an elite high school background, many students like Lexi struggled with identifying the right approach toward engaging with the social landscape at their colleges. Tiffany, a White third-year at Midwest College from an underresourced school, arrived at college with dreams of Greek life and getting involved in student government. She was met with resistance from her affluent peers. Instead of matching with a sorority or finding friendship in student leadership—an activity she had been deeply involved with in high school—she spent the bulk of her first year confused and heartbroken. She noted, looking back, that her strategy had been destined for failure: "When I got here, I had this idea in my mind of what a student from my school should look like and act like. I had watched a lot of movies [laughs]. So, I tried my best to fit that part. I dressed like the rich girls I had saw on my visit and came in thinking that it would be easy enough. But it totally didn't work because everyone knew I was on scholarship."

It is important to note that Tiffany's status as a low-income student was not what locked her out of participating in these predominantly affluent communities on campus. As prior research[94] has established, students from across socioeconomic backgrounds have the opportunity to actively participate in campus social scenes—albeit to varying degrees of success. Instead, it was her lack of knowledge and experience around what it meant to be a low-income student in these spaces, a lack of a socially mobile habitus, that made her affluent peers see her performance as illegitimate. A number of other students also described their first attempts to access these elite groups as trying to mimic, or pass as, a wealthy student—a strategy that quickly failed. Without access to the knowledge needed to produce a socially mobile habitus, first-generation students like Tiffany often lost out on opportunities to engage in entire social spaces on their campuses, limiting their access to the critically valuable social capital that these spaces bring to the table at selective colleges and universities.

While experience and time eventually enabled some students like Tiffany and Lexi to produce an acceptable socially mobile habitus, the learning curve was notably steep. Most students reported abandoning these efforts and switching strategies for engagement—noting that they did not have the time or energy to continue pursuing initial visions of how their college life would take shape. For some students, this meant limiting their friendships to other low-income and first-generation students and engaging primarily in student groups and programming that targeted students from historically underrepresented backgrounds. Other students described how the frustration and low self-esteem they experienced after trying and failing to integrate into social groups on campus led to experiences with isolation.

Nicki, a multiracial third-year at East College, had excelled both academically and socially at her underresourced high school, and arrived at college excited about forming friendships with students in her women-only residence hall. However, she found it hard to connect with this community of young women who were largely from affluent and highly educated backgrounds. She spoke at length about how she struggled to find her place in college and how the radical differences between her poorly funded rural high school and her elite college in the Northeast impacted her ability to understand and connect with her classmates. Halfway into her third year, she noted, "I'm still struggling to feel like I belong here. I have one very close friend—but I don't feel connected here. I just couldn't ever break into a group here, I couldn't figure out how these people worked . . . what they wanted. So, I stopped trying."

Like Tiffany, Nicki did not have the experience or capital needed to produce a socially mobile habitus and struggled to find community within more elite circles on her campus. Early experiences like these often formed persistent social hurdles for low-income students without elite educational backgrounds. Although Nicki was able to form at least one significant friendship on campus, the fact that she continued to feel isolated and disengaged from her campus community well into her third year of college is of concern. As prior research demonstrates,[95] this kind of isolation has direct impacts on student achievement and outcomes and is often a major contributing factor to why Nicki and students like her struggle to keep up with coursework and experience below-average GPAs. In addition, this kind of isolation—whether intentional or not—prevents students from forming relationships with other students across their campus communities and accessing the valuable social capital contained in those networks. These relationships and social capital matter even for students who manage to achieve academic accolades and graduate—as their limited networks may have long-term impacts on the shape of their trajectory of upward mobility.

THE EASE TO PUSH BACK AND ACT UP

Not all students with a socially mobile habitus chose to use it to navigate elite social circles in the same way. In contrast, some students reported that they knew how to move in those circles, but preferred to distance themselves from their more affluent peers. These students often joined or formed student groups focused on identity-based activism, and often led efforts to expand resources and support for marginalized student groups on their campuses. They often regarded themselves as part of grassroots efforts on campus and vocally critiqued the elite aspects of their campus cultures and the orientation of the administration toward low-income and other students from underrepresented groups. Yet, at the same time, many of these students cited their development of a socially mobile habitus as the reason they were able to successfully craft and assert this particular embodiment of their identification as low-income on campus. For these students, it was the development of knowledge, capital, and ease on campus that gave them the confidence and comfort they needed to push back on their campuses—often in ways that mirrored those of their more affluent peers. Andrea, a multiracial fourth-year at East College who had attended a preparatory school, said explicitly:

> You know, I learned how to play the game of this kind of place a long time ago in prep school. I speak the language and have the knowledge that rich students do. That gives me power and confidence. Power to say "fuck it" and wear my hoops and my kicks when I want to. Because when it comes down to it, I know what it takes to succeed here. I can be the well-behaved scholarship student, but I can also try and make the space for people like me a little bit larger and more authentic.

Like Will, who drew on his experiences in private day school to help him secure a position in his school's elite investing club, Andrea drew on the knowledge and capital she had gained while attending an elite prep school to inform the way she chose to embody her position as a socially mobile low-income student attending an elite college—though she chose to engage in building a community outside of this world rather than fit herself within it. In many ways, the capital she had gained during high school gave Andrea the confidence she needed to actively participate in long-standing facets of selective higher education in the United States—protest, activism, and nonconformity.

It is important to note, however, that students like Andrea and Will were not confined to a single strategy. In fact, having command of the requisite cultural capital along with the knowledge of their position in the social field of their college often allowed these students to pivot between different communities and strategies of embodiment with ease. For instance, Andrea explained that not only did she feel the confidence to assert her authentic self on campus while pushing for structural change via protest, she also credited her experiences in prep school as the source of her comfort in navigating institutional structures and engaging campus leadership in partnerships and initiatives. This comfort and skill at being an active and engaged socially mobile first-generation student on campus opened up valuable opportunities for students like Andrea to gain access to further resources and to build meaningful ties with students, faculty, and staff from across their campus communities.

In contrast, some low-income and first-generation students' lack of comfort, confidence, and ease in their campus spaces constrained their desire to participate in political activities like protests on their campuses. Even when these students expressed oppositional ideas or affects, they often viewed the kind of oppositional collective action that some students engaged in as an activity out of bounds for most low-income students. David, an Asian American in his second year at East College, noted:

> You know, there has been some protesting and activism on campus around financial aid and low-income students and also about racism. And like, I support that, but I can't be in there doing that shit. I have a scholarship, and if I lose it, I'm done. A lot of the students that are really active are rich, so they don't have to worry . . . but my friend Andrea is part of it too, and she went to a fancy school. She's way less afraid than I am.

As David highlighted, low-income students can experience a tension between their desire to support efforts around social change and their need to maintain their financial aid and enrollment status. Many students from these populations feel like they must weigh their desires around activism with the potential impact it might have on their status as minority students on financial aid in a way that their peers may not. Unlike Andrea, David did not have the experience or exposure to know how to manage these competing desires in a way that balances meeting the expectations around his positionality as a low-income student and pushing the boundaries of elite academic space through activism and protest. Because of this, he was faced with far more limited strategies for engaging and navigating his place on campus—missing out on the opportunities that students like Andrea have to build further capital and actively shape and change their schools through activism and protest.

THE IMPACT OF CREATING CONCEPTS

The experiences highlighted above align with prior research on the notion that not all first-generation and low-income student experiences at selective colleges and universities play out the same.[96] As established in Anthony Jack's research,[97] students who make up the "privileged poor" come to these colleges from private boarding and day schools with knowledge and capital that their counterparts from (mostly underfunded) public schools included in the "doubly disadvantaged" do not have. This produces bifurcated experiences as these two groups of students navigate central aspects of college. There are real advantages to having gone to prep school, and as I show, additional advantages to having the support and resources of an outside organization to guide you through these critical first moments in college. Perhaps even more than realized. These divides in knowledge, experience, confidence, and ease produce lasting disparities in how students navigate a college's organizational spaces, their academic confidence and outcomes, and the relationships and communities they form.

This divide between the exceptional experiences of a select group of elite students and the majority of first-generation students became important in a number of ways for the students I talked to. First, many students were aware of differences between themselves and other first-generation students, but they could not pinpoint why they were having experiences and outcomes that were divergent from other first-generation students they considered their peers. For instance, as Nicki struggled with classes and finding friends at East College, another first-generation multiracial student in her year, named Wesley, appeared to be finding quick success academically and socially. Nicki explained that she knew Wesley was on the same scholarship as her, but was confused at why they were having such different experiences at East. She said, "Wesley really has everything figured out. I don't get what he's doing right and I'm doing wrong. Sometimes I think that East is just hard for first-gens, but then I see Wes doing his thing and I think maybe it's just me?" For Nicki, Wesley was the comparison group that she was measuring her success against, and without the knowledge that Wesley had gone to a private boarding school that prepared him for the academic and social aspects of college, she assumed that the differences she perceived were due to personal failure and not structural inequality.

A number of upperclassmen who went to public schools told me that they didn't even know that selective private boarding schools and day schools existed in the United States until they came to college. They assumed that schools like this were exclusively European or the construction of television and novels. These moments of realization that the internal comparisons within a campus first-generation student community were not completely equal helped students understand the differences they had noticed. For instance, Angel recalled how he felt when he learned that the other two first-generation students he knew on campus had gone to private boarding schools:

> I had no idea that schools like that were even out there! When I found out they [his friends] went there [private boarding school]—it made so much more sense. I get that they're still first-gens, but really they're, like, way closer to the rich kids than they are to me . . . Like, they're part of the Canada Goose[98] crew and I'm just an ugly duckling. Okay, maybe not part of the Canada Goose crew, but totally Canada Goose Adjacent.

However, as Angel's explanation shows, this knowledge not only helped him understand differences, but also became a way to differentiate between the type of first-generation student he was versus the type that his friends were.

This process of making distinctions between subsections of the first-generation population was something that I found across a number of the campuses I visited. Interestingly, on some campuses this divide within the first-generation and low-income student population ended up becoming concretized through the adoption of Jack's concepts as a way to think and talk about differences within their own communities. Jack's article that predates *The Privileged Poor* came out in 2016, with his book following in 2019. Jack's major arguments were making the rounds across college campuses, higher education platforms, conferences, classrooms, and popular media while I was doing fieldwork for this project. By the time I was in my last stage of fieldwork, I noticed that some students had begun using the central concepts of the book as part of their own understanding of their experiences and the experiences of others in their campus communities. They were drawing lines around who they perceived as the "privileged poor" and the "doubly disadvantaged" on their campuses. And, while this dichotomy is a useful analytical tool for understanding variation in low-income and first-generation college student populations, it is just that—an analytical tool that is perhaps more useful for thinking sociologically about a complex process than it is for students to use as a means for dividing up a community population that contains far more individual nuance than a dichotomy can encapsulate. And yet, they do.

I found that the ways some student communities used their interpretation of these terms to make distinctions often left other students feeling alienated, attacked, or misunderstood. For instance, some students noted that their peers' interpretations of first-generation status and privilege did not always take into consideration the full spectrum of an individual's background or experience. In particular, students felt that characteristics like coming from an immigrant family or having an unstable family life could essentially be erased because they had attended a school with high resources. For instance, Will had attended an elite boarding school for high school but had experienced periods of homelessness during his childhood and teenage years. Going to boarding school certainly gave him the education and experiences he needed to be academically successful at Midwest College, but, as he explained, his peers could not see past this privilege and understand that he faced other challenges, such as living a deeply erratic and uncertain life. He explained, "Right now I'm not sure where my mom and my little brother are. Her phone is turned off, and the shelter they were at hasn't seen them in a few days . . . So, I have to figure that out before break so I can find them—that's what my end-of-semester wrap-up looks like." Will went on to further explain that he had tried to form friendships with many of the first-generation students on his campus, but felt like he was treated like an outsider due to his boarding school status. Although he had friends at Midwest College from across socioeconomic backgrounds, he wished that he had more friends who could relate to his experiences at home. He said, "They treat me like I'm not actually firstgen, and that hurts. Being first-gen is at the center of my experience, and I'd love to connect with them about that, but I don't feel like I have the space to do that right now."

Will's frustration with the narrow lens through which the firstgeneration student experience was defined by some of his firstgeneration peers was shared with a number of students who came to college from well-funded public high schools. Although not defined as part of the "privileged poor" by Jack, the resources and rankings attributed to these schools were considered substantial enough on some campuses to differentiate these students from their less advantaged peers. Angie, a multiracial second-year at East College, moved in with her aunt in order to go to the highly ranked public high school in her district. "I had to leave my family, my home, to go there. My dad is on disability, and my mom works in a cannery. I'd hardly say I am privileged. But they [the students who consider themselves the "doubly disadvantaged"] have their little club, and I'm not in it." In many ways, Will and Angie's status as students from well-resourced schools trumped every other aspect of their backgrounds—by being marked as part of the "privileged poor," the legitimacy of their first-generation status was called into question and effectively denied by the peers they needed the most. These students' experiences highlight both how the divides within low-income and first-generation student populations operate interpersonally as well as the role that academic sociological concepts have had in impacting students' frameworks around these divisions. In many ways, the work of sociology is to explain and give name to complex social processes that people experience in their daily lives. It is rare, however, to also see how these terms come to hold meaning and begin shaping the actual discourses of those communities.

The Polishing Process

On a particularly cold afternoon at the beginning of the spring semester, I accompanied a group of first-generation students to an event on networking and navigating career fields. The event included a panel of local early career professionals in the areas of business and finance followed by a "happy hour" style event where students would mingle with guests from these industries. The posters that could be found across campus advertised the event as an opportunity to learn from, meet, and talk to professionals in these fields while honing your "networking and schmoozing skills." Admission to the event was free, and the required dress code was advertised as "business dress." As our group wound its way across campus, the students and I chatted about what we were hoping the event would include. Whittaker, an Asian American student in his second year of college, enthusiastically listed off the different hors d'oeuvres that he hoped would be there, taking the time to describe the taste and texture of a tart (as if he were a TV-personality chef) that he had had at a similar event a few months earlier. The group chuckled at his description while Luis, a Latinx student also in his second year, backed Whittaker up by saying, "Yo, you know the food is going to be lit! I'm about to learn *at least* [his emphasis] three new food words today!" This turned the group's chuckle into uproarious laughter as Luis turned to his friend Kristen, a White student in her fourth year, and asked her what she was hoping to find at the event. To which she simply replied, "A job, duh!"

A number of the students in the group echoed Kristen's desire to find a job or an internship at the event, with Alicia, a Latinx student in her first year, chiming in that she was feeling stressed out about the networking aspect of the event. "I always get too sweaty at these things. I don't ever know how to talk to professionals. I just feel so awkward and out of place. Don't y'all?" A few of the younger students nodded at Alicia's admission of nervousness about the event as Kristen put her arm around her, saying, "You're going to do great! Just remember what Angela [a staff member] covered in the workshop. Follow their lead and ask open-ended questions. Make eye contact and connect with them about common interests. Just breathe." Alicia nodded her head along as Kristen continued to list off the pointers from the workshop they had attended the week earlier on networking and connecting with professionals and seemed to visibly relax as she quietly whispered to herself on repeat, "You've got this. You can do this. You know what you're doing," as we walked through the main doors to the event location.

It was a beautifully decorated space with a table-length charcuterie spread flanked by a dessert table, both gorgeously decorated with local flowers at the center of each elaborate arrangement. Bite-sized foods sat in waiting for the reception. Bartenders stood in the back behind a full bar, and servers finished their setup while event participants filed into the adjacent lecture hall. As our group started to file in, Whittaker peeled off and jogged over to the group of event staff. He embraced a friend who was a student worker with catering services and had a quick conversation before he came jogging back to us, his tie bouncing across his chest. He smiled widely and mouthed, "They have the tarts" at the few of us who were watching him as we waited to enter the room. This got a good chuckle out of all of us as we headed into the room and settled in for the panel about transitioning into early professional careers after college.

Events like the one described here happen weekly at selective colleges and universities across the United States. Many of these are developed as a way to explicitly improve and increase the skills, resources, and knowledge—or varying forms of capital—of first-generation and other marginalized students.[99] The investment in this kind of programming by higher education comes in large part from social scientific research that posits that it is deficiencies in economic, social, and cultural capital that are the primary engine behind documented disparities in outcomes and experiences for marginalized students and their more advantaged peers.[100] These concerted efforts to develop underrepresented students' cultural and social capital found in exclusive higher education spaces—be it colleges and universities or scholarship organizations—have become a highly effective "polishing process" that works to fundamentally change these students. It provides students with new forms of knowledge, skills, and experiences that they need to successfully navigate and belong in the worlds of selective higher education and, eventually, the upper-middle class. But it also begins to take some things away. If you imagine the relationship that selective colleges and universities have with first-generation students as akin to the relationship that a processing plant has with raw minerals like diamonds and other rare gems, the effects of this process start to become clear. Just as diamonds enter these plants in their raw form, with rough edges, unwanted blemishes, and mineral deposits that must be removed in order to be valuable, first-generation students arrive at selective campuses with ways of speaking, thinking, acting, and seeing the world that—from an institutional perspective—must be changed in order to succeed on campus. And, while this process is not inherently a bad thing—in fact, it is part of the constellation of reasons that many of these students choose selective institutions in the first place—its role in shaping the experiences, outcomes, and trajectories of first-generation students is critically important to consider.

In this chapter, I will detail the most common forms of programming and resources that make up the structure of the polishing process and describe the capital-centered institutional narratives that colleges and educational organizations have about their role in student support and success. I will demonstrate that these programs that undergird much of the polishing process are quite good at what they set out to do—which is rewrite first-generation students' forms of capital in order for them to better align with their campus communities, cultures, and expectations. This ultimately improves students' social experiences and academic outcomes as designed, but it also fundamentally changes their perspectives, tastes and preferences, frameworks, and identities. Finally, I will provide a window into the different ways in which first-generation students think about and experience these forms of programming, contrasting students who see the polishing process as either a welcomed, neutral, or even novel side effect of attending a selective college with world-class amenities, resources, and opportunities with students who struggle with, and at times push back against, programming that they perceive to be erasing or devaluing their backgrounds, experiences, and identities as first-generation students and members of their campus communities. These students' experiences, and the experiences of students in the remaining chapters of this book, will provide a critical lens for considering the complexities of the polishing process and its full impact on first-generation student experiences, outcomes, and trajectories.

PROGRAMMATIC INTERVENTIONS FOR CAPITAL DEVELOPMENT

A significant amount of social scientific research has demonstrated that first-generation students struggle during their transitions to college.[101] As I have shown in chapter 2, the hurdles that students face are tied in many ways to the gaps in resources, knowledge, and skills—or forms of capital—that they arrive at college with relative to their more affluent and continuing-generation peers. A significant investment in higher education in the enhancement and restructuring of programming and resources for marginalized students emerged out of the findings of this research—starting with efforts to eliminate gaps in these students' economic capital.[102] Selective colleges and universities across the country have developed special scholarship programs and tuition waivers to increase access to students with family incomes that were institutionally considered low-income. Many of these programs saw a positive impact on first-generation student enrollment and ensured that these students would graduate with minimal to no student loans.[103] Subsequent research coming from the social sciences then indicated that even with tuition waivers, many first-generation students struggled to meet even their most basic financial needs during college.[104] This spurred an additional wave of programs and support that—at the most well-resourced campuses—included living stipends, cold-weather outfitting, waivers for costly campus events, travel stipends, financial and housing support during academic breaks, and support for other vital resources. These programs have had a net positive impact on student experiences and outcomes during college and continue to develop and expand on the campuses that have the financial means to provide them.[105]

Although these initial interventions that focused on providing funding and financial resources—or economic capital—to first-generation students were widely successful, continued research indicated that disparities in the experiences and outcomes of first-generation students and their peers continued to persist even with these financial supports.[106] This set of findings spurred a new argument from higher education researchers—that these students did not have the valuable cultural capital they needed to easily navigate the academic demands, social expectations, and cultural nuances found at selective colleges and universities. This lack of capital has been seen as holding them back from fully integrating into their campus communities, impacting their success and outcomes, and preventing them from forming the valuable social connections that come from attending schools with the most elite student and alumni communities.[107]

These arguments produced an explosion of programming, resources, and staffing across selective campuses nationwide in an attempt to infuse formal opportunities for building cultural and social capital into the college experiences of first-generation students.[108] Many of these campuses now offer their first-generation students mentoring and bridge programs, free and subsidized cultural programming and outings, formal and informal social events, workshops on building skills to aid in their academic development, opportunities to network and build connections with influential alumni and community members, and countless other resources. All are designed to give them opportunities to build skills, knowledge, experiences, and relationships needed to thrive as socially mobile first-generation students. These opportunities form a layer of intentional programming that overlays the more organic ways of developing cultural and social capital that come from merely living and going to school in these elite environments[109]—coming together in an effort to "level the playing field"[110] for these students.

It is important to note that much of this programming (and the research it is rooted in) has historically taken what is referred to as a "deficit" approach when framing the purpose and need of this capital-building work. Researchers, policy proponents, and higher education administrators who operate within this framework focus on how gaps in capital between underrepresented and normative student populations produce difference, and often frame these gaps as students being at a deficit or lacking the capital they need to succeed.[111] The deficit perspective remains widely used in social science research and policy development and has become a primary framework for guiding the development and deployment of programming for marginalized student populations—most notably first-generation students and students of color.[112] While the inequalities in resources that are central to this research are critically important and significant factors to consider, the deficit perspective has been heavily criticized as normalizing the dominance of elite forms of capital over capital readily available to marginalized communities.[113] And, as the experiences and perspectives of students in this chapter and the one that follow will demonstrate, an assumption that this kind of programming merely adds to the existing capital a student has when they arrive at college misunderstands the transformative properties of the work that colleges as "people-changing organizations"[114] are doing and the impact that this is having. Instead of merely providing students with something more, this programming comes together to form a polishing process that fundamentally changes these students.

ORGANIC CAPITAL DEVELOPMENT ON CAMPUS

It is important to first note that social scientists have pointed to the somewhat organic process through which students gain capital during college by interacting with wealthy peers and faculty, attending classes, and living on campus.[115] And, in many ways, this semi-organic process of absorbing capital through interaction is still central to the first-generation student experience. For instance, Jasmine, an Asian American third-year at East College, noted, "If you spend enough time around rich kids, you start to pick things up. Their language, their mannerisms. If you pick that up, you end up less outside the loop." Similarly, during Whitney's second year at Midwest College, she talked at length about how she had framed her first-year experience as one of learning inside and outside the classroom. She described coming into college feeling like an outsider. To resolve this feeling, she worked to find ways that would help her fit in better with her wealthy peers:

> I think I was the only first-gen on my floor as a first-year. Everyone had a lot of money, and—and it made me feel like I was from a different planet or country or something . . . I spent most of that year just listening and watching, you know? The less I gave away about myself, the less out of place I seemed . . . and the more I learned from them, the more I could act like I belonged and knew those things all along.

In many ways, the experiences that Jasmine and Whitney described align closely to classic sociological theories of how identities are interactionally produced and maintained.[116] Whether they knew it or not, the students in Whitney's residence hall gave her the crucial information she needed to begin aligning herself more closely with what she saw as being a normal student at Midwest College. While this informal accumulation of capital is part and parcel of the highly selective college experience for many first-generation students, it is enhanced significantly by formal institutional programming designed for gaining access to the skills, knowledge, and experiences—or capital—that these students need to be successful during college.

PROGRAMMING APPROACHES AND STAFF PERSPECTIVES

The campuses that I spent time on boast extensive programming that aims to increase the academic skills, cultural capital, and social capital of its most marginalized student populations—with some campuses having programming designed exclusively for first-generation students. The staff and administrators in charge of developing and producing this programming are well informed on the social scientific research about higher education and understand the critical value that these forms of capital have on student experiences and outcomes. They often described the work they were doing on their campuses explicitly in terms of reducing gaps or deficits by promoting the formation of capital and skills. For instance, when Linda, a student services staff member, described a new program her office had developed around making office hours more accessible to first-generation students, she referenced some of the more recent social scientific literature on the subject as the impetus for the project and talked about how the design of the program was informed by other efforts around capital promotion: "We tried a new thing this year where we had select faculty members hold office hours here in the student center . . . We were trying to break down the barriers around going to office hours for our marginalized students. They just don't have the capital to know they should go—and a lot of them are afraid to go even after we tell them what to do. So, we brought the faculty to them." A number of staff members discussed how they tried to pair opportunities for increasing social capital via specialized networking

events with "teachable moments" around how to prepare for and be-
have in these situations. Carla, a student services staff member at a different college, described one such event: "For a lot of our students, this
is the first time they will interact and network with professionals in their
potential fields. We see it as a practice run for the future and take this
opportunity to have real conversations with the students about how they
should dress and hold themselves and interact with folks in these situations." She went on to explain that many of the students she worked with
described being uncomfortable in more formal settings. Part of her job
was to try to help them achieve the same kind of embodied and casual
"ease"[117] that their peers have in a variety of contexts.

Programming designed to produce this ease or sense of belonging and comfort in different university spaces was heavily represented
across the campuses I spent time on. A lot of them focused on ease in
classroom and academic spaces. For instance, I accompanied a couple
of students to a workshop aimed at new students that focused on how
to feel confident and comfortable in class discussions. This 90-minute
session covered the nuances of navigating the Socratic-style classes,
delved into norms and expectations around tone and approach when
disagreeing with classmates and faculty interpretations of materials,
and included an overview of some terms on concepts they were likely
to encounter. At the end of the session, there was an informal reception
with snacks and beverages, and I had the opportunity to sit down and
talk to Jennifer, a student services staff member, about the idea behind
this workshop. She explained that this was the first time they were running this particular workshop, and that it had emerged out of watching
some underrepresented students struggle with academic content and
a classroom setting that their more affluent peers were more familiar
with. She noted,

> Some of our students come out of their first week of classes shell-
> shocked. They're thrown into the deep end of the pool here and ex-
> pected to be able to swim. It turns out a lot of them are drowning . . .
> I had a student tell me last year that he felt like he was learning a sec-
> ond language—and this was in his *required* [her emphasis] first-year
> courses. I started thinking about the foundations of this workshop after
> that conversation. I thought of it like "If we provide tutoring for French
> and calculus, which are both languages our students need to learn,

then why not provide tutoring in learning to speak elite academics?" and voilà! This workshop was born [laughs].

As Jennifer's language analogy highlights, programming like this has the ability to mitigate unnecessary setbacks by demystifying social and academic norms on campus, giving students the knowledge they need to better navigate these situations as they adjust to college.

In many ways, capital programming has become part and parcel of program development for underrepresented students at selective colleges and universities. This extends into providing opportunities for underrepresented students to have the same cultural experiences as their more affluent peers. During my fieldwork, I saw countless flyers and emails that advertised off-campus outings for first-generation students and students from other marginalized backgrounds. These programs ran the gamut from museum trips, theater shows, and architecture tours to mountain climbing, fine dining, and chocolate-tasting demonstrations, and are a common facet of life at a selective college. When I was a first-generation student attending a selective college, I benefited from a significant amount of programming like this. At the time, I simply saw these trips—like museum tours and getting to eat at a Michelin-star restaurant (which I had no idea what that was at the time)—as the perks of attending a school like this. What I didn't realize is that these opportunities were part of a much deeper project to expose me to experiences that would give me the cultural capital I needed to thrive alongside my more affluent peers on campus and into my postgraduation career and life.

The staff I spent time with emphasized that these programs were in fact designed to have a dual character of fun and learning. Hannah, a student services staff member, described a recent theater trip in this way: "The *Hamilton* event was more than just about getting to see an amazing show. It was about getting these students into that space and exposing them to the beauty of theater—and giving them the capital they need to feel confident in those contexts." Winston, an administrator at another college, echoed Hannah's framework and described an institutional desire for outcomes around student programming in this dualistic fun/benefit perspective: "Of course, in many ways we want the students to have fun—to take a break from studying and get out in the world. We also want them to be exposed to art and culture and experiences that are new for them—things they wouldn't have had a chance to see or do before coming here." As these staff perspectives highlight, the dual nature of this programming is intentional and seen as adding valuable cultural capital for these students that will aid them in their trajectories through college and beyond.

Enhancing capital in order to produce a sense of ease or comfort in social interactions and network building was another major focus of the programming on the campuses I spent time on. One variety of this is represented in the events detailed in this chapter's opening vignette. This multifaceted event included a pre-event workshop where staff walked students through the basic tenets of networking, including where to place a name tag so that it would be directly in your interlocutor's line of eyesight, how to join and exit conversations, standard questions to ask, balancing providing information and avoiding oversharing, and even breathing techniques for soothing social anxiety. This how-to session was followed by an opportunity a week later for these students to apply their newfound skills and knowledge in an applied setting at the early career professional panel event—inclusive of fancy dessert tarts.

During the reception part of that event, I spent some time chatting with the college staff and administrators that had put the event on. Everyone expressed how pleased they were with the evening and the student turnout. Trinity, a staff member who worked with underrepresented student populations on campus, including first-generation students, noted that her students had been both nervous and excited for the event, and that it had been the primary topic of discussion in the days leading up to it. She went on to express how great an opportunity events like this were for students, but especially students who might not have access to settings like this otherwise. And she noted that an event like this was simultaneously about the experience and the potential for making connections for opportunities like internships. Bridget, an administrator, nodded in agreement to her assessment and said, "Events like these are a win-win all around. The students who need this exposure get what they need, but all of the students can benefit from it, which makes it an easy yes." The group agreed as we moved on to a rousing discussion of ranking the desserts we had each sampled.

Trinity and Bridget's perspectives not only highlight the perceived value this kind of programming has for underrepresented students, but also provide an albeit brief window into the constraints that staff operate within when developing and justifying this kind of programming on campus. A number of them expressed stress and tension over institutional frameworks around programming designated for students from marginalized backgrounds. Many of them noted that programming like this had become an expected cornerstone of the work done in student services, but that it was difficult to get approval for new or enhanced programming without (1) being able to demonstrate the benefits and takeaways—like the cultivation of cultural capital—that underrepresented students will gain as part of attending a given event or program, and (2) preferably being able to merge specialized programming with an event that could demonstrably benefit the broader student body. These constraints left some staff feeling stymied in their ability to develop new or experimental programming that pushed the boundaries of best practices and trapped in replicating programming that had been deemed the most cost- and impact-effective by administrators who were often removed from the actual application of this programming.

Parallel Programming from External Organizations

Campus administrators weren't the only ones hoping to provide opportunities for first-gen students. In fact, many external education and scholarship organizations provide the students they serve with similar and overlapping opportunities, resources, and experiences, thus adding to the capital-accumulation efforts. For example, about a third of the students who I spent time with were recipients of a Jack Kent Cooke Scholarship, and as a result benefited from ongoing programming from this scholarship organization. This included attending a "Scholars Weekend" during the summer before matriculation and often again during the summer between years in college. This multiday event includes an introduction for new Scholars to the ins and outs of how their scholarship works, workshops and information sessions on navigating the demands and expectations of college, and social events designed to build community within the scholarship community. Many of the workshops mirrored the ones I found on campuses across the country, with a focus on providing panels and instruction on understanding academic expectations, navigating interactions like office hours and classroom discussion, and pursuing networking and career opportunities. Like colleges and universities, this scholarship foundation frames this kind of programming as an opportunity to fill in the perceived gaps in knowledge, experience, and capital that these students are coming to college with. Eliza, a higher education staff member at the Foundation, reflected on the purpose of this programming by noting,

> As you know, it's all about capital. Most of our Scholars come from backgrounds that aren't going to give them what they need to have smooth transitions into college. There are a lot of gaps in what they know compared to other students coming from wealth and education. So, we have a series of programming that is basically designed to make up for that. They're not getting it from their high schools or families, so we step in to provide it for them. And the idea is that this will help close the gap between them and their peers and make it easier for them to thrive on campus.

Eliza's framework around this kind of targeted programming mirrors the frameworks expressed by staff and administrators at the selective colleges and universities I spent time with. In many ways, this is due to the fact that staff across these different organizations in the sphere of higher education are all actively engaged in staying up to date with best practices for supporting first-generation and other marginalized students. The research coming out of the social sciences and education fields demonstrates the importance of capital and the push for programming and interventions that aim to improve capital among marginalized student populations.[118] This, in turn, influences a continued investment in this programming as well as the frameworks and language that staff and organizations use around their efforts—creating a uniform perspective and approach across institutional actors in higher education.

In addition to these forms of more targeted programming, Scholars Weekend includes a formal banquet where incoming scholarship recipients, returning Scholars and alumni, staff, and invited guests don formalwear for an evening of celebration. The night usually includes a reception with passed canapés, followed by a formal banquet featuring a guest speaker whose ranks over the years have included Arne Duncan, Jesse Jackson, and Colin Powell. Individuals are preassigned to their tables of 8–10 new and returning Scholars and staff who are often sorted by academic interest. This is a white tablecloth affair with a multicourse meal served by an enormous team of waitstaff that winds their way through the tables effortlessly as the evening progresses. The energy in the room at these events is electric, and you can feel the celebratory, yet nervous, energy wafting off many of the newest additions to the Jack Kent Cooke community. Jessie, a higher education staff member at the Foundation, reflected on the banquet in an interview by noting:

> The banquet is such a great event! Everyone gets dressed up, we do a photo shoot, people connect at the reception, and then we have a beautiful meal with a speaker. It is a time to really celebrate our Scholars. It's also a great way to introduce our Scholars to events like this and give them an opportunity to get comfortable with formal events and spaces like this that they'll encounter in college and on internships. A lot of our incoming Scholars are headed to Ivies and other highly selective schools, where a formal event or outing is pretty commonplace. Giving them exposure to what that is like before they arrive on campus makes it less intimidating and alienating, I think.

As Jessie's comments highlight, whether intentionally designed this way or not, programming like formal banquets and fine-dining excursions gives students exposure and an opportunity to learn and gain valuable capital in environments that are relatively low-stakes. In fact, when I was an undergraduate, I had taken to referring to this banquet as the *Pretty Woman*[119] moment for Jack Kent Cooke Scholars. As an alumna of this scholarship and a sociology student, I had homed in on the deliberate yet awkward character of hosting a formal banquet for hundreds of students who had likely never experienced anything remotely resembling it before. I remember sitting at the banquet in my first year with the Foundation anxious and unclear of the rules at the table as I scanned the numerous utensils and glasses in front of me. Sensing my unease, a staff member seated next to me quietly explained what drinks were assigned to each glass on the table and then covertly gestured to each of the unfamiliar utensils, explaining when and how they would make an appearance during the multicourse meal.

Fast-forward eight years to the banquet during one of my years of fieldwork at Scholars Weekend, and there I was sitting at a similar table watching a newly minted Scholar furrow her brow at the table set in front of her. I watched as she covertly pulled her phone out and started googling in her lap, glancing up at different items on the table and returning to her screen to search for more information. Even with a world of information at her fingertips on her phone, she still looked confused as she went to select a glass to pour water into. In that second, the staff member seated to her right merely said, "Water?" and poured a glass for her from the pitcher as the Scholar nodded in affirmation. I then watched quietly as this staff member kindly explained the different glasses, smiling warmly as the student nodded along. A few minutes later, I struck up a conversation with this new Scholar by joking that it was a good thing I was thirsty, because they had certainly given me enough glasses. She responded with a laugh, and we started talking about our shared perceptions about the banquet. She shared that she had been nervous about the banquet portion of the event for weeks leading up to Scholars Weekend, and that it was more formal and extravagant than she could have even imagined. She explained that coming from a small town in the Midwest, her extent of experience with a banquet had been the end-of-year sports banquet held in her high school gym, and that the crepe paper decorations and BBQ buffet served on paper plates were a far cry from the opulence of our current backdrop. I nodded in agreement, sharing my own story as a first-time attendee of the event, and assured her that it would get less stressful over time. She smiled at that and said, "Well, I know what a butter knife is now, so I'm already at least 50% more ready for the next one."

Much like Barney, the maître d'hôtel who coaches Julia Roberts's character Vivian in *Pretty Woman* on the ins and outs of fine-dining utensils to prepare her for a formal dinner out, these staff members gave me, my dining companion, and likely countless other new Scholars impromptu lessons in the props and performance of formal dining spaces. This first introduction did exactly what Jessie hoped it would do—it prepared us for countless dining situations during our time in college and beyond. And, while this first introductory experience certainly does not carry enough capital to match the more affluent students on campus, it is a very important start in producing the confidence needed to navigate those situations as first-generation students at selective colleges and universities.

STUDENT PERSPECTIVES ON PROGRAMMING

A number of students I talked to emphasized how much they appreciated the experiences and knowledge they gained from these kinds of direct programming efforts at their colleges and scholarship organizations. Many of them spoke at length about the impact that early programming on interfacing with faculty and understanding norms inside classrooms and other academic spaces had on their experiences and perspectives. Whittaker, an Asian American student in his second year at West College, pinpointed a workshop he had gone to on interacting with faculty and the importance of office hours as a turning point in his academic experiences and confidence in his first year. He noted, "Before that workshop, I was freaked out about office hours and didn't really know what they were for, and didn't know how to talk to my professors about problems I was having or even about things I was excited about in the class. Having the staff and faculty there to explain everything and just talk us through it changed everything for me. Now I'm in office hours all the time and feel so much more confident in everything." For Whittaker and students like him, having this kind of programming available helps them begin to decode opaque and unwritten expectations around this element of their college experiences.

Other students focused on the impact of social and cultural programming in the form of outings and campus events. David, an Asian American student at East College, had been particularly involved in programming with his peer mentor group as a first-year and felt that experiencing unfamiliar settings and contexts with his peers made them seem less intimidating. He explained, "I went on a bunch of outings my first year or so with my mentoring program. We saw a play, went to nice restaurants, saw a traveling exhibit at the modern art museum, a bunch of stuff. It was super exciting and didn't feel too intimidating because we were all in the mentoring program together." Tiffany, a White student in her third year at Midwest College, echoed David's sentiment, noting that the experiences she had had as part of programming for first-generation students on her campus had been an accessible way to engage with unfamiliar topics, saying,

> We did all kinds of things my first year that blew my mind. And I am glad I got to do it with other first-gens because it was like "no judgment," you know? I remember this contemporary dance show we went to that felt so strange at first. I had never seen anything like it, and I kept having to keep myself from giggling for like the first 15 minutes of the show. But then I just kind of really got into it. And afterward we got

to talk to some of the dancers about their art, and it was super laid back, you know? I learned so much that night.

As with David, Tiffany's experience highlights the important quality that attending social and cultural programs with peers from similar backgrounds can have for students. What is also important to note is that these programming experiences can begin to directly impact students' experiences on campus. During this conversation, Tiffany went on to further describe an interaction she had had not long after her first-gen group went to this dance performance. She said:

> And you know what's crazy? A couple of days later, I got to class early and was sitting there listening to these two people in my class I'd never talked to before discuss the same show I'd been to, and I just busted into their conversation like "Wasn't it the best! I just thought the commentary on the dynamics of aging and sexuality was so beautiful and well expressed." And you know what? They dug what I was saying, and we had this whole conversation about it. That was no shit the first time I felt like I ever connected with anyone from my classes. It was like I could suddenly talk to them, you know? Totally crazy.

As Tiffany's experience here demonstrates, these programs are in fact doing what they set out to do. Not only did Tiffany and her first-generation peers gain experience and knowledge around this form of performance art, but Tiffany was also able to translate that into recognizable cultural capital in her interaction with classmates. In that moment of interaction, Tiffany was able to signal to her peers that she had not only seen the same performance, but was also engaging critically with the subject matter in a way that signaled her legitimacy and belonging on campus.

While many students spoke to their appreciation around these experiences, many others had different perspectives. For some, these attempts to increase and improve student cultural capital were perceived as efforts from the university that were perhaps well intentioned but nevertheless seen as an indication from the institution that they needed to change in order to belong or succeed on campus. Quinn, a Black third-year at Midwest College, had a take that aligned with this perspective. He recognized that these events were meant to expose first-gen students to new experiences, saying: "I think the [student] center knows that most of us haven't been to a lot of the places they take us. I'm pretty sure that is intentional. It's expected that students here know about art and films and things like that—it comes up in classes all the time—so making sure we know those things too is what I think they're trying to do." He went on to further explain, however, that he did not agree with the ideological perspective that first-generation students and students of color needed more cultural capital:

> They always say that we need more cultural capital, but I think maybe a little more honesty around all this would be good . . . We don't need *more* [his emphasis] capital, we need the capital they want us to have. Those are two different things . . . I get that I need to learn, but it would also be nice if they ever considered what I have to offer . . . I do have to say, though—knowing what fork to use and everything else ended up being really useful when I was on my summer internship in DC. There were a lot of dinners that I think I would have freaked out about if I hadn't already done it before.

This dual critique leveraged here by Quinn was a common sentiment among a number of the students I talked to, particularly (but not exclusively) of students of color. For many of these students, the intentional programming on campus designed to promote capital development was seen as a dismissal of the forms of capital they arrive on campus with. As prior research asserts,[120] students of color at predominantly White institutions—like the ones these students were attending—often experience institutional attempts at increasing their capital as a rejection of their race and ethnic identities and cultures. This is due in large part to the fact that the interactional currency at these institutions is one of an upper-middle-class White culture that demands particular ways of being to be seen as legitimate members of the community.[121] Elias, a multiracial student in his fourth year at East College, noted,

> By expecting me to talk and act in ways that align with the historical wealthy White norms of East, East is saying that this is the only acceptable way to be a student at East. And anyone who doesn't do this as expected is discounted and socially punished. So, it makes it nearly impossible to completely reject the norm here. And because you can't

completely reject it, you are reinforcing that it is the norm, you know? It is a nasty cycle that will eat you up if you're not careful. You have to find the right ways to push back.

As in prior research,[122] students like Elias are cued into this aspect of higher education and have developed significant critiques of the ways that these practices continue to support a structure of inequality within their schools and across higher education. What is interesting to consider here is that further into my conversation with Elias, he credited East College with exposing him to the concepts and ideas that initially helped him build his critiques of higher education's orientation toward marginalized students. He explained that a combination of materials from his courses, conversations with older students, and guest lectures had "opened his eyes" to the "positionality of underrepresented students trying to achieve social mobility" at schools like East College. He went on to further credit East College with giving him the language and confidence he needed to take his ideas to the next level and try to enact changes on campus. He explained,

> It's kind of funny, actually, when you think about it. If I hadn't come to East and gone through everything they do to change you, I wouldn't have what I need to critique it. I had to start becoming the quintessential East College student before I could critique it and be taken seriously . . . It makes it complicated because I am glad that I have had this opportunity, but I am also glad that I might be able to change it for folks that come after me.

As Elias points out, in many ways schools like East College provide first-generation and other marginalized students with the vital knowledge, skills, and experiences—or capital—that they need to not only fit in and thrive on campus, but also actively critique this system that they find themselves situated inside of. This produces a complicated perspective for many of these students, where they simultaneously appreciate the opportunities and capital they've gained during school, but also see that process as one that attempts to suppress or change aspects of their identities and capital that do not fit within the normative expectations of students on their selective college campuses.

PERCEIVING POLISHED PERSPECTIVES

I found that many students talked about how participating in direct programming and gaining the capital it intended to produce for them had unexpected consequences that often took them by surprise. In particular, students described experiencing changes to their perspectives about the world, their knowledge around new topics and cultures, their preferences in media and food, their behaviors and mannerisms, and their patterns of speech and ways of expressing themselves. In essence, the programming that makes up the structure of the polishing process at their colleges had done its job well. These students had changed in specific and targeted ways that aligned them closer to their peers from more affluent backgrounds, thus enabling them to navigate expectations more smoothly in upper-middle-class and elite spaces. In many ways, the changes that the students I talked to described are what occur when an individual gains significant amounts of embodied cultural capital and undergoes habitus transformation.[123] Just as Bourdieu describes a country peasant taking on the foreign mannerisms and tastes of the city as he experiences them, the students I talked to described shifting and changing to become more like their elite college environments.

Students who I spent time with spoke extensively about ways they had changed during college that could all be grouped under forms of habitus transformation[124] that come from shifting and expanding cultural capital. Many students discussed how their vocabularies were shifting to incorporate terms they had learned during class, at workshops and info sessions, at on- and off-campus programming, and in conversations with faculty and peers. Sarah, a White student in her third year at East College, reflected in a conversation while she gave me a tour of her campus about the changes she'd noticed in her vocabulary, saying, "Sometimes I wish I had kept a journal or a log of all the new words and concepts I've learned. It's pretty astonishing, really. I mean, I knew nothing about neoliberalism before coming here, and now I am thinking about how I can incorporate it into all of my final papers." Similarly, a number of students reflected on how their cultural references to literature, film, history, and music had shifted during their time in college. Jamison, a Latinx student, noted during a conversation in his third year at South College that he was surprised at how many references to outside sources and cultural touchstones he understood in class that year compared to his first year. He explained: "When I was a first-year, I was pretty sure that I missed about half of what was being said in class because I either didn't know the words or didn't know the things and places and events that were being talked about. And now I am nodding along with everyone else, actually knowing something about all of the different books that are *not* [his emphasis] on the syllabus that they are referencing. I didn't think that would ever happen."

For Sarah, Jamison, and students like them, the time they spent inside and outside the classroom gave them the knowledge they needed to literally speak a language on campus that the majority of their peers were already fluent in. This significant increase in knowledge and skill is ultimately what these students, and many of their families, hope they will gain during college. And, while all students are learning and growing inside the classroom, I found that many first-generation students were acutely aware of the intellectual distance they had traveled from semester to semester compared to their more affluent peers. Although many of these students expected to learn a significant amount during college, they were often surprised by the depth and breadth of how their vocabularies and knowledge had expanded.

A number of other students spent time detailing the ways their tastes in food, clothing, media, and extracurriculars had changed. For instance, students spoke at length about learning about new cuisines and trying new foods that they had believed to be undesirable in the past. A memorable conversation I observed with Veronica, a White student in her final year at East College, and her friends while trying to decide where to eat dinner stands out in this regard. The group was at a standstill on where to go, and Veronica looked sheepishly at the group, saying, "We could always get . . . sushi . . . ," letting the suggestion hang in the air before two of her friends threw their arms in the air, groaning loudly and complaining that she always suggested sushi. Veronica laughed and retorted, "I can't help myself! I'm making up for lost time. This delicious treasure was hidden from me my whole life, and now I've got sushi fever! I'm a verifiable sushi monster." Her friends laughed uproariously, with one smirking back at her, saying, "You're a verifiable something!" This got an even larger laugh as they kept debating where to eat. When asked about this interaction a few hours later, she laughed and commented, "They love teasing me but it's really true. I honestly can't get enough of the stuff ... I never would have thought this would be me, though. I went to one dinner with my mentor group, and it was sushi, and man, was I freaked to try it. But it was so good! Changed my life."

Veronica had grown up in a small town in the Midwest and had never tried sushi prior to coming to East College. Now in her final year there, she was a regular at a small sushi spot near her off-campus apartment. This was a contrast that she saw as significant and representative of her time at East. While a shift in tastes around something like food might seem unimportant or part of the normal evolution of taste as one gets older, a number of students contrasted changes like this as a way of measuring the distance between their pre- and post-college selves.

Some students took a somewhat self-deprecating or comical approach toward describing the changes that they had noticed in their tastes and behaviors. For instance, Braiden, a Black second-year at East College, used his knowledge about cheese to describe the unexpected ways that his tastes had changed: "You want to hear some crazy shit? I can tell you the difference between different cheeses. I don't think I'd even had a soft cheese before I got here. In my house it was a bag of shredded cheddar every day. Now I'm sitting over here like 'Mmmhmm, yes, that was a particularly good triple-cream.' Jesus." Braiden's reflection on his evolution in cheese knowledge and taste highlights the tensions many students felt over the changes in their tastes. Although Braiden has embraced his newly found knowledge around cheeses, his self-effacing approach toward talking about it uncovers the discomfort he felt with becoming the type of person that knows about and prefers exotic cheeses over a simple bag of cheddar shreds. This kind of discomfort was evident in many of the interviews I had with first-generation students.

Instead of cheeses, Zane, a White fourth-year at Midwest College, used his knowledge around art as a way to talk about the changes he perceived in himself: "I don't really think people actually like modern art. Everyone is just standing around lying saying things that sound smart like 'This piece really evokes the precarity of space and time.' That doesn't mean anything [laughs]! No, really, though, I think it's all bullshit, but I do it too now. It's ridiculous." Like Braiden, Zane felt an internal conflict around his shifting tastes and social mobility. He went on to further explain that he was struggling with feelings around legitimacy as a first-generation student. He said, "Am I even working class now? I don't have any money, but I've got all this knowledge that no one I know does. What do I even do with that?" For Zane, gaining enough cultural capital to be able to appreciate (and critique the appreciation of) modern art also meant gaining enough cultural capital to call his working-class identity into question. This kind of internal struggle over his core identity was something that he noted was difficult to consider and beyond the scope of what he could manage under the pressure of the impending finals he would be taking the next week. Zane's experiences here hint at the deeper impacts and weight of considering changes brought on by college that I will focus explicitly on in chapters 4 and 5.

Some students described how the institutional programming designed to promote cultural capital had the unintended consequence of putting their lives in stark contrast to their families at home. Putnam, a Latinx fourth-year at East College, described an outing that he took with a student group to an apple orchard in the countryside near his college: "They took us apple picking once. We went out to this farm and paid them money to pick apples from a tree. My friend and I couldn't stop laughing. It was our group and a bunch of rich White people out there paying to do what a lot of people in our families do for a living every day. I guess it was a really good intro into how our lives were always going to be different now." And while Putnam tried to initially laugh off this eye-opening trip to the orchard, he ended up using this experience twice more in our interview to illustrate how alienated he felt on campus as a first-generation Latinx student from an immigrant family. While he knew that this field trip was probably meant to give the students in his group a chance to experience something new, he was saddened by the fact that administrators had not considered how it might be received by students whose families do agricultural work for a living. This moment on the apple farm stuck with him throughout college as a pivotal moment in his development. "I think about that day all the time. If my life was a movie, that would be the day the narrator said some cheesy shit like 'In that moment his past and future selves met.' Or something. Know what I mean?" For Putnam, this moment encapsulated his understanding of when the trajectory of his social mobility began to tick upward—an experience that not only came as a surprise, but made him reflect on the ways that attending East College had begun to fundamentally change him as a person. Putnam's thoughts here begin to highlight the deeper effects the polishing process can have on students. In many ways, it is not merely about having a new vocabulary, trying new foods, and learning social rules. It is about gaining the skills, knowledge, and experiences needed to change a student's social and economic trajectory. It is about rewriting students' futures, but perhaps also about planting the seeds that will fundamentally change who they are.

This chapter has detailed how the development of extensive targeted programming and resources for low-income and first-generation students has created a highly effective system of providing students with the experiences, support, and opportunities they need to develop the forms of cultural capital seen as valuable and necessary to succeed in elite educational and social spaces. This system of resources, and the polishing process it produces, is not inherently a bad thing. In fact, it is exactly what draws many students to these schools in the first place. And, as many of these students' experiences showed, the development of the forms of capital it produces is demonstrably beneficial for student success and experience. Even with these benefits, however, it is critical to consider how this process works and what effects might have been overlooked. In many ways, first-generation students are seen as diamonds in the rough on selective college campuses, which with the right amount of programming and instruction can be polished up enough to become the impressive and rare specimens they have the potential to be. And, while this is all done in the name of student support and improving experiences and outcomes, the critiques of some of the students here should give pause and a reconsideration of whether this is the right approach.

Is it fair to demand this kind of intensive transformation of first-generation students? Is pushing students to change in this way actually leveling the playing field, or is it merely giving them a crash course in how to play a game that their peers have been learning since birth? In a world where innovation and change often come most notably from diversity and difference, is trying to produce uniformity for the sake of upholding historical expectations the right path forward for higher education? And, finally, have we stopped to consider what these efforts to rewrite first-generation students' capital and social locations do in the long run, outside of economic gain and career placement?

In the remaining chapters of this book, I will explore how the efforts that make up the polishing process designed to change these students' capital, frameworks, perspectives, and tastes also significantly impact their relationships to themselves, their campus, and their families and communities at home. In many ways, first-generation students must buy into the polishing process in order to fully integrate into their campus communities. And, while polishing gives students the capital they need to succeed academically and socially, it also changes them and provides them with the framing that the communities they came to college from, and the capital they brought with them, are undesirable and poorly fitted for the elite spaces that they are learning to call home. The unexpected impacts and outcomes of this process cause some students to reconsider their college choices and begin to fundamentally question the costs associated with becoming socially mobile through an elite education. I will show that in many ways, selective colleges provide all the resources that first-generation students need to build extensive amounts of capital, but they do not provide students with the tools and support they need to navigate the complicated process of change that they experience as a result. And, while this has not historically been the purview of selective colleges and universities, neither was providing programming and resources around cultural capital, prior to a few decades ago. Perhaps it is time to evolve institutional approaches once more.

· 4 ·

Unexpected Impacts and Contentious Conflicts

It was the first day back to classes after winter break at West College, and the Student Center was abuzz with activity. Students sat chatting in the common area, reconnecting with friends, signing up for events, and eating the cookies that the staff had set out as part of a welcome-back event. Two second-years, a young Latinx man named Gabe and a White student named Xavier, discussed their trips back home for the break as a small handful of other students listened in. Gabe recounted each meal his mother cooked for him in great detail, describing the flavor and texture of homemade tortillas much in the style of a television host on the Food Network. Andie, a multiracial upperclassman, slid backward over the top of the couch, landing on her head and grasping her stomach, groaning, "I'm already having withdrawals, man. The food here is just for rich White people, it's quinoa and seitan as far as the eye can see!" Andie's culinary observation produced an eruption of laughter from everyone in the group except Rachel, a White first-year sitting next to me who had been quietly staring into her lap at the same page of Plato's *Republic* for the better part of an hour.

While everyone continued to laugh and joke, Xavier leaned over to Rachel and said, "Hey, what's got you so quiet over here?" Crinkling her forehead, she responded, "I don't know, everybody seems to have had such a good time at home, and that is not what my break was like." Xavier stretched his arms out, sighing, "Let me guess, you went home excited to see your family and all your friends from high school, and once you got there everything felt off, like you were out of step or in an alternate universe." Rachel looked at Xavier skeptically and said, "Yeah, that's exactly what it was like." Andie turned her head to Rachel and laughed. "Welcome to the Upside Down! Home to the Demogorgon[125] and First-Gen Students!" Everyone around her erupted in laughter as a look of relief, as if she had just been seen for the first time, crept onto Rachel's face.

In many ways, college is designed to change the individual,[126] but as I will show, the concerted efforts of colleges and universities to "level the playing field" for low-income and first-generation students that make up the polishing process produce changes that are far beyond what is considered standard adolescent development during college. As demonstrated in chapter 3, the polishing process—or the intentional programming, resources, and opportunities that colleges and universities employ to infuse students with critical forms of capital—is often a notably successful endeavor. It provides students with new forms of knowledge, skills, and experiences that they need to successfully navigate and belong in the worlds of selective higher education and the upper-middle class. What is crucial to consider, however, is that this process does not simply add to a student's tool kit, it also changes and takes important pieces away. The experiences and opportunities they gain during college, and the resulting social mobility that comes with them, ultimately begin to rewrite their capital and social locations. It changes these students' frameworks, perspectives, and tastes, and in doing so shifts their relationships to themselves, their campus, and their families and communities at home.

For many students, these changes produce experiences that mirror those of Rachel and her peers as they begin to confront the unexpected impacts of attending a selective college and wrestle with what this means for their identities and futures. Critical moments on campus or, in most cases, the initial visit home from college becomes a moment of renegotiation and change around ideologies and expectations around attending and becoming socially mobile during college. Although most students I talked to had maintained digital contact with their family and high school friends throughout the school year, coming home and reengaging these relationships within the physical and social contexts of home unearthed both expected and unexpected outcomes. For many students, this first trip home brought with it the full weight of the divide between their college lives and their home communities. This unexpected divide forced them and their families to grapple with and reinterpret the costs and benefits of pursuing social mobility through attending a selective college.

And, as these students' experiences will demonstrate, simply assuming that students can easily develop a "cleft habitus"[127] or "culturally straddle"[128] in order to navigate the tensions and competing demands that arise out of this situation fails to fully consider how complex it is to navigate the competing demands that emerge from social mobility as a first-generation student. Instead, I will show how the incomplete rewriting of students' capital that arises out of the polishing process makes it hard for students to reorient to their home communities while also complicating their positionalities on campus. For many, this means reframing their own expectations and understanding of attending college as a first-generation student. For others, it means renegotiating these frameworks with their families. And for some, this means facing significant conflict over the real (or perceived) changes that college has brought. This chapter considers how students navigate these critical moments, the impact they have on their experiences and trajectories in college, and the double bind that many of them find themselves in as they try to meet the expectations of their campus and home communities.

CAMPUS (DIS)CONNECTIONS

Some students pointed to interactions and experiences during their first year on campus as the first moments the deeper impacts of attending a selective college began to become apparent. For instance, some students described feeling surprised and unsettled by interactions with their peers that challenged their internal conceptualizations of self as working-class and first-generation students. Evie, a multiracial second-year at East College, talked at length about how their relationship to the students on their residence hall floor evolved over the course of their first year at school. Coming into college, they saw themselves as very different from their peers and felt very alienated from them. Evie was from a working-class family, was the first in their family to attend college, and was on a full scholarship at East. They noted that they were slow to make friends on campus, but eventually formed some bonds with students on their residence hall floor. They described how a conversation that occurred not long after winter break upended the way they saw themselves in relation to their peers:

> I remember I got really upset during a conversation with some of the folks on my floor—I said something about being working class and Deidre laughed it off and said, "Yeah, but you're not like, really like that, you're one of us." Or something like that. And in my mind I was like "Bitch, please! My daddy didn't buy my way into here, and I don't have a maid and a giant house like you do." . . . I just sat there quietly and then went back to my room and cried a lot . . . Because in a lot of ways I realized that she was right. I was way more like them than I realized I was.

Like many of their first-generation peers, Evie came into college with a particular frame around their identity as a working-class student, and they used that frame to inform their choices and to understand their relationships to other students, their family, and college. When another student suggested that Evie was something other than working class, she also ruptured the frame through which Evie understood their identity and positionality at East College. This left Evie with the difficult work of grappling with the realization that they had started to become more like their affluent peers than they realized, and sorting out what that meant more broadly for their identity as a low-income and first-generation student.

Moments of rupture around students' identities like Evie's were difficult to navigate and produced significant stress and anxiety for a number of students. Elijah, a Black fourth-year at South College, explained that when he went through an experience similar to Evie's, he began to question how much college would change him in the long run and whether it was worth it or even possible to avoid that kind of change. "The thing about this, you know, is that you've got to pay to play. Nobody is going to be letting me into law school if I don't fit the part. And to fit the part, I've got to keep changing. And if I keep changing, well, I don't know what that will mean." For Elijah, the prospect of continued change through college had become an expected but not necessarily accepted aspect of social mobility. He knew that to achieve the goals he had set for himself, he would need to conform to the normative expectations around membership in the educational elite, but he had not yet decided whether this potential erasure of his identity was worth it.

HOMECOMINGS

Many students I talked to focused on their first visits home as their first moments of grappling with the ways that college was changing their identities and positionalities. In addition to negotiating old curfews and expectations around chores and family obligations, many students struggled to transition back into the pace and culture of their communities. And, when confronted with the often unnoticed and unexpected differences that had begun to transpire during their time away at college, many students reported internal and external tensions that left them feeling stressed, confused, and unclear of what the right pathway forward should be.

Returning to Precarity

For some, returning home from college often meant a move back into the precariousness of poverty and the chaos of tightly shared spaces that placed the differences between their college lives and home in stark relief. Camila, a Latinx second-year at South College, talked about this difference: "Even with a roommate, I have the biggest and nicest room I have ever had in my life [at college]. I have so much space! And that space is mine. It was weird at first, but now I hate going back to sharing at home. It's so suffocating, I just *need* [her emphasis] more space, you know? Oh my God, do you hear me? I sound like *such* [her emphasis] a brat!" As noted in prior research,[129] the juxtaposition of home and school life can be difficult for low-income students to reconcile and navigate. For Camila, residence life was the first opportunity she had to take ownership over a space that was wholly her own, and returning home on breaks to a small room shared with three younger siblings put her two lived realities into stark comparison. In many ways, expressing this newly developed preference produced complicated feelings around change and entitlement that Camila did not feel equipped to process.

Similar to Camila, Whittaker, an Asian American student in his second year at West College, focused on the entitlement that he felt around food when returning home the first time and how that made him contend with the changes he was undergoing at college. He explained that he and his four siblings had grown up on food stamps, and that eating in the dining hall at West was the first time in his life that he had had access to the kind of selection and volume of food that a well-funded dining hall at a highly selective college could offer. He noted, "I hadn't forgot, but like, it was almost like I forgot, you know? When I got home, it was back to making it stretch and mostly empty cupboards and no pocket money for extras at the store. My mom's food is amazing, and it's not like I was starving. Don't get me wrong. But I guess I had gotten so used to having whatever I want whenever I want that I kind of was a jerk about it." Whittaker went on to explain that after a week or so of being home, he had a moment of reflection about his changing expectations and orientation toward food. He explained, "Here I am home for the holidays and I am bitching about snacks like an ungrateful asshole and then my mom cooks this beautiful meal. And when she put everything on the table, I just kind of had a moment and I just kept thinking, 'Who the hell am I? Is this who I am becoming? What a douche.' You know?"

For Whittaker and students like him, moments like this pushed them to recognize and consider the ways that their college experience had begun to shape and change them. As is the case for many first-generation students, attending a college like West College had given Whittaker an opportunity to live a life characterized by opportunity and choice as opposed to constraint and limitation. And, while this is arguably often seen as a positive and desirable gain that comes from social mobility, when juxtaposed in a way that puts a life of necessity lived by your family in stark relief with the relatively lavish life of preference that you've become accustomed to, it can lead students to question if these changes are ultimately a good thing. The weight of this adds an invisible layer of emotional work that these students must grapple with while also trying to focus on exams and forging friendships.

For some students, the divide between home and school was more extreme. Bren, a White second-year at East College, explained that instabilities in her home life made going home on breaks difficult: "Breaks have been a nightmare for me. My mom moves around a lot, so I actually don't know where I'm supposed to go in a couple weeks. And I don't know who will be there living with her or what the, like, grocery or lights situation will be . . . I save up for breaks just in case I have to cover things [bills]." She further explained that her most recent trip home had involved a fight with her mother over whose responsibility it was to make sure the trailer they were staying in had electricity during winter break. Citing her elite status as a student at East College, Bren's mother, a semi-employed domestic worker, had mounted an argument that Bren was in the best financial position to cover the bills. Bren in many ways agreed with her mother but wished her situation was different. "I know it's not her fault, but recently I've been super annoyed about all of it. My breaks are so different than my friends', and I am having a hard time reconciling it . . . I guess it wasn't until I made friends and stuff that I noticed how strange my life is." For students like Camilla, Whittaker, and Bren, being away at college and becoming accustomed to a different way of life challenged what they had previously understood as mundanely normal. It wasn't until their lives before college were juxtaposed with their lives in college that they were able to see some of the significant differences between themselves and their peers, as well as the differences in who they had started to become during college. This provided them with a new perspective on their lives that impacted the ways they viewed their families as well as the effects that college was having on their relationships to them.

Unexpected Criticism and Concern

While not all students came home to living arrangements that were precarious, this new perspective on the formerly taken-for-granted was a common experience. For many of these students, unexpected experiences with families and friends during their first visits home produced crucial moments of conflict or recognition around their social mobility and class embodiment that forced them to reorient their perspectives, or frames, around college and their increasingly embodied social mobility. These moments of forced reorientation were often prompted by what students described as a process of noticing and recognizing either startling changes that had occurred in their communities or unexpected differences between their new college lives and the lives of their families and friends.

During Rena's first winter break home from college, she learned that two of her friends from high school were getting married and another was expecting a baby. Her thirteen-year-old brother also had gotten into trouble at school for smoking weed in the bathroom. She said, "I guess I didn't think about what their lives would look like staying home. Even though I know that babies are what it means to live your life there." She went on to further explain that learning this information "forced me to really, like *really* [her emphasis], reconsider how college was going to change my life. That messed me up for a minute. Like, I knew it was going to change me—that's what I wanted. But I never thought about that compared to my friends [at home], I guess." She went on to further explain that while she knew that she could not have changed what had happened, she felt guilty for not being home to look after her brother and felt a "deep sadness" that she was attending one of the most selective schools in the nation while her friends were "cementing their lives as mothers and wives" in their small town.

For many students like Rena, the first trip home from college often complicated their framing of college as an economic pursuit with primarily financial benefits by revealing the significant ways in which they had begun to change and embody the social and cultural capital they were gaining in college. Without the distance of being away at college, students could see clearly their future trajectories juxtaposed against the trajectories of their friends and families for the first time. This recognition challenged their understandings of their suspended community identity—producing what Erving Goffman refers to as a "frame break"[130]—and caused many students to experience a crisis as they attempted to reorient their experiences and identities.

For Tyson, a White third-year at West College, it was the juxtaposition of his daily routine in college and that of his high school friends that forced him to contend with the unanticipated ways he had become upwardly mobile. He spent the beginning of his break sleeping in and working on internship applications—typical college behavior on his campus. But, after a few days of watching his cousins and friends come home exhausted after working ten-hour days in construction, he started to feel ill at ease. "It's pretty hard to think your life hasn't changed when you go home and everyone around you is working themselves to the bone doing hard labor when you spend your days in college writing papers and hanging out in coffee shops." He further explained, "I wasn't sure what to do with this for a while. I just kind of sat with it spinning . . . eventually I guess I told myself a new story about what I was doing. Because that's what we do, right? Tell ourselves stories." Like many of his peers, Tyson struggled to reconcile his belief that his life had changed very little during college with the realities of the widening gap between his life and the lives of the friends and family he left behind at home.

Nolan, a White third-year at Midwest College, who described initially approaching college with a desire for some kind of abstract change and personal growth, was shocked to find that he had little control over how that change was received. He described his surprise over feeling "distance" from his family on his first trip home: "It really took me by surprise, actually. I was expecting to change in, I guess, general ways, but I didn't expect to feel disconnected from my family and friends. Especially so quickly. It was just different. I wanted to talk about Herodotus and experimental film, and my family wanted to talk about the *Survivor* season finale. That was hard. I kind of went into an identity crisis, I guess." He further explained that he and his brother fought for the majority of the break, with his brother leveraging insults about his "snobbiness," and most of his family mocking him in a British accent as a means of emphasizing that his new status as an elite college student made him an outsider to his community. He spent the entirety of his winter break "angry and depressed without any idea of what to do." Thinking back on it, he said the problem was that he had not anticipated a real change in how he carried himself. "I hadn't even thought about it that way—like, about class, I guess. That college would make me different than my parents, my background."

Students who had left for college with a positive view about social mobility reported a sense of shock over the conflicts they experienced during their first visits home. Many of these students had entered college with the perspective that personal change would aid in their upward mobility—a perspective that they believed was aligned with their parents' views. Yet, returning home called that sense of shared belief into question. Chris, a White fourth-year at South College, described his first winter break home from college as "far more difficult than expected." He described an awkward video game session with his younger brother and a friend who was attending a local community college. Before Chris had left for college, the three of them had regularly played multiplayer shooter games, and they were excited to resume their activities. Scheduling time for this became a problem, however, as Chris was balancing the demands of applying for internships with finding free time at home. Although he had assured his brother and friend that spending time together was a priority, it was an entire week into the break by the time they found time to play—which created tension:

> We were sitting there playing Battlefront II, I think, and my friend Drew turned to me and was like "I didn't think Mr. Future Stock Market was going to find time for us, what with finding internships and taking over the world." I remember my brother laughed and threw an M&M at me, saying, "Yeah, he thinks he's hot shit now." I remember that moment because it hit me hard. I froze. I just sat there thinking about what that meant while a Storm Trooper shot me over and over. Looking back, it was like some ridiculous metaphor.

On the surface, Chris had returned home from college with new priorities and demands around finding an internship that made it difficult for him to shift smoothly back into his old routines. And, while he had initially framed it this way—as merely a new set of responsibilities on his plate—they were representative of a deeper set of changes that his brother and friend were reacting to. In many ways, the Chris who had existed prior to attending South was as gone as his on-screen avatar was. And, unlike in the game, he could not simply respawn and start over. He had to figure out a pathway forward as this new version of himself who was expected to meet the often disparate demands of both college and home.

Many students described similar moments of recognition that their friends and family did not always see their personal transformation in college in a positive light. Violet, an Asian American first-year at East College, returned home at winter break with countless stories of her experiences and was excitedly sharing everything she had done and learned with her parents. She remembered being hit by surprise when her parents expressed unhappiness with aspects of her college life: "My parents were so excited when I came home for break. We talked for hours about college and my experiences—even though we had been talking on the phone a bunch of times a week. One night at dinner, though, this weird thing happened. My dad looked at me and said, 'Don't stray too far or you will be lost forever, Violet.' I didn't know what to do with that." As she was cleaning up after dinner, her mother stressed to her that she and her father were still very proud that she was attending East College, but they were concerned that she was rapidly changing without stopping to consider whether those changes were ultimately what she wanted. Violet noted that this unexpected moment was pivotal for how she thought about her social mobility. "I didn't see that coming and feel like I spiraled for a while trying to rethink what I was doing—who I was—and what everything meant." Her parents' concern disrupted the way that she understood, or framed, her mobility and identity in a way that forced her to reconsider her choices and seek a means for realigning and reframing her mobility.

In many ways, Violet's parents' shift in orientation toward her social mobility is a reflection of the gap between standard perceptions about mobility as being about gains in economic capital and the realities of the role that social and cultural capital play in the process. Violet's parents, like many of the parents of students in this study, enthusiastically supported her attendance at a highly selective college because of the promise it held for upward economic mobility in the form of a stable career with a high-paying salary. However, their own social location as low-income laborers limited their perspective on the full range of how college would change their daughter. In many ways, they simply did not have the cultural capital needed to understand how and why the cultural capital Violet would gain at a school like East College would begin to fundamentally change her.

Challenges and Conflicts

Students who approached the potential changes of social mobility by creating suspended identities, as detailed in chapter 2, described experiencing the most heightened levels of conflict with their friends and families during breaks. This group of students had families that were explicitly opposed to the aspects of higher education that they associated with class change and mobility—with many parents quick to pick up on and interrogate changes they perceived in their children. Even students who believed they had adequately managed to protect their home self from their college identity reported abrupt and unexpected conflicts over winter break. Jake, a multiracial student at South, assumed that he was succeeding at living a split life and anticipated being able to easily transition back into his pre-college life without his family perceiving any changes. However, as he later explained, he received an early "reality check" that he was not managing changes as well as he thought:

"I thought I was so slick, honestly. I had been talking to my parents throughout the semester, and I didn't think anything felt different. I was at school doing my thing—I joined the crew team [laughs], I had friends in Greeks. And then I went home and probably, oh, I don't know, 15 minutes into the ride home, my dad looked at me and said, 'So you're a fancy motherfucker now, huh?' My stomach totally dropped."

While Jake had gone to great lengths to hide his involvement in school activities associated with elite colleges and the affluent friends he had made at school, he was unable to hide the more nuanced changes in his embodiment, such as the way he held himself or his mannerisms and pattern of speech. Jake went on to further describe this interaction with his dad, saying he immediately denied the changes his father was objecting to. To this, he explained that his father laughed and began listing off his evidence that he had changed—including the way he was wearing his hat, the "proper" way he was talking, and the amount of gesturing he was doing with his hands when he was talking. The ability of his father to uncover and articulate the particularities of the ways he had changed in such a short amount of time shattered Jake's frame of both the personal identity he held about himself and the social identity he was attempting to project onto his family. "I remember being in the truck just thinking, 'Okay, fuck. If I can't be the Jake I want to be and I can't be the Jake they want me to be, then what fucking Jake am I going to be?' It was terrifying. Everything was upside down." He went on to explain that that winter break was fraught with conflict as he attempted to reframe his social mobility and identity both for himself and also for his family and friends.

While Jake may or may not have actually changed in perceivable ways, his father believed he did, and that was enough for him to challenge Jake in that moment. In fact, it is possible that Jake's father did not actually notice any differences in the way he was talking or the way he was wearing his hat. Instead, he may have simply been primed to perceive these changes—looking for something to confirm his worries and anxieties that could help him cement his negative perspective about how college was changing his son. But, whether imagined or real, Jake was vulnerable to his father's assessments and suffered extended anxiety and stress from these continued moments of conflict over his upward mobility.

Gillian, a multiracial first-year at East College, described a similar conflict, the aftermath of which took her months to process. "I really thought I had it [identity management] figured out, and oh, man, was I wrong! It took me into the summer before I was able to start reconciling who I was becoming with who my parents wanted me to be in a way that made sense for both of us." Chloe, a White first-year at East College, had also returned home over her first winter break to a warm welcome, but, over the course of the first few weeks, her family slowly began to critique her personality, new clothing choices, and interests:

> It was like every time I turned around they were like "Chlo, why is your hair like that? What's that book you're reading? Did you just say 'hegemonic'? What the fuck does that even mean?" They insisted that I had changed so much, and I just kept telling them that I was the same Chloe. That I had always changed my hair and clothes, and that I had to read these things for school. It was hard because I didn't really think I had changed that much, but they saw it in everything I did. That made me rethink a lot of things about college.

This constant insistence that college had changed her in meaningful ways was enough to prompt Chloe to reconsider her own perspective on the personal impacts of college. Like Chloe, many students noted that these conflicts at home left them with the task of not only reconfiguring their own personal framing of their social mobility, but also trying to reframe their college selves for their families.

Delayed Disruptions

These contested homecomings did not always materialize on the first trip home. When I interviewed Darien, a multiracial student at East College, during his first year, he was insistent that his winter break had been uneventful, and that he had "picked up where I left off" with friends and family. However, when we followed up during his second year, Darien told me that his summer had been notably different: "By the summer I had totally changed and, man, that caused real rifts between me and my parents. I didn't expect it. Before college it was all 'Oh, honey, you gonna be so fancy soon! A college man!' and we all meant it.

In a good way. But I don't think any of us were prepared for what that actually meant and, let me tell you what, my parents didn't like what they saw. That messed me up for a while for sure." While he had initially perceived that the effects of his social mobility were not impacting his relationship with his family, he later was confronted with the disconnection between the positive framing he had around his social mobility and his family's negative reception of changes to his habits, interests, and personality that they tied to changes in his priorities and the core of his identity and authenticity. Darien's experience highlights that students experience the unfolding process of social mobility in college not only in different ways, but also at different speeds. For some students, change is immediate and readily visible by their families and friends—for others, change is slow and cumulative, requiring time to take shape. Regardless of speed, these first moments of conflict and reorientation were often just the first in what would become a constantly evolving and contested process of social mobility and identity change during college.

It is a well-known notion that college is a time and place for change, exploration, maturation, and evolution.[131] In fact, this is one of the three primary ways that many colleges and universities market themselves to prospective students and their parents. College commonly brings changes like the adoption of a new diet like veganism, the use of alcohol and other drugs, a realignment of political beliefs, or sexual activity. All of these can be contentious, and they are often framed as a normal part of adolescent development and/or rebellion. And many, but not all, parents and families write off these changes as a phase of young adulthood and begrudgingly accept them as a temporary detour on their expected pathway of development.[132] In contrast, some of the changes that are part and parcel of the social mobility that comes with attending a selective college as a first-generation student are often seen as having higher stakes. They are framed as more permanent changes that directly contest the classed identities and lives of first-generation students' parents and families. Instead of being seen as a phase or a natural part of adolescent development, these classed changes are perceived as aberrant and dangerous. Even further still, many of these students' families have built their identities in opposition to the educated upper-middle class.[133] To have a family member begin to evolve and change into what is seen as the personification of everything they are in opposition to is likely at least part of why some families' responses are so intense.

THE BENEFITS OF EXPERIENCE

That so many students return home from college to conflict and grief around their changing class identities goes against the normative assumptions embedded in the popular imaginary around embracing upward mobility and college at all costs.[134] It is generally assumed that low-income students attending the most selective colleges in the nation hold on to positive ideologies about higher education and social mobility throughout the course of their college experiences. And, while I have shown that expected and unexpected changes can complicate the perspectives of even the most positive families, there were in fact some students and families that were relatively unfazed by the changes and details that incited conflict in other households.

The Preparatory Advantage

A small number of students in my study had attended elite boarding schools during high school, and each of these students reported very smooth first trips home. Typically, these students had been away from home for the entirety of high school, only seeing their families during breaks in the academic school year. These students attributed the relative lack of conflict with their parents as a result of having had to navigate these tensions and conflicts with their families at a younger age. By the time these students reached college, in other words, the personal impact of social mobility had been contested and recontested to the point that, save for minor disagreements, it had become an expected (if not accepted) aspect of their education and trajectory. Sebastian, a Latinx second-semester first-year attending East College, is exemplary of this group of students. Sebastian had received funding from the Jack Kent Cooke Foundation to attend high school at an elite private boarding school in the Northeast. When I asked him about his relationship with his parents, he said they got along relatively well and he felt like they had less conflict than some of his peers had with their parents:

> My friend Oliver is always in an argument with his parents about what he is doing here. He was in the common room yesterday fighting on the phone about his priorities for like an hour. It gets really bad— sometimes I can even hear his dad yelling at him through the phone,

and then he ends up crying . . . we've talked till like 3 in the morning a bunch of times about what he's going through. It's kind of crazy, but even though I'm younger than him I end up being like a mentor because I have experience he doesn't. When I was boarding, I fought with my parents like that all the time, and going home the first few years was miserable. But that's not a problem anymore because we are basically on the same page. We all get what's happening now, and I think even my mom is okay with it.

Unlike Oliver, Sebastian and his family had already gone through the process of contesting and recontesting many of the major personal impacts of social mobility before he even began school at East College. It is possible that this was also made easier by the fact that these students and their parents went through this process when they were in junior high and high school, and that instead of framing these changes as being tied to a classed identity, they were wrapped up in familial frameworks around normal boundary pushing and adolescent development tied to this life stage.[135] And while Sebastian's experience was rare, the students who had gone to elite high school boarding and preparatory schools benefited greatly from having already negotiated the personal impacts of social mobility and elite education with their families before college.

Low-Income but Not First-Generation

With the exception of two students whose absent fathers had advanced degrees, every low-income but not first-generation student reported that their family's perspectives about college as an engine for social mobility and career growth remained positive throughout their college careers. These students had at least one parent that had earned a bachelor's degree (and in some cases advanced degrees) but worked in low-paying professions, worked part-time, or were on disability. Molly, a multiracial first-year attending South College, whose mother was a part-time special education teacher at a public school and whose father was on disability after an accident at work, exemplifies the low-income students I interviewed. Her parents had both been first-generation students, met each other while attending a well-regarded public four-year college, and married soon after completing their bachelor's degrees in

engineering and education. They were both excited that Molly was attending South and saw college as a great opportunity for their daughter to achieve her desire to become a public-interest lawyer. During her
first year, Molly described to me how she and her parents felt about her
going to college by saying, "My parents and I were super excited about
me going to college when I got into South. It's such a good school and
a great opportunity for me to move up, to get a prestigious education
that will get me to law school and then to a good career as an attorney.
It's all I've ever wanted." While Molly had some difficult experiences in
college, like struggling in her introductory chemistry class and failing to
find a home in a sorority, she and her parents continued to see college as
a positive endeavor that would increase her chances at social mobility.
Reflecting on her first return home for the summer, Molly said: "I spent
the summer doing an internship at the Southern Poverty Law Center. It
was amazing. My parents were so excited . . . I was home for a few weeks
at the end of the summer and we spent, like, every night talking about
my classes and internship, and my friends and our plan for a break trip
to their ski cabin. It was great."

Molly went on to explain that she felt like she was at a major advantage over her first-generation friends because her parents could relate
to her experiences. For instance, while her mother was not the biggest
fan of her attempts at joining a sorority, they were largely on the same
page as she made choices and began changing as a result of her experiences during college. She did acknowledge that having friends from
more affluent and privileged backgrounds was difficult to manage, but
emphasized that she saw her parents as a resource for dealing with that.
She explained, "I mean, my parents basically did this before me. I'm just
taking it to the next level. They were first-gens back when first-gen was
not really a thing so, like, all their friends were better off than them."
Because of their familiarity with the process of becoming socially mobile through college, Molly's parents could serve as a sounding board as
she tried to navigate the "bougie culture" at South. Instead of describing initial visits home filled with conflict and anxiety, Molly, and other
second-generation students like her, chronicled these first trips back
home as opportunities to recharge and a chance to go to their parents for
advice. This was due in large part to the fact that while their parents did
not have the same level of economic capital as the parents of their affluent peers on campus, they did have the vitally important cultural capital

needed to be able to anticipate, frame, and embrace the experiences and resultant changes that their students were going through during college.

For Wyatt, returning home to his family was a welcome respite from the stressors of attending East College and navigating an elite culture among students he felt were disingenuous and lacked a critical lens around their own positionality as privileged people in a deeply stratified society. Wyatt had reached out to his mother for advice and counsel when first dealing with his mixed feelings about the trade-offs of being at East and felt that her own experience as a first-generation student made her a well-informed sounding board around his own experience. He described his first trip home from break as something akin to a mindfulness retreat, where he was able to become recentered and refocused on what his purpose was. As he described his visit home in this way, he actually began chuckling to himself. He explained that he remembered describing the visit in the same way to his mom and uncle during a family dinner, that his uncle had been confused by the somewhat naturalistic framing that he was using to describe his visit home, and that his mom had laughed about the interaction and equated it to her own experience. He said, "It was hilarious, I'm on one side of the table talking about rejuvenation, and my uncle is across from me looking at me like I just grew another head. So, my mom starts laughing and says [to the uncle] 'Oh Eddie, come on! This isn't even that out there. Remember when I came home and declared myself a Taoist? How about when I was a lesbian for a semester? It's all part of the college experience. He's just happy to be home!' It was hilarious!"

For students like Wyatt and Molly, having a parent who had attended college mattered not just in terms of how they experienced their breaks at home, but also in terms of how perceived changes to their personalities and identities were framed and received by those closest to them. Even in moments like this one described by Wyatt, where his uncle was unsure about his Buddhist-informed approach toward explaining his experiences, Wyatt's mother's familiarity with the college experience smoothed over a potentially tense or uncomfortable moment by equating it to part of a natural process of development. Having a shared frame around social mobility, college, and change with parents reduced the likelihood of conflict for continuing-generation students, which resulted in lower reported levels of stress and anxiety around their relationships and expectations at home.

The Role of Majors

While I expected to see some differences with students who were low-income but not first-generation, I identified another pattern in my interviews that I did not see coming—the possible protective function of major. Students majoring in STEM fields—particularly men—were the least likely to discuss experiencing these moments of rupture or renegotiation with their parents during visits home from college. Fred, a White third-year, was representative of many of the men in STEM fields whom I talked with. He was a low-income first-generation student attending East College on full scholarship, majoring in chemistry with the intention of going to medical school and eventually becoming a doctor. His parents were fully behind his decision to attend East and, as he explained, had envisioned his future as a doctor for as long as he could remember. Fred described visits home as pleasant and mostly spent participating in relatively mundane family activities, doing extra reading for school, and studying for the MCATs alone in his room. When I later asked him to reflect on whether and how he had changed during college, he focused primarily on academic growth, but also discussed feeling more "refined" and like he had "learned to be more East." When I asked him what that meant, to "be more East," he expanded by saying, "Well, if I had to say, I would say I am more like my wealthy peers now. I think my intelligence always fit in. I didn't have any catching up to do. But now I think my speech, my dress, my everything fits in. That's where I had makeup work to do." Fred detailed changes similar to many of his first-generation peers, but asserted that he did not feel like he experienced conflict with his parents or high school friends around these changes. He explained, "My parents certainly noticed that I started wearing button-down shirts more regularly and that I was eating healthier than our normal meal choices. But it wasn't a problem." Instead of producing arguments about change and losing his sense of self or identity, Fred noted that when his parents would bring up changes in his dress, diet, mannerisms, or interests, they were cosigning these changes as positive and associated them with a "natural part of fulfilling my potential and becoming a doctor."

The way that Fred's parents framed these changes as part of the "natural" path of mobility necessary to achieve the goal of having a prestigious and stable medical career was something I only found in a small number of students who were planning to become doctors. This, of course, may potentially be linked to the personalities and relationships these students had with their parents, or even their lack of exposure to ideas about the salience of identity that are more often taught in the social sciences and humanities. They were often the most academically focused students I interviewed—opting to focus as exclusively on STEM courses as their institutions would allow them—including two students who chose to opt out of nearly all social aspects of college in favor of focusing on academics and interning in labs, a choice that may have also negated the accumulation of cultural capital from programming, events, and socializing, thus reducing the magnitude of observable changes. It is difficult to pinpoint exactly what aspects of being a STEM or pre-med major matter the most, but they are all relevant and interesting aspects to consider as mechanisms for protecting these students from the conflicts described by their peers. However, the experiences of students who started out as prospective doctors majoring in STEM fields who then changed majors and career trajectories midway through college provide more depth to understanding how a student's major and perceptions about the role or career they are striving for may inform how parents frame changes when they happen.

Zane, a White fourth-year attending Midwest College, had started school much like Fred. He spent roughly his first two years as a biochemistry major and had plans to go to medical school and eventually become a surgeon. However, Zane described growing tired of constantly struggling to keep up in his STEM courses and not having time for anything outside of P-sets and labs. After talking things through with his academic counselor, he decided to change his major to political science and pursue a career working for an international environmental nonprofit. He explained that he had gone abroad over a summer to intern with a health nonprofit and was surprisingly drawn to the nonmedical work that was being done around international rights and politics. When he began considering a shift in majors, he went with the one that would best fit his new career goals and that had the lowest barrier to entry. He recalled being very excited about the change, saying, "I felt excited and alive for the first time in as long as I could remember. I couldn't wait to tell my parents."

When Zane went home during that winter break of his third year, he remembers being surprised with how upset his parents were about his change in major. He commented, "Man, they really were pissed. It's not like I was changing to modern art or something. I wanted to help people! I had to talk them through it for hours." He went on to explain that in addition to being upset about the switch, his parents became hypercritical of many of his other choices, including things that they had not objected to prior to this period of conflict. He described an interaction with his mother that occurred in the kitchen after a particularly tense and long dinner conversation.

> I was standing there in the kitchen cleaning up the dishes, and my mom came around the corner clicking her tongue at me like "Tsk tsk." And I was like "I'm sorry, Mom!" and then she went into this whole thing about my pants being too nice for a weeknight dinner and how I was acting "all high and mighty like I was better than them" [his air quotes]. And I was like in my mind, "Uhhhh, what? You bought me these pants. There's a picture of me wearing them to a BBQ on the shelf like four feet away." I was so confused. All of a sudden everything I did was wrong.

The emotional exchange that Zane described between himself and his mother was clearly not about whether or not his pants were appropriate attire to a Tuesday night dinner. In many ways, the critique on his clothes and attitude were essentially collateral damage from the larger rift caused by his unexpected divergence from a taken-for-granted trajectory into a prestigious medical career.

What is interesting, however, is how these shifts in his parents' attitudes highlight how particular majors and careers may influence the way that parents perceive and interpret changes in their students. Once Zane chose to change majors, he was no longer on the path toward becoming a doctor, and his family began to see him through a different lens. Unlike Fred's parents, Zane's mom and dad could no longer frame his actions and choices as part of becoming a doctor. Without an imagined medical career to continue anchoring their understandings of his growth, the distance that had emerged between Zane and his family became a symbol of unwanted changes that threatened to turn their son into something unrecognizable. Although perhaps a relatively rare experience, the shifts in Zane's family that occurred after he changed majors are illustrative of how ideas around what changes are considered normal or acceptable are often influenced or framed through beliefs about particular majors and career paths—and behaviors that may be considered legitimate for a student on the path to becoming a doctor are no longer acceptable once they deviate from that path.

This aligns with the idea that the average American recognizes pursuing the professions of doctor and lawyer as legible and legitimate routes toward economic mobility, and other careers are understood and accepted with less certainty.[136] The loss of the ability to apply the convenient and broadly recognized cultural script for "doctor" to situations like Zane's matters for the families of first-generation college students. When Zane and other students like him were on the track to become doctors, the changes their families observed were framed as legible and legitimate aspects of becoming a doctor—a preapproved career associated with very specific forms of capital. Whereas once they changed courses to majors that were tied to unfamiliar career paths, those same changes became decoupled from the cultural imaginary of "doctor" and as a result lost their legitimacy and became unwanted and undesirable. In many ways, these examples demonstrate that acceptance and endorsement of the changes a student is going through during college may be directly informed by parents' and family's ability to produce a narrative framework that normalizes and legitimates those changes as critical aspects of the career or role they are attending college to achieve in the first place.

THE DOUBLE BIND

While these examples demonstrate that some low-income or first-generation students can make it through the initial changes associated with the social mobility that occurs from attending a selective college or university relatively unscathed, the majority of students I talked to faced some sort of complicating conflict around the ways they were changing during college. For some, this was an internal conflict that was activated through experiences on campus; for others, it was an external conflict that emerged during an early trip home to friends and family; and for many, it was a combination of both of these experiences accumulated over time. What is particularly important to note, however, is that regardless of the source of this conflict, an overwhelming number of students I talked to discussed that these conflicts led to feeling ill equipped to reconcile the incongruencies in the messaging that they and their families had internalized around the value and purpose of a selective college education. Violet, an Asian American student at East College, explained that after the conflict she had with her parents during her break, she was left confused about how she should move forward in a way that would satisfy the seemingly contrasting expectations coming from her parents. She explained,

> I felt very lost. My parents had been so supportive, maybe even demanding, that I attend East College and become a doctor. But once I started to walk down that path, they didn't like what they saw and critiqued who I was becoming. But they're the ones that wanted me to do this, to get rich and move up and all that, in the first place . . . Later on when I tried to explain that this was all part of it, they couldn't, they wouldn't hear me. And, like, how am I supposed to do both? Climb the ladder, but also not? It's so confusing.

For Violet, and students like her, trying to reconcile the mismatches between how their parents initially framed the purpose and value of a selective education with their newly reinterpreted frameworks left them confused and questioning their own decisions around college. Angel, a Latinx student in his first year at East College, echoed Violet's confusion after his first visit home and noted that he felt as though his family was asking him to do something inherently contradictory. He explained,

> So, it's like my family wants me to go to East and become successful but also wants me to stay exactly the same. Which, bro, that's impossible. I am pretty sure that's at least half of why people go to East is because it makes you successful, it makes you into a person that's successful. Pretty sure something about that is probably on the website right now. So, like why did you send me here if you didn't want that? What am I supposed to do? Just be like "Nah, I'll pass" on learning anything new or different? Then why am I even here?

Violet and Angel's confusion and frustration with the conflicting messaging they were receiving from their families were echoed by a number of students I talked to. Even further, a significant number of students connected this frustration to a growing tension they felt between meeting the expectations of their families and friends and the expectations

of their campus communities. This led these students to feeling significant stress over what was described as trying to balance competing pressures to "buy in" to the elite educational context without "selling out" in
the eyes of their home communities, which aligns with some of the findings from philosophical work[137] on the costs of social mobility in college
as well as prior investigations[138] of the choices first-generation students
make when under pressure.

For many students, this tension produced what I refer to as a "double
bind," which emerged as they struggled to make sense of and navigate
these competing demands. Inherently informed by Du Bois's notion
of "double consciousness,"[139] or the internal conflict felt by a subordi-
nated group in an oppressive society that arises out of their membership
in two categories with irreconcilable expectations, the "double bind" is
the sense of being stuck between two worlds with the pressure of meeting competing (and often irreconcilable) demands that I argue many
first-generation students find themselves in at selective colleges and
universities.

Arnold, a multiracial student in their fourth year at Midwest College,
explained that after a difficult first quarter at Midwest and a tumultuous
trip home to visit their family, they found themselves "trapped in the
middle of two super-intense sets of expectations." Arnold went on to describe their experience of the emergence of this double bind by saying,

> I was in the dining hall one morning, and I just sort of realized that what
> Midwest and my parents were asking of me were in complete opposi-
> tion. If I wanted to be seen as a legit part of Midwest, I needed to let my-
> self become more "Midwest," more refined, you know? But if I wanted
> to be seen as legit by my fam, I needed to stay true to myself. And whoa,
> that hit me hard because how do you do that? How do you do both?
> I felt stuck. Like I knew I couldn't do both, but I also couldn't just do
> neither and still succeed, you know? It was a heavy thing to start work-
> ing through while jamming on a breakfast burrito, you know [laughs]?

As Arnold highlights here, many students find that what it will take to
be successful at their selective college or university and what it will take
to maintain positive relationships with their families and friends are at
odds with each other in a way that complicates their path forward. As
I will show in chapter 5, Arnold and the many students like them turn

to their colleges and universities seeking support and guidance around how to navigate unexpected changes, contentious conflicts, and an emerging double bind. However, for the most part, standard campus support for low-income and first-generation students does not include programming or resources that cover these critical student needs. This gap between what universities and colleges offer, and the support that these students need, often leaves these students alone to find and build support systems, navigate strategies for managing these demands and tensions, and cope with the mental and emotional health impacts of these processes.

· 5 ·
Making Sense
of Social Mobility

One of the student groups that I spent a lot of time with during my field-work worked for an entire year on putting together a conference for low-income and first-generation students attending colleges in the Midwest. A year before, a couple of the student leaders had the opportunity to attend IvyG, a conference for first-gen students attending Ivy Plus schools, and wanted to bring the sense of community and empowerment they felt at that conference to their peers. Students from over a dozen schools across the region attended the conference, representing elite privates, regional privates, liberal arts schools, and public four-year institutions. They brought with them a diversity of backgrounds, experiences, and perspectives on what it means to be a first-generation college student in the United States. Throughout the conference, students shared their stories and pushed each other to expand their frameworks beyond their individual experiences and university contexts.

Toward the end of the second day of the conference, I was cofacilitat-ing a breakout session with one of the student leaders, Lucy, a third-year from Midwest College. Our small classroom was packed with nearly 20 students, who were eagerly chatting away as we prepared for our session. Lucy sighed heavily as she unpacked a box full of index cards—it had been a long couple of days, and the demands of planning and running an entire conference with little help from staff or administrators were beginning to show on her face. I told her to hang out in the back and take a break—I had done this kind of presentation before and figured that covering the nuts and bolts of low-income first-generation event planning would be a straightforward process.

After doing introductions around the room, I asked if anyone had any questions before we got into the workshop. Trevor, a White student from a school in the area, raised his hand and asked if we could briefly talk about what people's campus communities looked like. His voice hitched as he said, "Because I gotta say, we don't got anything like this [at my school]. I've never had people to talk to about all this." Next to me, an Asian American second-year from another school in the area nodded her head in agreement, adding: "Like, my college has tons of programs, but none of it's real. Sure, yes, teach me how to network. That's important. But I'm like 'What about the soul-crushing pain I feel on campus and at home? What about that? Oh, you have nothing for that? Cool cool cool.'" Her voice trailed off at the end of this comment as she looked down at her notebook, tears dripping onto her handwritten notes from an earlier session about accessing and understanding financial aid. I could feel the oxygen leave the room as she finished speaking. As I scanned the room, Lucy caught my eye and she motioned for me to do something in response to the emotionally charged moment we had stumbled into. In that moment I took a deep breath, pressed my palms onto the table, and said, "Okay, so let's talk about that. Who wants to start?"

Moments like this were very common during my fieldwork. The experience of struggling to understand and contextualize the unexpected changes brought on by social mobility during college without formal institutional support is part of a larger pattern that appeared across my interviews, focus groups, and conversations with students. Even at schools with extensive first-generation resources, many students had a hard time finding formal support when moments of rupture and conflict occurred on campus and at home.

This chapter details how first-generation and low-income students navigate and cope with the unexpected changes and conflicts that I highlighted in chapter 4 and considers the gap between the support that these students often feel they need and the institutional programming available to them at their selective colleges and universities. I argue that highly selective colleges and universities have yet to understand the full impact that the polishing process has on its first-generation students, and that although they frame themselves as people-changing organizations broadly, the kinds of intensive change that this portion of their student population is grappling with require more resources and support than they currently realize. Ultimately, I show that in the face of mismatched support on campus, many low-income and first-generation students must navigate the effects of the polishing process, the demands of the double bind, and the full costs of social mobility during college on their own. And, as a result, first-generation students often face intensive stress, anxiety, and alienation that have significant impacts on their experiences and outcomes during college. As I show, this pushes some students into making very difficult choices around how to navigate and alleviate the stressors and tensions they feel as low-income and first-generation students going through social mobility at a selective college.

UNIVERSITY-SPONSORED SUPPORT PROGRAMS

When low-income and first-generation students begin grappling with these unexpected experiences and contentious conflicts, they often look to their colleges and universities for support. And while many selective colleges and universities have poured significant resources into supporting their first-generation student populations,[140] I found that the majority of these resources and support are part of the polishing process itself and focus on developing the skills students need to thrive in college or cover generalized concepts like "impostor syndrome" as a psychological roadblock that they can overcome, or "cultural straddling" as a strategy for fitting in on campus. While these resources help build the capital students need and can be helpful for students as they navigate life as a first-generation student, they do not directly address navigating and dealing with the challenges and conflict that arise as a result of the polishing process.

The majority of campuses I spent time on offered workshops and skill sessions for first-generation and other minoritized students around talking to faculty and how to use office hours. Interestingly, a number of the students I spent time with not only critiqued these sessions; they also emphasized their desire for alternative programming. For example, Arnold, a multiracial student at Midwest College, said, "Look, I really appreciate everything the student center does, I really do. But they don't have anything that I really need. I went to a workshop on how to talk to professors last week, and that's cool, I guess, but like, I need a workshop on how to talk to my mom about my life, you know what I mean? Where's that workshop?" As Arnold notes, an important gap exists between what the college was offering and what they needed as first-generation students grappling with social mobility. And, while it can be argued that what Arnold is asking for is less the work of a college's student support division and more the work of a private therapist, it is important to note that access to consistent and affordable mental health services is a documented challenge for marginalized students[141] in a way that is far less pronounced for their affluent peers. For Arnold and students like them, their college is often the only resource they have to turn to in moments of crisis and the unknown. Having programming available from student services or counseling centers that addresses strategies for grappling with challenges like these could make a remarkably significant impact on their experiences and trajectories during college.

Another popular branch of programming and workshops found on selective campuses across the United States focuses on understanding and combating impostor syndrome. Coined by Clance and Imes, "impostor syndrome"[142] is a concept that is used to encapsulate when individuals—particularly those inhabiting marginalized identities— have feelings of doubt about their legitimacy or belongingness. It has gained a lot of attention and ground in higher education student affairs as a way to talk to first-generation and other minoritized students about their experiences.[143] A number of students I talked to discussed that impostor syndrome workshops had become a popular student services go-to for helping first-generation students feel at home on their college campuses. And, while a number of students noted that they appreciated the idea of impostor syndrome as a way to contextualize their feelings of inadequacy and aloneness on campus, others critiqued its use. Garrett, an Asian American first-year at East College, expressed his frustrations with the way that impostor syndrome was used so readily to explain the problems he and his friends faced on campus: "You know what's bullshit? Impostor syndrome is bullshit. I mean, it's a real thing for sure, I think everyone feels like impostors sometimes. But, it's just what ends up being used to explain what can't be explained. You know what I mean? It's like 'Oh, you're going through something that I can't cover on my PowerPoint? That's gotta be impostor syndrome. So, like, get over that because you belong.' Easy enough, right?" On Garrett's campus, the notion of impostor syndrome had become a catchall for any kind of experience or problem that did not neatly fit into a category that could be easily be addressed. For Garrett, and many other students like him, invoking impostor syndrome felt like a way for their colleges to absolve themselves of the responsibility of trying to unearth the root causes behind the problems they were facing. In many ways, Garrett's experiences highlight how impostor syndrome frames student challenges as a psychological one via using the medicalized term "syndrome" rather than a symptom of a structure that actively excludes students. This produces an environment that not only ignores the deeper needs of students, but also shifts the focus in a way that institutionally and culturally frames student experiences as a personal trouble instead of a public issue.[144] Instead of having their complaint addressed, these students were being told that the confusion, stress, and anxiety they were feeling around their social mobility were an internal issue that they alone could overcome. This left many students like Garrett feeling unheard and disregarded by the very institutions that they had worked so hard to become a part of.

"Cultural straddling"[145] and "code-switching"[146] are additional concepts that the students I talked to (particularly students of color) discussed as being integrated deeply into the programming offered to them as marginalized students on their campuses. Coined by Carter and Haugen, respectively, these concepts encapsulate strategies that individuals use to navigate and interact in two different social worlds. Haugen's early sociolinguistic work considered how and when people switch between two different languages or culturally relevant ways of speaking. It has been used to highlight the ways that minoritized students juggle interactions across education and familial contexts as they move back and forth between the linguistic demands of each space. Carter builds on the idea of code-switching with the introduction of cultural straddling as a way of explaining the strategies employed by K–12 students as they navigate the contrasting social expectations and demands between their school and home communities. Both Haugen's and Carter's concepts have been considered in many K–12 settings as well as applied to the experiences of underrepresented students in higher education.[147] Like impostor syndrome, these concepts are favored by student affairs staff in higher education as a way to talk to first-generation and other minoritized students about their experiences and can be found in the content of programming and social science coursework across campuses nationwide. Because of its popularity as a tool for aiding students in making sense of their experiences, I found it commonplace to have students bring up the concept in discussion and talk about how it was worked into programming on their campuses.

During his first or second year, Elijah, a Black fourth-year at South College, had tried to access support around making sense of the changes he was experiencing. While the student services staff had been very welcoming, they merely suggested that he attend an upcoming brown-bag talk on code-switching that a multicultural group was hosting on campus. Elijah said that he attended the workshop and found the topic interesting, but not particularly useful for explaining his actual experience. He explained that code-switching was something he was familiar with and thought it was a useful way to think through potential strategies for balancing his school and home lives. However, he also noted that it did not aid him in working through the questions he was developing around whether he had made the right choice in attending South and what he was questioning in terms of his identity. For Elijah and students like him, the relevance of code-switching was limited to efforts around navigating contrasting social settings and interactions and was seen as less useful for making sense of the internal challenges they faced or the changes they saw in themselves.

Nicki, a third-year at East College, relayed a similar experience where she had been referred to a workshop on cultural straddling and code-switching strategies for students of color at East College. While she was familiar with the concept as a multiracial person (Black and White), these strategies did not work as well when trying to navigate across classed contexts. In many ways, she attributed this to not having enough capital to be able to effectively do the work of code-switching: "I've read a lot about code-switching and I went to a workshop on it, but that's not working for me. I think maybe I don't know enough of the code yet." Unlike her experience growing up in two different communities, Nicki was just beginning her journey into social mobility. She had accumulated enough capital to begin thinking about her new contexts, but not enough to have the level of fluency required to effectively straddle or switch between the two worlds.

This gap in the programming available to students and their ability to deploy its techniques matters. Students are turning to their campuses (which are often the only resource they have access to) in their moments of need and are walking away empty-handed. Concepts like

cultural straddling and code-switching are being used as primary strategies for aiding first-generation students through their bifurcated experiences in higher education, and yet, as I have shown, this should not be
a catchall resource for this student population. As is the case with impostor syndrome, colleges and universities are merely giving students
the language they need to describe a feeling (of being an impostor or
having to switch dialects) that that kind of programming does not teach
students practical skills or interventions that they actually need to manage those experiences. As I have shown, many students require different and deeper programming that can address the tensions and conflicts
they are experiencing due to identity transformations and social mobility during college. Without the means or networks to access the support
they need on their own, students like Nicki and Elijah will continue to
silently struggle on campus and potentially face significant impacts to
their mental health and academic development.

In many ways, this set of student needs was a programmatic blind
spot for the majority of staff and administrators. And, in cases where
staff were attuned to some of these student needs, they cited a lack of
support and funding at the administrative dean level around this kind
of programming. Janette, a staff member, explained that in the time
she had been working at her college, she noticed that many of the first-
generation students struggled with how college was changing them.
When she proposed new programming around this topic, it failed to gain
traction with upper-level administrators because they did not see that
kind of specialized work as a good use of resources. She said,

> The first-gen students worry about identity erasure, and we don't have
> anything to address that. I proposed new programming around that,
> but they told me it was too specialized and that I should just lump it in
> with existing programming around racial identity or try and include it
> in the impostor syndrome workshops. So, I do my best to help students
> one on one, but that is hard because I am a team of one, and even when
> I can help students, I am sure I am missing so many others out there
> that I don't know.

For staff like Janette, colleges' larger institutional frameworks for understanding student experience plus an overreliance on a cost-effective one-
size-fits-all approach often stymie program development and institutional

progress. Janette and other staff like her expressed their frustration with this situation. Tristen, a senior staff member in student services at her college, described a situation on her campus similar to Janette's and noted that "many first-generation students suffer because no one can decide whose responsibility it is to take care of them. They basically get left out in the cold on a lot of issues." As Tristen and Janette's assessments highlight, schools as elaborate bureaucracies are often slow to develop, and many student needs are unmet in official capacities. In addition, the expanded set of programming required to support a student population that is often without significant financial capital, private insurance, or experienced social networks is something that contemporary colleges and universities are reluctant to take on as part of their bureaucratic repertoire. Because of this, when these students seek help from the only institution they have connections to that has significant resources, they are often left empty-handed, frustrated, and disregarded.

BUILDING CAMPUS COMMUNITIES OF SUPPORT

On many selective campuses, pre-college bridge programs and peer mentor programs play an important role in creating community for first-generation and low-income students. These intensive bridge programs and peer mentor programs became an important element of many first-generation students' first-year survival tool kits by providing valuable information about college and connecting them to a community of students from underrepresented backgrounds that they could rely on. These programs did not, however, offer formal programming around contextualizing and navigating the unexpected changes that occurred as a part of becoming socially mobile during college. Understanding and grappling with what it means to become upwardly mobile—and the shifts that this creates in perspective, habitus, and identity—were not included among the lengthy list of workshop topics and program focuses at any of the schools I visited. Although these programs do not provide formalized programming that addresses these aspects of low-income and first-generation student experiences, they do have the function of producing a dense community of peers that students can rely on to form vital informal peer support networks. Finding these peers was made easier for students on campuses with low-income and first-generation student groups or diversity programming that was inclusive of first-generation students.

For example, Rachel, whose story about winter break opened chapter 4, was part of a program designed to support the needs of underrepresented students. This program served as a community space for many low-income, first-generation, and students of color on campus. While she was reticent to speak up initially about her experience, being able to connect with older, more experienced students who had been through similar experiences became her first step in tackling the difficult task of understanding and reconciling the ways that social mobility was impacting her identity and experience during college. When she divulged that she was having a difficult time processing her negative experiences during winter break, the older students around her became the central resource she drew on to begin understanding her experiences and reframing her own ideas about her positionality as a socially mobile first-generation student at a selective college. Not only did Andie provide Rachel (and the rest of us) with comic relief by equating being a first-generation student with being trapped in an alternate-reality dimension filled with monsters, she followed up those jokes by helping Rachel understand that hers was a shared experience that she had control over.

In that very crucial moment, Andie looked at Rachel and explained, "Seriously, though, that shit is real, and we've all been through it—we're all going through it . . . This place does things to you. If you're not careful, you'll get lost." Rachel responded tearfully, "That's what I'm afraid of. Everything feels weird now. My mom said I've changed, that I'm different." Taking a far more serious approach than before, Andie replied, "Look, everyone changes in college. It's not a question of *if* you change—it's a question of *how* you change. And that's something we get a say in." In our follow-up interview the next year, Rachel referenced this interaction as a turning point for reimagining her relationship to her education and what upward mobility actually meant to her and her family:

I don't have it all figured out yet, maybe I never will. But it's gotten a lot better since freshman year. It's still changing all the time, but I get what's going on now. It's funny now to think that I thought I could go here and do this without changing at all [laughs]. Can you believe that? But I guess it makes sense. No one talks to you about this, like, ever. Not in high school, orientation, workshops. Never in classes. It's like you have to have a breakdown before anyone thinks, "Oh yeah, we should probably let her in on this." And then it's like only other students and it's such a, like, lottery . . . Did you know that Andie and everyone and I weren't even friends before all of that? Yeah, we all just happened to be in the center at the same time. Yeah. They're not even in the mentoring program anymore. They used to be. No one told them they should help me. They just did that. It's very random, really.

Like many other students, Rachel found support and guidance from her older peers that were loosely and informally connected through current and former membership in more formal college-sponsored programming. As Rachel's experience highlights, support does exist in the form of peer community on many campuses. However, finding and fostering this kind of community support takes a lot of initiative on everyone's part and requires significant emotional labor from students who are already overwhelmed with their own lives. Finding this support is also never guaranteed and is left far too up to chance. There were no formal workshops or brown-bag discussions at West College that covered these aspects of the lived experience of being a first-generation student that Rachel could reach out to for help. Instead, she ended up finding community in a group of unknown students who were common fixtures in the student center at West. And, while this worked out well for Rachel over time, the uncertainty that she felt in those moments where she felt like her world was unfolding was not inevitable. Much of her turmoil could have been eased if the institutionally supported mentoring program she was a part of framed this kind of support as just as central to her success as having access to extended tutoring support and other resources.

Similarly, when Elle, a White student at Midwest College, returned to school from her first visit home during her first year, she sought the help of her older peers to help her process the conflicts she had had with her father around perceived changes to her tastes and personality. The Bridge group chat had been relatively silent during break (an occurrence that Elle now framed as many of her friends not knowing how or wanting to bring up their own conflicts), and she was convinced that she was alone in her experience. A Bridge student named Audrey who was two years ahead of Elle ended up reaching out to her after she saw Elle looking distressed in the dining hall. The two quickly became close, as Audrey provided Elle with a sounding board for processing her experiences while using her own story as a way to teach her that her experience was normal and something that could be worked through over time. When discussing this influence on her well-being and trajectory through school, she noted:

> Without Bridge, I don't know if I'd be here. No, for real, though. I probably would have gone home and gotten a gig at some place my friends from high school were working at or something. It's not easy to have your family tell you they don't recognize you anymore and to feel like maybe you don't want to go back to them . . . That's absolutely not part of the "official" [her air quotes] Bridge programming, but it grows out of it. Bridge isn't ready for all of that and all of our problems. Their speed is more making sure we don't fail classes or starve during the summer—which is cool, you know. But the Bridge crew, they've got your back no matter what.

For Elle and many of her peers, they saw the official Bridge program as an important resource and part of their support network at Midwest College. But they saw the more organic peer network that existed in varying levels of formality as their only resource when navigating the difficult spaces and questions that emerged as a result of their social mobility during college. While peer support is well known as a valuable aspect of bridge and peer mentor programming,[148] the depth and content of this support was by and large not on the radar of most administrators and staff. Because of this, instead of being officially recognized and fostered through training and programming, this intensive peer support around the unexpected trauma of social mobility operates as an unofficial and often hidden safety net for students who are lucky enough to find it. This not only puts the burden of support on students, it also creates an environment where the only framework available to students for processing their experiences is coming from their peers. And while these peers are certainly a valuable resource, they lack the critically valuable experience and credentials that a trained professional could provide to these students.

While it is not the perfect solution, having peer support is a valuable resource for many first-generation students that their peers at other institutions cannot count on. In contrast to students like Elle and Rachel,

Chloe, a White first-year student at East College, attended a school that had very little in terms of a first-generation community. When she returned back to campus after her first winter break, she struggled not only to contend with the ways that social mobility had impacted her identity but also to find support from peers that she could connect with over shared experiences. She noted, "I really didn't know anyone because there wasn't a first-gen group. I had friends, but it turned out that they were all middle-class or rich kids. That second semester was really alienating and lonely, to be honest." She further explained that she spent a great deal of her second semester of her first year of college in turmoil over the conflict she had experienced with her family during winter break. It was not until she made friends with a low-income fourth-year at her on-campus job that she started to feel like she was able to talk through her experience and begin to "think through how changing and being mobile was a part of college that couldn't be avoided." While it is possible that Chloe would have managed to work through this on her own, having at least one friend who had already experienced this process provided her with an additional perspective for understanding her experience.

In addition to bridge and peer mentor programs, a number of first-generation students of color discussed the role that student groups organized around race or culture played in connecting them to the less visible network of low-income and first-generation students. For instance, many of the schools that the students I interviewed attended did not offer programming directly tied to first-generation student status, but did have established groups for Latinx and Black students. Aligning with prior research,[149] these programs and groups became a social home base for many first-generation students of color where they could develop friendships within an often densely connected network of students of color from across class years. For many of these students, the friends they made in cultural organizations filled the same kinds of support roles as the students in Bridge did for Elle.

However, some first-generation students of color had mixed experiences when it came to expressing their class identity within these spaces. For Yesenia, a Latinx third-year at South College, being a part of her campus chapter of MEChA (a nationally recognized student organization for students from Hispanic/Latinx backgrounds) meant having access to a group of students who shared her experience as a first-generation immigrant woman. She was happy to have found community around her Latinx identity in MEChA, but she struggled to find support and camaraderie when it came to questions of socioeconomic class. She explained,

> Having MEChA and other cultural groups helped a lot in my first year, I think. Buuuuuuut [her exaggeration], then I took a class on stratification and was like, "Wait. This isn't just about me being Latina, there's some class shit going on in here too . . ." But, [MEChA] is a really mixed mostly rich group, and people weren't really open to the class thing. The focus was about not losing our cultural identity. Which is great and all. But I was losing my class identity, and no one cared.

For many students, programming for cultural groups can be a great resource for finding the valuable peer networks that will support them as they navigate the complexities of being both a student of color and a first-generation student at a selective college. However, whether that happens or not can depend on a significant amount of variability that is tied to what kinds of cultural programming are available and the ratio of affluent students of color to low-income students of color on a given campus. From a 30,000-foot view, students like Yesenia appear to be well supported and embedded deeply in a tight-knit group of students with similar identities and experiences. However, upon closer inspection, these students potentially feel just as alienated and alone as their peers not involved in these kinds of programming because they still lack access to peers from similar class backgrounds with whom they could connect.

BUILDING OFF-CAMPUS SUPPORT NETWORKS

Because of the frequent gaps between the resources that colleges offered for first-generation students and the support these students felt they actually needed, many people sought support from their peers, from their families (when available), and from communities that were external to their campuses. These extra-institutional resources and communities often could provide the space and support that students needed to make sense of the unexpected ways that becoming upwardly mobile in college was shifting their identities, behaviors, and frameworks for understanding the world. However, finding and navigating these extra-institutional spaces takes added time and effort that can compound the burdens these students feel.

Families with Experience

Some students I talked to had family members that had graduated from (or at least attended) college, and this was seen as a valuable resource to turn to throughout their college experiences. For instance, Wyatt, a low-income White student attending East College, felt lucky that his mother had attended college. He spent much of his first year talking to her on the phone and processing his experiences. While he did not feel isolated on campus, he remembered being surprised by some of the negative interactions he had with peers and faculty early on. Wyatt came from a working-class family and recognized what a gift it was to attend an elite college—a perspective that he felt was in stark contrast to the more entitled approach that many of his peers took toward their education. Wyatt had struggled a great deal with how to respond to classist remarks made by students and faculty during classes and in casual conversation with the students who lived on his floor. He described the importance of his conversations with his mother in this way:

> I had some friends that I talked to that were—I guess sympathetic is the word—but my mom knew me and knew what it's like. She was my go-to champion big-time that year. I think I was on the phone with my mom maybe every week, going off about these classist assholes [laughs]. She'd been through it way worse than me when she went to college. She was first-gen from the middle of nowhere. So, she would walk me through how to handle it right. How to see myself in relation to all of this [gestures across campus].

For Wyatt, having a parent who had experienced classism and rejection during college became a valuable resource for helping him process his own experiences during college.

Other students had older siblings they could draw on for support as they made sense of their college experiences. These relationships were particularly helpful when siblings were also enrolled in or had graduated from college. Lucas, a White first-year at East College, noted that having an older brother who was a third-year at another selective college on the East Coast was an invaluable resource for him during his first year of college. He explained, "Cristobal was already in college, so when I started at East College he was my go-to for basically everything. He got what I was going through and he, like, knows me better than I know myself, I think." For Lucas, having an older sibling that had navigated similar experiences was an invaluable resource.

Students with older siblings who had also attended an elite college also emphasized the important role that being able to observe their sibling's progress played in their ability to process conflicts around their social mobility. Maya, a Black first-year attending Midwest College, noted that although she was initially stunned by her first conflict with her parents over changes they associated with her social mobility, she quickly remembered watching a similar interaction between her parents and older sister Danielle two years prior. "I remember her fighting with my parents too—about having changed . . . Having Dani do this before me has been everything. She's gone through the exact same situations. It really helps with perspective." And, while Maya struggled to reframe her perspective and understanding of her mobility and identity in a way that was very similar to many of her peers, her experience was eased by her ability to seek help and advice from her sister in order to smooth out her relationship with her parents. For students like Wyatt, Lucas, and Maya, having close family members who had gone through similar experiences during college helped them process their experiences and contextualize their positionality as low-income and first-generation students undergoing social mobility while attending selective colleges.[150]

What is important to note is that for the majority of these students, the availability of campus resources designed to meet these particular needs became less important than it was for many of their first-generation peers. Because they were able to turn to their social network and family for these kinds of support, they viewed campus resources as primarily for building skills, providing material resources, and cultivating opportunities and experiences. This, of course, aligned with the way that colleges and universities frame their initiatives for supporting underrepresented students and, thus, generally led to these students expressing relative satisfaction with the ways their colleges were supporting their needs as low-income students. And, while this kind of satisfaction does not mean that all of these students' needs were met by the colleges they attended, it is illustrative of a substantial divide between these students and their peers who do not have college-educated parents or siblings to draw on. Having parents, siblings, and family members that are able to draw on firsthand experiences with college as a means for helping contextualize experiences matters for students. And, in many ways, this familiarity with college and the experiences and changes it can bring is what set returning-generation low-income students apart from their first-generation peers.

External Organizational Support

Some students were able to draw on an external community of low-income students to find support when trying to contextualize their experiences at highly selective colleges. These students cited having a community of people with similar backgrounds who were connected through the same scholarship organization as a major way they dealt with the challenges of being a first-generation student at a highly selective school. Some Jack Kent Cooke Scholars noted that having other students who were Cooke Scholars at their schools or at schools nearby helped them form a community of mutual support on campus. This was particularly useful for students who were at campuses with very little in the way of formalized programming for first-generation students. The majority of Jack Kent Cooke Scholars that I talked to, however, were either the only Cooke Scholar on their campuses or were not aware of other Scholars nearby. Some of these students described being relatively disconnected from the Foundation and Cooke Scholar community, whereas others noted that they made and maintained contact with other Scholars through online communities and texts. Nina, a White fourth-year at West College, noted that although they were the only Cooke Scholar on their campus, the active online Cooke Scholar community became a source of support, information, and validation. They explained, "I am the only Scholar here at West, but I am really close to a lot of my cohort mates. We text all the time. The Foundation also has a major online presence, so if I ever have questions I just go to Facebook and ask, and I swear it only takes seconds before the replies start rolling in." Although physically isolated from fellow Cooke Scholars, Nina felt like their membership in the Jack Kent Cooke Foundation gave them much-needed support and perspectives that they were not getting on campus.

Nina went on to explain that West College provided very few programs specifically tailored to their identity as a first-generation student. They did have first-gen friends and friends from other underrepresented groups, but they didn't relate to them in quite the same way they did to other Cooke Scholars. They said, "I'm pretty sure that I am trauma bonded with some of my Cooke cohort mates. They're the only other people that understand what I've gone through both to get here and to stay here. It's way rare, you know, this whole ridiculous thing we're doing." In many ways, having a peer network of other students who were simultaneously going through the same rare experience gave Nina a perspective that very few other first-generation students at highly selective colleges have access to. For Nina and students like them, the experience of becoming socially mobile during college becomes a group experience that, while still unsettling and difficult, is one that can be better understood and managed through hearing about the experiences and strategies employed by trusted peers and mentors.

It is important to note that one reason Nina felt so empowered to reach out to their scholarship peers is because it has become a part of the Cooke Scholarship culture to openly discuss many of the challenges of being a first-generation student attending a selective institution. Social media spaces associated with the Cooke Foundation frequently feature students and alumni sharing stories of their personal struggles and asking for the advice and help of peers—or, as many people prefer, their "Cooke Cousins." And while this public discourse around college and mobility is not central to the mission of the Jack Kent Cooke Foundation, the idea that Cooke Scholars are part of a community that is so close they might as well be considered family is deeply rooted in the programming and messaging that Scholars receive once they are selected for support from the Foundation. So, when students like Nina are faced with uncertainty or are struggling to reframe their trajectories as socially mobile first-generation students, they tend to feel empowered to reach out to fellow Cooke Scholars and alumni for support.

The Foundation also formally structures the way they interface with and support Scholars, and this comes with some very valuable and needed informal support as a byproduct. For instance, each incoming

College Scholar is assigned an advisor that they interface with in group and one-on-one meetings covering the gamut of topics from registration for classes and changing majors to coping with parental divorce and identity change. While most of the advisors were not first-generation, they had intimate knowledge of students' families and experiences in a way that is uncommon for staff at a college to have about students. In the case of Cooke Scholars, many of these students cited the close relationships they had with their advisors as a key source of emotional support in college. Gillian noted, "I'm pretty sure Brett [a staff member at the JKC Organization] is just a White dude from a wealthy background, but he knows my parents and my life. He gets what's going on with me, so I can talk to him about the hard stuff." For many students, this familiarity served as a proxy for shared experience, and provided the bridge needed to find support and a knowledgeable sounding board as they worked through the "hard stuff" of considering the full implications of college and social mobility on their lives.

In effect, the Foundation, much like colleges, often perceives their interventions to be impacting students in a particular way—such as giving them individualized advising to guide them through formal requirements and hidden curriculum. They perhaps do not always realize the depth of this important benefit: that this same intervention also gives students access to a knowledgeable adult who has intimate knowledge of their personal biography that can help them think through and contextualize unexpected conflicts and challenges along their mobility trajectories.

Off-Campus Communities

While family and external scholarships can prove to be an important resource for some students, the majority of students I talked to did not have college-educated parents, older siblings already attending college, or intensive scholarship communities to turn to for help, advice, or perspective around the unexpected aspects of social mobility and experiences on campus. These students often sought support in communities off campus. For religious students, finding community through churches near their campus was a common way of remaining embedded in a community of support during college. Some families saw a student's connection to a church of their denomination as a critical part of their college support network, with some parents going so far as to contact local pastors ahead of their child's move to make sure the local church community was ready to receive and support their student. This kind of immediately available support from a community off campus could produce feelings of continuity and be a grounding force that allowed students to maintain an important aspect of their identities during this transitional period. Angie, a multiracial second-year at East College who came from a religious family that helped connect her with a church before she had even arrived at college for orientation, noted, "I was annoyed at my mom at first for calling Grace [church], but I gotta say, having that stable force in my life—especially last year—really mattered. Everything else was up in the air, and I felt rocked to my core and alone at school, at home, with my friends, but not at Grace."

Having this outside community provided a constant for these students that allowed them to ultimately feel like they could maintain stasis over at least one aspect of their identity during a time of major flux. This desire to maintain stability or routine appeared to draw students to the church even when they changed or reevaluated their faith in religion. As Elijah, a Black fourth-year at South, explained, "I'm not even sure I believe anymore. My ideas have changed a lot around God and the universe. I think now I go for the people. The community. The routine of it too, I guess." Like many college students in the United States,[151] a number of the young people I talked to had begun to reconsider their faith during college. As Elijah's comment shows, however, this reconsideration did not always stop them from participating in their church communities because the benefits of community often outweighed the disconnect between their developing beliefs and the beliefs of the church.

It is important to note, however, that none of the religious students I talked to cited their church communities as a resource for navigating the unexpected parts of social mobility that they had to navigate during college. Even Angie, the most outwardly self-identified religious student in this study, expressed frustrations around the limits to her church community's ability to understand the kind of support she needed as she grappled with her social mobility. She explained:

There's limits to it, though. Nobody at Grace could actually help me with the tailspin I was in—that maybe I'm still in [laughs]. When I was like "I'm really second-guessing college," or when I came to the women's group for advice about the pressure I felt to change and how that made me feel . . . I felt like a traitor to my family and community, and the response always turned it into something about my faith. After a while I was like "Uh, I dunno if that's what's going on here, fam. Like, okay, maybe God will guide me there, but this isn't about God per se." Which then made me think I was having a crisis of faith for a minute [sighs]. But, it's okay. At least I have this place where I can come and reflect and eat and be with people.

Angie's experience highlights that while there are often limits to the support that comes from outside communities, having any community place to feel a sense of belonging and embeddedness during college becomes important and valuable for students. This is particularly important for underrepresented students like first-generation students, who may otherwise feel alienated and disengaged from their campus communities,[152] regardless of where they are in the process of managing the double bind of social mobility during college.

A number of students sought stability and support in the working-class communities surrounding their college campuses. Much like their more religious peers, these students reported that finding peers and elders from backgrounds that aligned more closely to theirs became an important part of navigating their positionality as a first-generation student attending a selective college. Having this network of off-campus peers to do activities with that were not tied to attending college became a central way for these students to feel more authentic to their working-class selves, something that was often wrapped up in the vague notion of being "normal." For instance, Evie, a multiracial genderqueer student at East College, moved off campus in their second year. It was important to them to find roommates who were "normal regular people" that "have jobs and do normal things." In particular, they emphasized the value of having a sounding board of friends not affiliated with their campus. "Finley and Nan [roommates] can't connect with everything I'm going through, but they for sure know what it's like to deal with rich assholes as normal people." For Evie, having a close friend group of people who came from working-class backgrounds and were not affiliated with their college allowed them to reassert their own working-class first-generation identity as "normal." This, in turn, enabled them to re-frame the unexpected and negative experiences they had had on campus not as a failure on Evie's part, but as a perceived character flaw of the affluent students they attended school with.

Strategies like Evie's, however, could become complicated and reproduce a renewed double bind over time. In a follow-up interview with Evie during their third year, they described feeling a lot of pressure from their roommates and friends to conform to their expectations around being working class. They noted that they were currently looking for new roommates and were considering moving in with another first-generation classmate at East because they felt that they may be more open to what they referred to as the "mismatch of high-brow and low-brow aesthetic" that they had cultivated as a socially mobile first-generation student attending East.

Reflecting on the potentialities of their future, Evie noted, "Maybe I need someone that can get all parts of what I'm going through. But, wow, I don't know what that means for the future. Am I only ever going to feel real with other college-educated first-gens? Whoa. That's a wild thought!" And, while Evie's questions may feel a bit extreme, they hit on the distinct challenges that first-generation students face when trying to navigate social mobility during and after college. These feelings of isolation and alienation, even when in a supportive community, extend throughout these students' trajectories and complicate the work of short-term strategies like code-switching and cultural straddling in a way that raises questions about how the tensions of the double bind can be eased in the long run.

ADDRESSING THE DOUBLE BIND

I found that even when students were able to form communities of support either on or off campus, many of them were still left with the onerous task of developing strategies for dealing with the realities of the double bind. They negotiated contrasting expectations and demands from school and home, reframed their positionality as a first-generation or low-income student going through social mobility at a selective college, and grappled with whether the socio-emotional costs of social mobility were worth it.

Straddling as a Long-Term Strategy

Prior research has asserted that part of what underrepresented students learn from their peers and support communities is how to employ code-switching and straddling strategies for managing the competing demands of living in more than one community or culture.[153] And, while I found that most students followed this trend—particularly in the earliest stages of their academic trajectories through selective colleges—I also found many students who felt like this social balancing was either ineffective or too much to handle over time.

Some students noted that instead of feeling like they had a foot in two different worlds that they could straddle, they felt trapped between the two worlds, unable to adequately navigate either. Quinn, a Black third-year attending Midwest College, summarized this when he said, "I don't really feel like I belong anywhere. When I'm at home, I am disconnected. When I'm at school, I am disconnected. It's like I'm trapped between two worlds and can't find a home in either one. It's total chaos." Quinn explained that he attributed this feeling of being trapped between home and school to changing some, but not enough, during college. He noted, "So, I've tried to fit in better because, you know, I'm first-gen, but I still stick out and all that. But that has changed me, so now I don't really fit in, I'm not the same as back home now . . . And that all puts me in this weird in-between." For many students like Quinn, the work of becoming a socially mobile college student, of learning, gaining, and embracing the capital needed to fit in on their college campuses, had the unintended consequence of creating distance between them and their families and friends at home. This not only produced conflict for these students; it also placed them in a somewhat liminal space where they were no longer seen as authentically aligned with their home communities and did not yet have the ease necessary to achieve full membership in their campus communities. This, in turn, made it difficult for these students to effectively straddle or switch between their two worlds, as they no longer felt like they belonged or had command over the capital needed to feel at home in either space.

Some students described trying code-switching and straddling techniques, finding them useful in the short run, but then more difficult to maintain as they continued to change during college. Some of these students reported that a feeling of in-betweenness arose from trying to straddle two identities and communities over time and asserted that it took a major toll on their emotional and mental health. Reece, a White genderqueer second-year at West College, explained their experience in this way:

> I've always been different, you know? The super-smart kid in class, the queer weirdo in town . . . but at least when people were calling me names I had the two other queer kids in town to retreat to. Now I am on an island, no, I am in the water. I'm in the water between two islands of people that I am trying to be like, but I am just out here, like, drowning and my therapist is, like, this cruise director that is trying to teach me how to samba or something, but she can't throw me a fucking life float or whatever those things are called . . . So, like, am I going to drown? Maybe I am. Or maybe I'll just pick an island and live there. I don't know.

Reece's island metaphor highlights the significant impact that this process of attempting to balancing multiple worlds has on students. It also hits on a gap between first-generation student needs and the services provided from campus-based mental health professionals that a number of students focused on in their interviews.

As prior research[154] demonstrates, campus mental health services are often perceived as inconsistent, understaffed, and unable to meet the needs of students in acute crisis. Reece and a number of other students noted that they had difficulty accessing mental health resources on campus, and that the triage approach toward counseling on their campuses limited them to just a few sessions and did not provide enough time to go in depth or build rapport with therapists. Additionally, many students felt like campus counselors struggled to understand their backgrounds and experiences as first-generation students, and that, much like research[155] has shown for students of color, there was a disconnect between the general training these mental health professionals received for treating the majority of college students and the needs of these specialized populations. This led many students like Reece to feel like they were alone in navigating the often dangerous "waters" of being a socially mobile first-generation college student.

Instead of alleviating or managing the double bind, the process of trying to straddle two different contexts, identities, and sets of expectations produced further conflicts and crises that amplified the effects of the bind for many students. Over time, many students found that as they continued along in their education, they continued to change. And, with each stage of changes, they often had to reenter conflicts with their families, friends, and selves in interactions that ultimately had much higher stakes than they ever anticipated. Instead of feeling like they had a handle on their divided identity, these students described undergoing a constant churning of conflict and alienation both at home and on campus.

For some students, this ended up becoming a long-term strategy for navigating the double bind that emerged out of their social mobility during college. When I followed up with students in their final year of college and postgraduation, a significant number brought up how code-switching and straddling had become a standard part of their lives. These students discussed facing the same problems as students like Reece and Quinn, noting that they struggled with balancing the demands of both sets of expectations effectively and that even when they felt as though they were achieving these expectations, they still felt like outsiders to all of the communities they were engaged with. Jeffrey, a White man and a recently minted East College graduate, was working in tech on the West Coast. He explained that while he had originally hoped that the work of code-switching would have ended after he graduated, he found that he actually did just as much if not more code-switching in his professional life. He noted,

> Code-switching is just part of my life forever now, I think? I try not to think about it much, though, because I get depressed as hell. I exist in a no-man's-land because I don't actually fit in or connect with my colleagues and friends, and I don't fit in with my family anymore either. No one I know, I guess except you and a couple first-gens from college, gets my experience or what this is like to be both and neither at the same time. It's just me rollin' solo. And when I think about that being the rest of my life, it gets very lonely and depressing. It's crazy.

For Jeffrey and first-generation students like him, the tensions of the double bind, the work of balancing them, and the in-betweenness this produces did not end once they graduated from their selective colleges and eliminated demands that were coming from their campus community. Instead, this process continued, and for many compounded and intensified as they moved forward in their social mobility trajectories into careers and social locations even further removed from their home families and communities. And, as Jeffrey's reflection shows, while continuing to balance competing demands, realities, and this sense of in-betweenness is feasible as a long-term strategy, it isn't without costs to these individuals' mental health, social networks, and further development of capital.

Leaving School

A number of students I talked to explained that the pressures of the double bind ultimately became too much, and that they ended up making the difficult choice of altering their relationship to their college campuses. For some, this meant transferring to a different college or university. For instance, Fiona, a White fourth-year, had transferred to West College after spending their first year at an elite liberal arts college on the East Coast. They described feeling out of place immediately at East and told me that they began working on a way to find a transfer by the time that orientation was over. They explained that they were a LEDA[156] Scholar and had an advisor that could guide them through the process and help them find other selective schools that might be a better "fit." They noted that they finally settled on West College because it was closer to their family and was known for having somewhat of a counterculture. Fiona was happy with their choice to transfer to West but still struggled to be a first-generation student living in such an elite setting. They noted, "I started out at East and really, really hated it. I didn't fit there at all, and there was a lot of pressure to conform . . . West is still a bit of a challenge socially as a first-gen student, but there's a little more space here to be different."

Fiona saw transferring as the best route to alleviating the pressures they felt at East to conform to a culture that they did not identify with as a first-generation student. Their ability to find an equally prestigious school that they could transfer to without losing their financial aid or earned credits was made possible by her LEDA scholarship, an advantage that most students seeking transfer did not have. Instead, the other students I talked to that eventually ended up transferring chose to transfer to public colleges that were closer to their home communities.

These students listed the proximity to family and a change in campus culture as the major reasons why they pursued a transfer. One student, a multiracial second-year named Logan, explained that he left East College because his parents were unhappy with him after his first year of school, saying, "They didn't like me bein' at East. It was too far away, and they kept sayin' that we were losing touch and that I was too distracted from my family. So, I figured why not leave?" Logan laid out the process he went through to transfer to the public state college that was only 45 minutes from his home. As we walked around his new campus, he described a renewed sense of connection to his family and community and asserted that he was happy with his choice to transfer. When I asked him about whether or not he felt like he was losing something by not getting a degree from East, he paused for a moment, thinking, and said, "No. No, I don't think so. My [new] school has a great engineering program. Sure, it's not as prestigious as East, but it will get me a good job just the same." Making the choice to transfer from an elite university with one of the top engineering programs in the world to a state college became the right choice when he was faced with growing tensions in his family.

Although there are real social and cultural advantages to attending selective schools, they can be overlooked or dismissed as unnecessary distractions to the primary purpose of degree attainment. For Logan, the central purpose of pursuing a college degree remained tied directly to career advancement, and this was something that he, and his family, felt could be equally achieved at nearly any school if the right programming was available. For Logan and students like him, transferring schools like this works to remove the unwanted social and cultural strains of attending a selective college while perceivably retaining desired economic advantages and career placement. Regardless as to whether that retention becomes the case or not.

Some students chose to take leaves of absence as a means for providing temporary space that they saw as necessary for processing their experiences and reevaluating their choices around college. After a long walk around his college campus during his third year, Hudson, a multiracial student at East College, opened up to me about taking a mental health break after his first year of college. During this conversation he emphasized how his Jack Kent Cooke advisor, Paula, had been a lifeline for him, saying,

I need you to understand that my advisor saved my life. My first year at East College was too much for me to handle. I came in thinking everything would be amazing and that I would have the time of my life. And that's not what happened. I didn't fit in at all, I felt like an alien. And I was trying to juggle my home self and my school self and everything unraveled. I didn't know where to turn to, and when I reached out, my advisor knew exactly what I was going through and was able to help me through.

Hudson's experience here highlights not only taking a leave of absence as a strategy for mitigating the pressures that can come with attending a selective college as a first-generation student, but also the critical importance of having access to the kind of one-on-one advising that can help guide a student through that process and connect them to the supports they need in moments of crisis.

Randie, a White second-year attending West College, described herself as a "loner by choice" and talked to me at length about how she had taken a leave of absence after her first semester. She had suffered from major anxiety after going through conflict with her parents and needed to find a way to regroup once she started feeling like she was "losing sight of who she was." When Randie returned to college her second year, she had adopted a strategy of disengaging from her campus community and was instead trying to find community off campus in a group of working-class people living in the area near her school. One afternoon on the way to the woodworking shop that she volunteered at, Randie commented, "I'm here to get an education and I am grateful for that, but I don't belong here. I know that, the rich kids know that, my parents know that, and the college knows that. So, I do my own thing and that seems to work." This strategy worked for Randie for a while, and she reported feeling far more empowered and happier with her life at school that first semester back. The following semester, however, Randie left school abruptly midsemester to return home to her family. In a follow-up email, she explained that she was working part-time in a convenience store and living at home while she helped her parents cover the bills. She had plans to return to West, but at her parents' request was looking into nursing classes at the local community college.

Randie's experience was in the minority, but I did find that students who continued to struggle with the pressures of the double bind over time were more likely to take a leave of absence than their peers who either developed strategies for coping through peer networks and advising support or effectively cut ties from people and communities. Students who experienced direct conflict with their parents about mobility during college were especially primed to take leaves from school and often framed their decisions to leave college as a means for eliminating the conflict with their parents. During a follow-up phone interview, Braiden, a Black third-year on leave from East College, connected his decision to take his first leave to the conflicts he had had with his parents and the pressures associated with making high-stakes choices with little guidance. He noted, "Well, I took a leave after my first winter break. Like, I didn't come back. My mom and dad and I fought so much during that break over what college was doing to me that I had to take a step back. I had to decide whether it was worth it or not. Is a college degree worth losing my family? Losing myself?" Like many of his peers, Braiden was faced with the herculean task of negotiating a minefield of competing expectations and desires as he navigated the often opaque experience of being a socially mobile first-generation college student. Instead of continuing down a tumultuous path with little guidance and support, Braiden chose to hit the stop button, hoping to use a break from college as an opportunity to reset his and his parents' expectations. He had graduated as salutatorian of his high school class and had always excelled academically, so to take a step away from college like that was a difficult but important decision. He explained that he returned after that first break with what he felt was a better understanding of his reasons for being in college. He was optimistic that he would still be able to pursue a degree without having to sacrifice his relationship with his parents or what he saw as the core of his beliefs and personality. This conversation, however, took place during his second official leave from East College, and at the time Braiden did not have a date in mind for when he planned to return.

Cutting Ties to Home

Through the course of follow-up interviews with a number of students, I found that one strategy some students took as a means for dealing with these recurring conflicts was to eliminate one set of pulls in the double bind by breaking off ties to home or their families. This happened to varying degrees, and many students started the process by eliminating friendships with the people they had grown up or gone to high school with. As prior research[157] has pointed out, falling out of touch with high school friends who stay home or attend college elsewhere is a common experience for college students. And, while some students were surprised when this happened, I did find a number who cut ties with their former friends after repeated negative interactions as a strategy for alleviating the pressures they felt to conform to a set of roles and behaviors that they no longer felt like they fit into.

For Chris, a White fourth-year at South College, the constant teasing from friends had become too much for him to handle, and instead of trying to continue managing that strained relationship, he chose to cut ties with his closest friends from high school. He explained, "At a certain point it just became easier to not talk to my [high school] friends anymore. Every time I saw them or snapped[158] or talked, I felt like shit . . . because they always had something to say about me and I was over it." Chris was tired of defending himself against the critiques that he was "stuck up" and too focused on his future and saw the tensions between himself and his friends as a major contributor to the struggles he faced with moving forward. "I feel kind of like, get over it, right? What did they expect? They're stuck in the past and I'm trying to move forward and, well, this sounds awful, but I can't have them holding me back. I'm sorry, but haters gonna hate, you know?" For Chris, walking away from these friendships helped alleviate the pressures he felt from them to resist change during college. Making this choice also allowed Chris to reframe his positionality as a socially mobile first-generation student. In doing so, Chris actively reframed these conflicts as the result of his former friends being "haters" and the aspects of his identity development that were under fire as a necessary part of moving forward.

Other students developed strategies of avoidance and the production of "busyness" as a means for avoiding continued conflicts with their parents. For Gillian, the pain she felt from the ways her family reacted to the unexpected ways she had changed during college was enough to prompt her to find reasons to stay at school during breaks. She explained, "Well, let's just say it's easier for me to be too busy to come home. They don't like it, but if I can say it's necessary for school, then they can't really argue against it." Like many other students, Gillian's family had bought in to the ways that East College could catapult Gillian's career, but did not support the other changes attending East had brought. Gillian lever-aged her family's belief in the importance of her education as a means for framing why she could not come home during breaks, thus avoiding further conflict. Gillian had eventually come to realize that the process of change she was going through was ongoing, and that she was not sure how to manage that in terms of her parents, noting, "I've changed so much at this point, if I came home right now I think it would be a total blowout." While Gillian had not chosen to cut ties to her parents com-pletely, her strategy of avoidance allowed her the space she needed to grapple with her own feelings around her social mobility without facing constant and often traumatic conflicts at home.

A small number of fourth-years I talked to had taken a similar strat-egy for the majority of their college careers and described uncertainty with how they would manage their relationships with their parents in the postgraduation stage of their lives. Zadrian, a Black fourth-year at Midwest College, is one example of this path. His family had immedi-ately struggled with what they saw as changes to his personality and beliefs. During his first summer, they had pushed him heavily to recon-sider whether his choice to attend Midwest was worth the cost of becom-ing a "stranger to the community." Bolstered by the support of an older cousin who had been the first in their extended family to attend college, Zadrian chose to return to Midwest after his first year—adopting a strat-egy of extended avoidance for the remaining three years of college.

Zadrian described having a lot of anxiety and stress in the months leading up to his college graduation, saying:

> I haven't been back home since my first summer, and I am about to graduate and will have a couple months before I start my [grad] pro-gram, where I will be home. I don't really know how that's going to go. I have stayed away "being busy" [his air quotes] to avoid the constant arguing and critiques. We talk on the phone, but that's usually "How are your classes? Are you eating enough?" It's pretty surface . . . I'm working on a plan right now for just in case it's too much.

Although Zadrian had been relatively successful in managing the pres-sures from his family via avoidance techniques, he was now faced with the unavoidable. He would be returning home after graduation and, while he had reframed his identity and habitus as appropriate, much of his family was likely going to have similarly negative, if not more pronounced, reactions as they did that first break. This left Zadrian feeling alone and without guidance from peers or his college as he headed into his graduation, a time that is generally meant for celebration and excitement.

Some students reached a point of animosity with their families that was so acute that they chose to cut off ties completely in an attempt to shut out the conflict that they saw as preventing them from moving forward. Olivia, a Latinx third-year at Midwest College, also chose this very painful route after her second year of college. She explained that her visits home were full of conflict, and that she and her mother had regular screaming matches about college and her becoming what her mother worded as "a stuck-up bitch." She said: "So, I don't really talk to my parents anymore. It's really just for the best. They can't get behind what I am doing here, and there was no way to find a middle ground. Believe me, I tried. Every time, though, it was a blowout and I was a traitor or a sellout . . . It's really fucking hard, but it's better this way." Olivia's choice to cut ties with her family was not easy. And even after having spent a significant amount of time away from her parents, she still felt much of the tension around her upward mobility that had arisen out of these conflicts. In many ways, this was due to the fact that she had internalized the narrative that her parents had expressed. She was constantly grappling with the idea that she had turned her back on her family. And although she thought her decision to walk away was for the best, sometimes she worried that she was the selfish person her parents said she was and that she had gotten her priorities mixed up while chasing her dreams for a better life.

Olivia's experience represents a small but important population of students attending selective colleges in the United States. The idea that a student might need to cut ties with their families in order to feel able to succeed during college is not a part of the conversation at most colleges and universities. The counseling services, advising staff, and faculty at Olivia's school did not have access to the language or framing necessary to adequately support her as she made this decision. And, without any alternative narratives available in her campus community, she struggled to frame her choice to cut ties with her family. By the time her third year came to a close, she was a former honor-roll student on academic probation and had noticeably withdrawn from the group of students she normally spent most of her time with. Ultimately, Olivia's crisis fell through the cracks of her college's administrative net.

The longer I continued to follow up with students, the more I found ones who were considering or had chosen to limit or cut ties to their families as a means for alleviating the pressures and conflict of the double bind. For example, in a follow-up interview I found out that Jake, a multiracial student who attended South College, had also cut ties with his family. We met Jake in chapter 4—he is the student whose father had called him "a fancy motherfucker now." Jake had not returned home again after that visit and had little contact with his family via text. He explained, "We text on holidays and say happy birthday and whatnot, but that is the extent of it at this point." He further explained that after returning to campus from that break his first year, he eventually realized that he was likely to never reconcile his family's feelings about his choice to attend South College and his continued desire to pursue his dreams of social mobility. This left him with a difficult choice to make, ultimately resulting in a decision to disconnect from his family. I talked with Jake often over the years of my fieldwork, and after he had made this decision he teared up each time his family came up in our discussions—saying,

I know I made the right decision for me. Well, I think I did—check back in ten years [chuckles]. But that doesn't make it any easier. Sometimes I cry at night when I am alone with my thoughts thinking about them. And pretty much every day I feel like I am missing something—like there is a for real hole in my heart. It's hard, you know? But it is what it is. I don't hate them [pause], and I know they don't hate me [pause]. We just can't understand each other anymore. You know?

For Jake, Olivia, and students like them, choosing to eliminate or severely limit contact with family and friends can be seen as the only viable way to eliminate pressure and conflict around the perceived impacts of social mobility that emerge while attending a selective college or university. While this difficult choice can certainly have positive effects for these students—allowing them to focus on their academic and social goals and perhaps even protecting them from intensive conflict and abuse—it likely also has important long-term effects on their mental health and life trajectories.

The students in this study are representative of the highest-achieving low-income and first-generation students in the nation. They were the valedictorians, team captains, student government presidents, start-up entrepreneurs, dedicated volunteers, and star students of their communities. They came to their colleges and universities just as qualified, excited, and full of dreams as their more affluent peers, and yet many of them faced a set of challenges and difficulties that their peers were free from. This is an important element to consider, not just because of the impact it has on these low-income and first-generation students, but also because of the ways that these kinds of intensive experiences potentially increase the gap between these students and their more affluent and continuing-generation peers on campus. The weight of grappling with and then attempting to resolve the unexpected impacts of social mobility during college—and the demands of the double bind that emerge out of this process—is something unique to these students. This hidden process has real consequences for these students' mental health, social networks, capital accumulation, academic achievement, and life trajectories. And it is potentially a significant element behind the enduring achievement and outcome disparities between these students and their peers at selective campuses across the United States. Because of this, we must not only consider how and why this occurs for some students, but also what it is that colleges and universities can do to effectively support these students' needs as they navigate this process.

Conclusion

In the winter of 2019, I sat in a coffee shop near Midwest College waiting for a student named Denver. We had agreed to meet at 2:00 p.m., but he was late. At 2:17 he texted to let me know, saying, "I don't know if I can do this today." Denver was in his second year at East College and was in the middle of a leave of absence. He was living with his parents in a suburb near Midwest College, and we had been meeting for semiregular coffee dates throughout his leave. When he came, he was usually late. But, more frequently, I got texts like these. Denver was in the midst of a crisis. He had stopped attending classes because he felt out of place and confused at East and preferred to stay in his room playing online video games. His parents had insisted that he take a semester off and come home after he was placed on academic probation for failing grades. They were pushing for him to leave East and transfer to the public university nearby, where many of their family friends had gone.

A week earlier he had walked me through the ins and outs of a video game called Overwatch and explained that he felt more comfortable playing online with friends he had made online and during high school than with his peers at East: "When I'm playing, I'm just the same Denver I've always been. I don't have to perform for anyone—I don't have to be anyone. I just am." He said that he felt an immense pressure to conform to the culture at East, a culture that was very different from his working-class neighborhood. Yet, during his first summer break, he had started to feel out of place at home. He said, "I think spending a year on a different track really changed me—and everyone else just kind of stayed the same." Denver was struggling to make sense of his place both at East and at home, and video games had become a neutral space where he was suspended in time—free from the demands of college and family and the pressures of the double bind.

On that day, I decided to wait for a few minutes to see if he might change his mind. At 3:00 p.m., I was just packing up my things when I saw Denver walking through the door of the coffee shop. He hurried over to my table and sat down—his cheeks were red from the cold, and his breathing was heavy. I laughed as I asked him how he knew I would still be at the coffee shop. He said, "I'm so sorry. I, I was in a fight with my mom. I told her I wasn't going back to East—and that I wasn't going to State College either. I got a job at this restaurant my friend from high school works at. I told her I'm going to do that for a while. And, well, and she freaked." We talked for the next two hours about his decision to leave school. Throughout the conversation, he kept coming back to his decision to leave, saying, "[I] just needed some time to get back to center."

As I have demonstrated throughout the pages of this book, the work that selective colleges and universities do to level the playing field for low-income and first-generation students is directly in line with prior ideas[159] about people-changing organizations. First-generation students often do not have the knowledge, skills, and experiences—or capital—that have been determined as necessary to be successful at selective colleges. This success—which is often defined in terms of outcomes like grades, graduation, and time to completion—is also defined in terms of finding a place to belong and be accepted as a legitimate member of their campus communities. The bulk of the programming and resources available at these colleges is designed to give first-generation students the capital they need to succeed and to provide a network of peers that they can form relationships with.

Interestingly, the work that selective colleges and universities do for first-generation students is much like the work social workers do with clients from stigmatized and marginalized communities. Social workers help their clients gain the formal statuses and capital they need to be seen as legitimate by landlords and community partners. When considered in this way, higher education and social work appear to be relatively similar. And, in many surface-level aspects, they are. A closer investigation of intensive people-changing organizations like social work highlights where colleges and universities may be missing the mark with their efforts around first-generation students. Perhaps the most crucial work that people-changing organizations do is the intensive one-on-one work of counseling individuals through transformations in their actions and self-images and then stewarding them through the often intensive and long-term process of taking on new roles and "becoming" a new identity.[160] This is where selective colleges fail their students. Selective colleges and universities see their directive as fostering social mobility for first-generation students, not providing them with resources and support once they begin to grapple with the real effects of this process. Instead, they focus all of their attention on offering a variety of robust programming and resources designed to raise students' varying forms of capital that come together to create a polishing process that very successfully changes these students—they give them the skills, resources, knowledge, and experiences they need to successfully navigate their elite college campuses and the upper-middle-class spaces and communities that their education is intended to lead them to.

It is this second step in the process of being a people-changing organization that selective colleges and universities have yet to master. What I have demonstrated through the experiences of students in this book is that the polishing process is most often where the formalized programming and support from selective colleges and universities stops. This leaves low-income and first-generation students on their own, often without private insurance or experienced and resourced social networks, to do the difficult work of either finding their own support or coping alone with multiple significant challenges. Such challenges frequently include the unexpected changes that emerge as part of going through social mobility at a selective college, the tensions and conflicts that often arise as a result of these changes, and the double bind that comes from trying to meet the conflicting demands and expectations of home and campus communities. As I have shown, this set of experiences are a major burden on many students and can lead to heightened stress, anxiety, and moments of crisis.

The impact of the double bind becomes particularly important in light of the fact that the majority of first-generation students and their families cannot anticipate many of the changes that come from attending a highly selective college because they do not have the experience needed to anticipate it fully. Instead, they tend to think about college in a way that is reflective of broader social imaginaries (and academic frames) around social mobility. Upward mobility is seen as a stationary thing or a goal that can be achieved, with a degree as a primary driver to that goal—a goal that is most often expressed in terms of economic gains and prestigious careers. The problem with this static view of social mobility is that it is devoid of the lived experience of people and their relationships to the communities that surround them. Because of this, most accounts of social mobility do not take into consideration what happens to individuals and their communities as they navigate the process of social mobility. We must shift academic and popular frameworks around social mobility to incorporate an understanding of it as a longitudinal experiential process. Colleges and universities must embrace this framework because they have the power to lead the way in reframing our cultural narratives and understandings about the relationship between social mobility and higher education to one that that is both process *and* student centric.

As I have shown throughout this book, the experience of becoming socially mobile during college can be a difficult, if not traumatic, experience for many first-generation and low-income students. In order to take full advantage of the elite education they have gained access to, they must "buy in" to the demands and expectations of elite educational culture. Buying in in this way irrevocably changes these students and produces shifts in beliefs, habits, tastes, and identities that are not always as welcomed as colleges assume. These unexpected and, at times, unwelcomed changes can cause moments of self-crisis for students and moments of rupture within families and communities. Many students are forced to rethink their choices around attending a selective college and must develop strategies for maintaining their upward mobility trajectories without being seen as a "sellout" by concerned friends and families. The pressure from the competing demands that arise from this process of navigating social mobility as a first-generation student at a selective college is difficult for many students to manage and can have serious impacts on their social experiences and academic outcomes. For some students, this double bind becomes too difficult to manage without adequate support—leading to difficult choices that can result in exiting school or cutting ties to home.

The deeply negative experiences that many first-generation students have as they become socially mobile during college can be avoided by shifting the ways that selective colleges approach their programming and support for first-generation students. While it is likely not possible to quell all of the negative impacts and experiences that I have high-lighted here, acknowledging that there is a significant problem that must be addressed is an important step. I argue that shifting and enhancing interventions around supporting first-generation students to include the full spectrum of components associated with people-changing organizations is key to closing the gap between low-income first-generation students and their more affluent and continuing-generation peers. It is critical that colleges and universities provide more than access to skills and capital—they must also support their students through all of the challenges and complexities that arise during the process of social mobility that comes from attending college.

This, however, does not mean that these schools must expand or further bloat their administrative ranks. Instead, a reconfiguration of programming and services that does less repetitive skill building and more targeted addressing of student experiences would be a strong start. Paired with this, identifying where the addition of staff that provide direct service to students would maximize the impact of these programs would be key. By providing well-funded and staffed programming and support for students (and potentially their parents) as they navigate social mobility and begin to transform their identities, selective colleges can come closer to ensuring their ultimate success. Focusing on the crucial one-on-one work of assisted identity management that is central in social services will teach students and their parents to anticipate changes and aid them through the often difficult process of becoming upwardly mobile. Perhaps more than anything else, I found that it is the unanticipated aspects of college and mobility that most easily derail students and their families. And, in many ways, this is logical. The unknown can be a frightening thing, and not being equipped with a set of lenses for interpreting and contextualizing change can result in confusion and conflict. Helping students and their families develop the frameworks they need to effectively navigate social mobility during college will not only aid them through a difficult process, but it will also promote their success in a way that the current approach cannot guarantee.

FUTURE DIRECTIONS FOR COLLEGES

The difficult work comes with trying to change the systems and processes that help produce the student experiences and outcomes that I have detailed here. The current approach toward leveling the playing field through programming and resources designed to increase student capital is certainly important, but it fails to support students (and their parents) through much of the difficult process of becoming socially mobile during college. If the ultimate goal is to further open up selective colleges to the nation's most promising students, regardless of social class, then we must reconsider what forms of support should be offered to ensure all students' success. Instead of solely investing in further programming around capital accumulation, I urge colleges and universities to explore how they can develop programming and resources that give students and their families the experience and resources they need to better anticipate and contextualize the changes that college will bring. Undertaking this work can begin immediately on most selective campuses, as the first step would be to develop or increase programming and support for first-generation students.

While it did not negate many of their struggles, I found that students on campuses with targeted first-generation student programming expressed feeling more supported and connected to their campus communities. Having a community, and in rare cases, a physical location to call home was critical for these students' sense of belonging and access to resources. Unfortunately, not all colleges and universities have targeted first-generation programming and support. Campuses that do not currently fully fund and staff first-generation student programming must invest in this foundational resource for the success of their students immediately. Although I take a critical eye toward the limitations of the existing programming and resources most often offered through these programs, I am not suggesting that they be eliminated or reduced in size or capacity. Quite the opposite, actually. Developing and expanding staff positions and the kinds of programming and resources described in this book that are dedicated to supporting first-generation student needs is a low barrier and essential first step toward closing the gap between these students and their more affluent peers.

A small number of campuses in this study had developed and invested in providing first-generation students with a physical space to find and build community within. On these campuses, the first-generation student centers were the epicenter of first-gen social life—creating a hub of activity, community, support, and resources. These spaces were often labeled by students as the only space that they felt fully comfortable on campus and were seen as a welcome respite in the draining and difficult work of performing their identities as socially mobile first-generation students on campus. Spaces like these for students of color, veterans, and queer students exist on campuses across the country and have been linked to increasing student belongingness and sense of community in ways that are associated with improved well-being and academic outcomes. The recognized benefits that come from having dedicated student space for these student communities would certainly translate to first-generation student populations. I encourage colleges and universities that have not yet developed campus spaces for their first-generation student populations to do so immediately.

Developing bridge programs in order to expose first-generation students to the academic, organizational, and social aspects of elite college life would be a critical next step in changing the ways that first-generation student support is approached at selective colleges. Although only a small number of the campuses in this study had well-established bridge programs, the students enrolled in these programs consistently cited them as an important resource that helped ease their transitions into college and produced a vital community that provided them with consistent support. I believe that the most optimal programmatic form would be to fuse the structure of a pre-college bridge program with the ongoing programming of a peer mentoring program. Like bridge programs, I found that students engaged in peer mentoring programs reported feeling more engaged and supported on their campuses.

I suggest that colleges and universities develop bridge and peer mentor programs that can serve their entire incoming populations of first-generation students each year. These programs should start a month before orientation and include academic and social experiences designed to develop a bonded cohort of students within an incoming class. At the onset of the program, incoming students should be paired with returning students who will serve as their mentors throughout the program and into the academic year. Incoming students should take micro classes from faculty that are designed not only to introduce them to academic expectations and norms on campus, but also to introduce them to interacting and connecting with faculty. Recruiting first-generation faculty into these positions would be ideal. Students should live on campus together or near each other in residence halls and have regular on- and off-campus programming during the bridge program that is designed to build community, knowledge, and skills. This programming should extend into the academic year, blending the bridge program into a peer mentor program. By taking the introductory aspects of a bridge program and pairing it with ongoing support and community formation that comes with mentoring programs, it would be possible to draw on and enhance the varied benefits that students described from both of these programmatic types.

The next crucial step is developing new programming and approaches toward supporting first-generation students as they navigate their experiences as socially mobile students during college. This can and should start with developing workshops that simply address the experience of being a first-generation student on campus. Feeling isolated and like there was not a space to talk about their experiences was a consistent theme for students across the campuses I spent time on. Even at schools with a robust first-generation student community, the consensus among students was that having a university-supported space to speak on their experiences was a missing but much needed resource. I suggest using this base-level programming as a springboard for a series of workshops about grappling with the more socio-emotional and relational aspects of being a first-generation student. As Arnold notes in chapter 5, workshops and resources that focus on helping students talk to their parents about their experiences are a missing piece to the university support puzzle, as are workshops on critical aspects of their experience like identity change or navigating and managing family conflict and resentment. Workshops like this should be built in collaboration with campus mental health services and incorporate first-generation alumni, faculty, and other community members whenever possible. No workshop will ever be able to fully encapsulate the entire first-generation experience, but we must begin to think more deeply and creatively about how this time-honored approach toward programming could better address all of the layers of experience that first-generation students have as they navigate college and the resulting social mobility.

The individual staff members doing the work of supporting first-generation college students in the United States are by and large deeply committed, creative, and passionate professionals. They are also under-resourced, understaffed, overworked, and stretched thin across the student populations they serve. Colleges and universities must invest in reimagining what staff and advising support looks like for first-generation students. And as part of this process they must invest in the individuals doing this important and direct work with students by fully staffing and funding the programs they offer. I suggest adopting an advising/coaching model that more closely mirrors social services than traditional academic advising structures. Like any other population that navigates unfamiliar organizational structures, bureaucratic demands, and personal transformations, first-generation students need intensive one-on-one support from staff as they navigate college. Colleges and universities should invest in hiring and training case managers that understand the experiences and needs of first-generation students. When students arrive on campus, they should be paired with a case manager or a case management team that they will work with throughout their entire time in college. These case managers should do the work of guiding these students through standard academic needs like choosing classes, meeting major requirements, and finding resources, but should also take on addressing the more intensive social and identity-based needs like the ones described throughout this book. Having sustained and regular support from staff in this way has the potential to ease the intensity of some aspects of the process of becoming socially mobile and provide a much needed, but unheard of, layer of support and guidance for first-generation students during college that will undoubtedly improve their well-being and academic outcomes.

None of the campuses that I spent time on had directed and extended programming or resources for parents. I suggest that colleges consider forming peer cohorts of parents, similar to the style of peer mentor programs for students. If the same relationship of mutual support and information sharing that is found in peer mentoring programs could be replicated for parents, it is possible that some of the tensions and anxieties around unexpected changes may be alleviated. Just as students look to their older first-generation peers to guide them through the tumultuous process of becoming socially mobile, parents of these students could benefit from their parent peers in the same way. Pairing parents with more experienced parent peers and supplementing these relationships with formal programming from the college would reduce the alienation that parents of first-generation students may be feeling in their communities and help them feel more connected and embedded in the larger community associated with their child's college. Investing in financial support to bring parents to campus at least once during their child's college career may further help familiarize and demystify college for these parents. I found that students reported that in cases where parents were able to physically see and interact with the space and people on their child's campuses, they appeared to feel more at ease with understanding their experiences. Providing financial support not only for students to return home, but also for parents to visit campus, may potentially help parents bridge the physical and emotional distance between students' lives at home and at school.

A separate but deeply interlinked charge for colleges and universities seeking to better support their low-income and first-generation students is to systematically rethink and deeply invest in campus mental health services for these students and entire campus communities. The United States is and has been facing a mental health crisis on college campuses nationwide.[161] The student experiences highlighted here are representative of a broader set of college students' mental health needs that are not being adequately met by campus administrations. In many ways, the structure of campus health and mental health services rests on the assumption that all students have access to private insurance and off-campus health care providers that can meet their specialized needs. While this may have been the case for student bodies that were historically very affluent, the diversification of these student populations on selective college campuses has changed the spectrum of physical and mental health needs of their campus communities. With this has come a shift toward a student population that requires access to comprehensive health care on campus because they do not have access to these vital services elsewhere. These students need high-quality, comprehensive, and culturally competent physical and mental health care that is readily available to them on campus without additional cost. Without this they will continue to not be adequately served by their institutions. Simply put, campus administrations must invest in and expand campus mental health resources if they hope to adequately meet the needs of low-income and first-generation students as they grapple with the complexities of their experiences as socially mobile students at a selective college.

So, what does this look like? The lowest-hanging fruit would be to provide professionally led support groups for first-generation students based out of student wellness and counseling centers. The support group/therapy model of providing services has already been embraced by many colleges and universities, particularly for gender-diverse and neurodivergent student populations. Providing a professionally supported space for students to collectively process and work through their experiences as first-generation students could make a major impact without requiring significant expenditure and resources. The next stage of reimagining campus mental health care and support for first-generation students would be to prioritize hiring and training culturally sensitive mental health professionals with knowledge and expertise in the experiences of first-generation students. This is an approach that some campuses have taken toward supporting and retaining their transgender students and students of color—a practice that should be expanded to first-generation students. Like their underrepresented and marginalized counterparts, first-generation students have experiences that should be addressed and served by knowledgeable professionals that are trained and equipped to address and understand their specific needs.

A much bigger, but critically needed, change in campus mental health would be to rethink the triage model of mental health that is the most common approach at colleges and universities in the United States. At most schools, if a student is in need of mental health support, they have access to a very limited number of sessions with staff on campus and are then referred to finding long-term counseling and other mental health care off campus. This may be the best (or only) way to meet the needs of a large campus population as a whole, but it is not currently meeting the needs of individual students—especially first-generation students. The success and viability of the triage model rests on a few crucial assumptions that do not take into account the lived realities of first-generation students. First, this model assumes that the students seeking help have access to comprehensive medical insurance that they can use for mental health services off campus after their requisite sessions have been used up. And, although colleges require students to have insurance, for many first-generation students this means taking the subpar university-sponsored health insurance that is often not accepted widely off campus or relying on state-sponsored insurance with limited range and coverage for mental health services. Students with these kinds of insurance cannot simply make an appointment with a private provider in the same ways that their peers with private insurance through their parents can. Second, the triage model assumes that students seeking help have the cultural and social capital needed to easily access off-campus mental health resources. Many first-generation students come to college with very little experience navigating complex health and mental health systems. When faced with the task of finding and connecting with a private counselor, they are often unsure and overwhelmed at how to go about it, and are not likely to have the resources and knowledge within their community networks that they need to figure it out.

The fact that the triage model relies on students' ability to access private mental health resources off campus produces a major barrier for first-generation students. They are limited to the resources on campus and must rely on their campuses to take care of their mental health in a way that their peers do not. This creates an avoidable gap in access to services between these student populations and significantly limits the help available to first-generation students in crisis. The best solution would be to expand mental health services to include consistent on-campus counseling and therapy for students throughout the duration of their time in college. This would admittedly be a very expensive and intensive undertaking that should be a near future goal for higher education in the United States. In the meantime, I suggest that colleges and universities develop relationships and partnerships with the mental health providers in their communities to build pipelines to service for first-generation students. It is not enough to refer them to private long-term counseling care. Schools must invest in creating the support systems and social safety nets that these students need to flourish academically and personally while in college.

It is critical that selective colleges and universities begin to reinterpret the work they are doing as people-changing organizations. It is not nearly enough to give students the capital they need to succeed at an elite college by "leveling the playing field." It is also imperative that colleges provide the intensive support these students need by helping them make sense of their social mobility and shepherding them into their new identities. This work must be put at the center of first-generation student programming and should not be relegated to counseling centers and off-campus therapists. The high-achieving hardworking first-generation students attending selective colleges and universities across the United States that the students in this study represent need and deserve cohesive and consistent programming and resources that come from dedicated staff who are trained to meet the full range of their needs as they become socially mobile during college. Elite colleges and universities have long prioritized the transformative character of the education they provide within their hallowed halls—and now the time has come for these schools to consider and address how these transformations emerge across their diverse student populations.

Finally, the very popular "playing field" metaphor should be unpacked. It is a misleading metaphor that obscures where the burden of change rests. Upon first consideration, it evokes the idea that it is the organization—the college—that is being changed through programmatic efforts meant to "level the playing field," with the field being the college and the players being the students. However, upon further consideration it becomes clear that the expectation for change rests solely on the low-income and first-generation students who have been given access to play on the most competitive playing fields in the world—elite American colleges and universities. It has been well established that the capital these colleges and universities provide to students as part of their efforts to level the playing field is an invaluable resource that become critical to their success during and after college. However, what has been less established are the costs associated with obtaining the social mobility that this process is designed to produce. And, although low-income and first-generation students are attending elite colleges at higher rates than ever before, what is asked of them once they arrive on campus for orientation is more than many of them bargained for.

More and more selective colleges are responding to the cry that first-generation students should be granted increased access to the highest ranks of higher education in the nation. And, while increases in space for the physical bodies of these students should certainly be lauded, it is hardly the case that these colleges and universities have made space for the ways in which these students physically embody their class as low-income and first-generation students. A reinterpretation of what it means to level the playing field is in order. Instead of investing in programming and resources that seek to change students to fit the mold of their selective colleges and universities, the time has come to imagine a campus culture and structure that is willing and able to make the meaningful changes needed to fully welcome these students—and the experiences and perspectives they bring with them—into their campus communities. Only then will colleges and universities be able to genuinely provide first-generation students with an environment where they can fully and authentically thrive.

Acknowledgments

The road to completing this book has been one of the great surprises of my life. I still look back to the start of this journey with a bit of wonder and astonishment that it happened at all. As a nontraditional first-generation student, I took a path to get here that was anything but conventional, and it was only because of the strength and support of my communities that I ended up making this far-fetched dream a reality. Each and every person that has been a part of my team along the way has my deepest and eternal gratitude—and I am going to do my best to express the smallest slice of that here.

Before I even knew what a PhD actually was, it was my community at Umpqua Community College that built my confidence to demand more and taught me the art of unapologetically toppling the barriers in my way. I will forever be indebted to the team of committed people at that small community college in rural Oregon. It was under their instruction and guidance that I somehow went from the most remedial classes to earning national accolades. If I can manage to develop even half of their skill, patience, and care, I will truly be an outstanding educator and mentor. While my journey began at UCC, Reed College is where everything began to come into focus. The faculty pushed me to critically engage the sociological canon and the world around me—building the confidence I needed to follow my gut toward research ideas that asked the big and difficult questions. The family I found in the Peer Mentor Program and the SAO kept me sane throughout the whirlwind of Reed and reminded me daily that the most important lessons I could learn were happening in the world around me. The six years that I spent at

UCC and Reed reshaped my identity and trajectory. It was not easy and would not have happened without these folks. My deepest thanks.

I conducted the majority of the research for this book while I was a graduate student at the University of Chicago in the Department of Sociology. I could not have asked for a better intellectual community and academic home that both challenged me and gave me the space to hone my skills at challenging institutions in return. From my first days of graduate school, John Levi Martin pushed me to think critically and creatively about what sociology is and should be. This project is far better for his encouraging me to take on more difficult, but more interesting, questions. I am deeply thankful for Anna Mueller's consistent encouragement to believe in myself and my data enough to make bigger, bolder claims. She helped me find my academic voice, situate it within the sociology of education, and use it to unabashedly argue my points. As an aspiring ethnographer, I could not have asked for a better methodological mentor than Forrest Stuart. He taught me the power of carefully constructed and doggedly pursued ethnography, pushed me to work through the most puzzling of puzzles, and gave me the space (both literally and figuratively) to cultivate my work. Having Kimberly Kay Hoang as a mentor in the latter half of my graduate experience gave me a role model for what a first-generation college student could accomplish as an academic and professor. I am forever grateful for her guidance and advice. It is difficult to express the depth of my gratitude for my mentor, advisor, and friend Kristen Schilt. Her mentorship is rivaled by none. I am undoubtedly a better writer, sociologist, and person because of her patient guidance and persistent support. I certainly would not have made it through this project or graduate school without her. She consistently believed in my work, always knowing when to push me further and having the wisdom to let me learn some difficult—and often hilarious—lessons on my own time. I will never be able to thank her enough for bringing me into the fold and showing me how to build the community I want and need in academia. I think this turned out to be a pretty good table after all.

I had the great fortune of finding and fostering a supportive community of colleagues, friends, and family at UChicago that showed up to celebrate every accomplishment and rally behind me to get through every setback. I feel very lucky to have found this group of people who will be my lifelong friends and partners in sociological mischief. I could not have done this without their brilliance, friendship, and support. My cohort was an interesting crew of people with a wide range of personalities. I am particularly thankful to have found Jane McCamant and Hanisah Abdullah Sani in this group. Their friendship, humor, and thoughtful insight have meant the world to me. Cayce Hughes's mentorship and friendship made this project and my experience at Chicago far better. Rebecca Ewert has consistently kept me grounded and reminded me that a love for teaching is something to embrace unapologetically. Sneha Annavarapu's wit and theoretical brilliance helped shape both the arguments in this book and my understanding of my positionality within it. Cate Fugazzola's seemingly never-ending energy and reminders not to take life too seriously have fueled me throughout this project. Jeffrey Parker has logged nearly as many hours with me adventuring for donuts as he has listening and providing feedback on this project. I hold a special place in my heart for my fellow first-gen Ice Wars Champion, Sarah Outland, whose commitment to building and sustaining community is something I treasure and aspire to. Grad school was a wild and unexpected journey for both of us, and I'm on the other side of all of it in no small part because of her. This project is far better because of her friendship, but also because of her brilliance. Finally, a huge thank-you to my larger community at UChicago, whose support, time, and humor made this book and my experience everything I could have hoped for and more. Thank you, Chad Borkenhagen, Alex Brewer, Meredith Clason, Pranathi Diwakar, Karlyn Gorski, Katie Hendricks, James Iveniuk, Alessandra Lembo, Linnea Martin, Nisarg Mehta, Shannon Morrissey, Moira O'Shea, Pat Princell, Alicia Riley, Yaniv Ron-El, and Brian Tuohy.

My colleagues at Western Washington University have provided me with the friendship and support needed to finish this book through the uncertainty of being a newly minted assistant professor in a global pandemic. I could not have asked for a better pair to start the tenure track with than Batool Zaidi and Cameron Whitley. I am forever grateful to Glenn Tsunokai, Liz Mogford, and Kristin Anderson for embracing my chaotic energy and giving me the support and space to begin thriving as a faculty member in our department. Ruby Ben has brought me the kind of empowering energy, support, and real talk that only a fellow first-gen could provide. Batool Zaidi will forever have a special place in my heart as my counterpart, coconspirator, and dear friend who kept me sane in the most bizarre of times. During my very first days at Western,

I met a small group of colleagues that would quickly become friends. I owe many thanks to the "yacht club"—Rebecca Borowski, Kristen Chmielewski, Lindsay Foreman-Murray, Mary Hunt, Lindsey Smith, Cameron Whitley, Felicia Youngblood, and Batool Zaidi. Building community, let alone friendship, is difficult in academia, and I find myself to be particularly lucky to count Kristen Chmielewski and Mary Hunt among my closest friends. The last two and a half years of working on the redraft of this book has been the wildest of rides—and I would not have finished it were it not for their fierce friendship and limitless support that both grounded me and gave me the confidence I needed to really shoot for the stars. I also want to thank my amazing students at Western. Their excitement for my project and consistent cheerleading throughout this process was a limitless source of energy that animated me on even my worst days.

Portions of this project benefited from the thoughtful insight, critiques, and suggestions of many of the most generous sociological scholars. I want to thank members of the American Sociological Association section on children and youth, the American Sociological Association Sociology of Education section, the Sociology of Education Association, the UT Austin Intersectional Qualitative Research Methods Institute for Advanced Doctoral Students, and the Chicago Ethnography Incubator, whose valuable feedback on early versions of this project helped shape its trajectory. Among those folks, I owe a particularly big thank-you to Irenee Beattie, Mary Gray, Laura Hamilton, Anthony Abraham Jack, Janice McCabe, Tiana Paschel, Laurence Ralph, Mitchell Stevens, and Iddo Tavory for helping me see the book I was envisioning with more clarity and giving me the feedback and encouragement I needed to make that a reality. A deep thank-you goes to the two scholars who anonymously reviewed this book at different points in its development; your thoughtful and critical insight made every chapter of this book stronger and clearer. This research was made possible with significant support from the University of Chicago, particularly the Division of the Social Sciences; the Center for the Study of Gender and Sexuality; the Center for the Study of Race, Politics, and Culture; and UChicago Urban. Additionally, this project benefited from the generous support of the Midwest Sociological Society, Sociologists for Women in Society, the Society for the Study of Social Problems, and the American Sociological Association.

This project would not have been possible without the Jack Kent Cooke Foundation. In 2010, the Foundation took a chance on me by awarding me an Undergraduate Transfer Scholarship. As an organization, the JKCF has given me all the tools I needed to flourish in every stage of my education. But, perhaps more importantly, the JKCF has given me a community of staff and JKC Scholars that I can call my friends and family. I owe a thank-you to each and every person in this community that has been there over this last decade. The support and access that the Foundation gave me became critical to the success of this project. My deepest thanks for their entrusting me to do this research and their willingness to allow me to take a critical sociological look at their programs, structure, and outcomes and the intentional and unintentional impacts they have on their Scholars.

I could not have asked for a better publishing experience than the one I have had with the University of Chicago Press. I am honored to have had the chance to work with Elizabeth Branch Dyson through the process of turning *Polished* into the book of my dreams. From our very first conversations, back when I was pitching the idea for the book, she came to our discussions with enthusiastic interest, critical engagement, and creative insight that made me feel the best combination of challenge and comfort. Her impressive publishing knowledge and experience helped me better understand my audiences and the nuanced stakes of my arguments. Getting to work with someone so creative and brilliant who was also a first-generation college student is something that made this book stronger, and something that I will cherish forever. The drafting and editing process for this book occurred during a global pandemic, and I owe additional special thanks to Elizabeth Branch Dyson and Mollie McFee for their patience, encouragement, and direction as my progress moved, at times, at a glacial speed. To the rest of the team at the press who have had a hand in making the book a reality, including especially Olivia Aguilar, Beth Ina, and Marianne Tatom, my sincere thanks for your invaluable work and commitment to this project.

When I decided to start this journey, most people were not quite sure what to make of it. I was the first in my family to go to college, and the idea that someone working as a dishwasher had any business becoming a doctor felt far-fetched. Nonetheless, my parents supported and encouraged me every step of the way—even when the steps became unfamiliar and ended up taking me most of the way across the country.

Thank you, Dad and Jimmie, Mom and Steve. And, although he never got to see me finish, my deepest thank-you to my brother Danny. I never would have considered this without his insistence that I could do it. He always knew I was meant for something different.

I am fortunate to have a community of found family that have been a constant font of encouragement and support throughout my journey with this project. NíAódagaín continues to be my most treasured mentor and coconspirator. I will never be able to express my gratitude for her friendship and the impact she's had on me by insisting that I believe in myself half as much as she does. Candie Solis is a cousin by happenstance but a friend by choice. Her humor, generosity, and capacity for listening made my time during fieldwork feel like home. Tom Louis is perhaps one of the best listeners I know, and I am grateful for all the times he has let me monologue about an aspect of the book I was struggling with or an argument I was trying on for size—offering the perfect encouragement or insight every time. Some of my very first stabs at understanding how people-changing organizations impact people were worked out in conversation with Kelly Reed when we were undergraduates. She has been a constant font of brilliance, humor, and steadfast support my entire career, and this book would not be what it is without her contributions. I cannot thank her enough.

My deepest thank-you goes to Osbornia: Hannah Osborne, Khristopher Osborne, and Madelyn Osborne. They have been my guiding force throughout all of this, and I could never have done this without them. I am grateful for everything they have sacrificed and for trusting me enough to lead us along this wild ride. I am also so very lucky that Mika Ozima and Matthew Ciolino have joined Osbornia—I could not have asked for better bonus children. Thank you all for always having my back and knowing when to put me in check. People often ask me how I have managed to get where I am today, and the simple answer is: these amazing people. Their love, patience, and humor are more responsible for my success than anything I could ever take credit for. Our little family has kept me balanced through the most uncertain times and reminded me that life is an adventure to be cherished. All of my love and gratitude. Also, this project would have been a far lonelier process without the Osbornian cats (Dr. Brian, Bill Seacaster, Durkheim, Godric, and Percival de Rolo III) that sat by my side, sometimes very late into the night, as I agonized over data and prose. You were the best RAs I could ever have asked for.

Finally, although I cannot name them here, this book is only possible because of the students and staff who welcomed me into their lives and shared their time with me. My sincerest thank-you for their patience, generosity, humor, and friendship throughout the stages of this research and book. I will forever treasure the opportunity to be a part of so many amazing people's lives. I hold each and every coffee, late-night meal, campus tour, walk, grocery store trip, party, event, meeting, lazy day in the quad, study session, and conversation near and dear in my heart. My sincerest thanks for trusting me with your words and to do justice to your experiences as first-generation and low-income students. I hope that what you have helped me build within the pages of this book will shed light on your experiences, honor your narratives, and lead to the change and support that our community deserves. Thank you.

Methodological Appendix

In this study, I draw primarily on in-depth interviews and participant observations I conducted with 150 first-generation and low-income students attending selective and highly selective private colleges in Illinois, Massachusetts, Oregon, and Texas between 2016 and 2021. My intention with the research design of this study was to produce a project that could provide an in-depth, multi-sited, longitudinal, qualitative perspective to my primary research questions: (1) How do low-income first-generation students navigate social mobility during college? and (2) How do institutions mediate those experiences? In this appendix, I discuss how I selected the populations and cases for this project, describe the methods I used for data collection and analysis, and provide a demographic description of my participants. Throughout these sections, I will discuss the challenges and limitations of my approach.

STUDY DESIGN

From the beginning of my research, I was particularly interested in why low-income first-generation students continued to have lower GPAs, higher attrition rates, and more reports of negative experiences than their affluent and continuing-generation peers. I ultimately chose the case of low-income first-generation students attending selective and highly selective private schools because this group of students represents the paradox in prevailing understandings about the relationship between support and success. These students attend school in institutional contexts that boast the most comprehensive support, and yet continue to see performance gaps between low-income first-generation students and their more affluent and continuing-generation peers. Focusing on a context where this persistent gap should not exist provided me with the opportunity to consider what might be negatively impacting students beyond a lack in different forms of capital.

My second interest was in how institutional interventions from outside organizations like scholarship foundations impacted or mediated student experiences and outcomes. I chose the Jack Kent Cooke Foundation (JKCF), a highly selective foundation that provides scholarships, support, and opportunities to high-achieving low-income students as they pursue their educational and career goals, as the primary case for this study. The Foundation currently operates a number of scholarship programs, including a Young Scholars Program that recruits high-achieving middle schoolers, an Undergraduate Transfer Program that offers scholarships for high-achieving students planning to transfer from two-year community colleges to four-year schools to complete their bachelor's degrees, and a Continuing Graduate Program open to current Scholars who wish to pursue graduate education. In the past, the JKCF has also operated a Graduate Arts Scholarship and a Dissertation Fellowship. For the purposes of this study, I focused only on the College Scholarship Program.

I selected JKCF as my primary organization for two central reasons. First, I had a working relationship with the JKCF as an alumna of their Undergraduate Transfer Scholarship Program (2010) and Graduate Scholarship Program (2013). Second, the Foundation had released a number of reports that demonstrate that their scholarship recipients tend to have academic outcome measurements that both outpace their high-achieving low-income first-generation peers and are more closely matched to peers from more affluent and continuing-generation backgrounds.[162] These data indicated that the JKCF was making a positive intervention in the outcomes and experiences of their scholarship recipients that needed to be explored. This shaped my initial strategy for recruiting student respondents. Roughly one-third of student respondents in this study are recipients of a Jack Kent Cooke College Scholarship, roughly one-third applied for but did not receive the scholarship, and roughly one-third neither applied for nor received it.

I designed the initial sampling strategy in an attempt to provide a comparison across relatively comparable high-achieving low-income students with differing levels of support from the JKCF. This distinction became less important than I originally anticipated, as the majority of students I recruited receive external support from other similar organizations, with many of them receiving support from multiple organizations at once. This funding landscape ultimately made it difficult to discern how many aspects of the support provided by the JKCF impacted student experiences and outcomes, as many other organizations provided similar and overlapping resources and support. Yet, there were some aspects specific to the resources and support provided by the JKCF that proved to be particularly important for student experiences and outcomes. I detail those points below.

STUDENT RECRUITMENT AND DEMOGRAPHICS

I recruited students in three ways: from campus-based low-income and first-generation student groups, through referrals from respondents, and from an email pool of student applicants and recipients of a College Scholarship from the Jack Kent Cooke Foundation. My first recruitment efforts were with Cooke College Scholars. The JKCF supplied me with a spreadsheet of active and incoming College Scholars, their demographic information, and contact information. I reached out to these potential participants via email, indicating that I was a JKCF alumna doing research on low-income first-generation student experiences and outcomes for my dissertation. In this recruitment email, potential respondents were given the option of selecting to participate in any combination of the following: a focus group, interview, fieldwork, or to not participate.

My second wave of recruitment efforts focused on students who had applied, but were not selected, for a Jack Kent Cooke Scholarship. Again, the organization gave me a spreadsheet with applicant names, contact information, demographic information and, for this group, their application scores. I reached out to these potential participants via email, indicating that I was a JKCF alumna doing research on low-income first-generation student experiences and outcomes for my dissertation. They were prompted to fill out a screener survey if they were interested in participating. This screener asked them if and where they were attending college in the fall and some additional demographic information. From this pool I selected applicants who were planning to attend college in one of my four regions and who had been ranked as semifi-nalists or within the top 25% of the applicant pool. This cutoff point was used as a means of selecting students who had academic profiles that closely matched students who had been selected. A follow-up recruitment email was sent out that gave students the option of selecting to participate in any combination of the following: an interview, fieldwork, or to not participate.

My third wave of recruitment efforts focused on students who had not applied for a College Scholarship from the JKCF. I recruited these students in two ways. First, through snowball sampling from my respondents.[163] At the end of interviews or during fieldwork, I asked respondents to refer me to other low-income first-generation students they knew who might be interested in participating. When put in touch with these students, I sent them emails that gave them the option of selecting to participate in any combination of the following: an interview, fieldwork, or to not participate. Second, I recruited students in person during fieldwork as I met them during activities and while shadowing my participants. After these initial meetings, I sent these students an email that gave them the option of selecting to participate in any combination of the following: an interview, fieldwork, or to not participate.

All of the students who participated in the study were low-income—with the majority of students having families with annual adjusted gross incomes of $30,000 or less. A total of 88% of students identified as first-generation—with neither parent completing a bachelor's degree. I included a broad range of students across class year—40% of students were first-years, 20% second-years, 20% third-years, and 20% fourth-years during their first interviews with me. I did not limit my investigation to students from a particular racial or ethnic background—35% identify as White, 14% as African American or Black, 20% as Latinx, 16% as Asian American, and 15% as more than one race. Finally, 48% of the students identify as female, 46% as male, and 6% as gender nonbinary and/or transgender at the time of my last interview with them. The pronouns used in this book reflect the pronouns respondents were using during our last interview or conversations.

I chose to include both low-income and first-generation low-income students in this study. Much of the research on low-income first-generation student populations neglects to fully parse out what separates

Table A.1. Description of student characteristics

	N (%)
Year in school at first interview	
First	60 (40)
Second	30 (20)
Third	30 (20)
Final	30 (20)
# of students in follow-up interviews (percent of first-years)	40 (66)
Jack Kent Cooke Scholarship status	
College Scholars	50 (33)
Applicants	50 (33)
Nonapplicants	50 (33)
Type of aid received	
Federal grants	148 (98.6)
School-based grants	150 (100)
Major external scholarship (>$10K annually)	107 (71.3)
Supplemental external scholarships	129 (86)
First-generation students	132 (88)
Race/ethnicity	
White	52 (35)
African American/Black	21 (14)
Latino/x	30 (20)
Asian American	24 (16)
Multiracial	23 (15)
Gender identity	
Male	69 (46)
Female	72 (48)
Nonbinary and/or transgender	9 (6)
Region of college in attendance	
East	87 (58)
Midwest	31 (20.6)
South	10 (6.6)
West	22 (14.6)

low-income first-generation students from low-income continuing-generation students. It has been widely established that having college-educated parents matters for student outcomes, but far less work has focused on how and why this might matter for student experiences. I made an effort throughout this manuscript to note how the impact of being first-generation in addition to being low-income produces differences among my respondents' experiences, frameworks, and trajectories.

FIELD SITES

The vast majority of qualitative research on higher education is bound to a single campus context, with many of the most well-known studies focusing on the same schools. Because of my interest in the college as a people-changing institution that explicitly works with its population to shape their identities and to build capital, I saw it as key to include as much institutional diversity as I could manage in order to elicit a comparison across institutional structures, resources, and programmatic interventions tied to different campuses. Because I knew that I would be initially drawing on the Jack Kent Cooke Scholar population for participants, I wanted to include states that had a large pool to recruit from. Massachusetts and Texas both fit these criteria (although when I settled on private schools only, Texas became less valuable in this regard). Being located in Illinois for graduate school throughout the duration of this project made recruiting students in Illinois a natural choice. Finally, I am originally from Oregon and still have ties to a number of communities there. Because of this, I traveled there frequently—which made recruiting for and conducting research there more accessible. While not entirely by design, but also not entirely up to chance, these locations ended up producing a nice set of geographical diversity, with schools from the East, West, South, and Midwest represented.

Although I built these states into my research design, I did not focus on specific schools within those states when recruiting participants. Instead, I attempted to recruit students attending any selective private college in the state. This resulted in a total of 18 schools, with 10 colleges in Massachusetts, 4 in Illinois, 2 in Texas, and 2 in Oregon. This cohort of colleges includes 9 liberal arts colleges and 9 research universities, with the largest undergraduate population being approximately 16,000 and the smallest being approximately 1,300. I assigned pseudonyms to the colleges and universities and grouped them by region when referenced directly—producing four composite schools: East College, Midwest College, South College, and West College. While this grouping does lose some of the granularity of particular place-based student experiences, I made this choice in an attempt to provide an adequate level of anonymity for respondents. The low-income first-generation population at any one of the schools included in this study is arguably small enough that simply providing the individual school with a pseudonym was not enough. In addition to being an ethically informed approach, I believe this choice fostered a more open dialogue with respondents.

I do provide information about the institutional structure of a college (i.e., liberal arts vs. research university) when knowing that information is integral to understanding a particular social process or series of events. That being said, I did find that while campus culture certainly matters for student experience, the diversity across these most competitive schools was less pronounced than originally expected. Regardless of the idiosyncratic quirks of a given institution, each of the schools represented here are well-resourced schools that have a long historical tradition of educating a predominantly White, wealthy, educated population of students and have only recently begun to recruit and admit low-income first-generation students at a significant rate. Because of this, the similarities between attending a large elite research university in the Midwest versus a small elite liberal arts college in the East were paramount for the majority of low-income first-generation students.

I selected private colleges and universities because they have the most resources available to support low-income first-generation students in terms of financial aid, academic support, and programmatic support. Yet they still see similar gaps in performance, outcomes, and experience between their low-income first-generation and non-low-income first-generation students that have been documented at less-selective and public institutions. This paradox, or puzzle, is largely what brought me to this project in the first place, and focusing on these highly selective private institutions seemed like the best way to begin understanding why. Low-income first-generation students at large public universities, community colleges, and less-funded regional schools face substantial, and different, barriers to success that need further attention outside of this study. Among other things, these students are far more likely to experience substantial economic precarity, homelessness, and food insecurity—all factors that have compounding effects on student outcomes and experiences. Data from focus groups and follow-up discussions with students who were not attending highly selective private colleges do provide evidence that the themes from this book could be a significant factor, albeit to a different degree, for low-income first-generation students across various institutional types. Because of this, I contend that while there are limitations to focusing solely on selective and highly selective private colleges, focusing on these more extreme contexts may bring to the surface effects and experiences that may be less pronounced or observable than in more conventional institutional settings.[164]

DATA COLLECTION

Student Focus Groups

I started the data collection for this project with a series of six focus groups in the summer of 2016. I completed a second round of six focus groups with a different set of students in the summer of 2017. In total, 69 students participated in focus groups, of which 22 went on to participate in interviews. Seven of the 12 focus groups included students who had just graduated from high school and were headed into their first year of college. Two focus groups included a mix of students who were transferring from community college to a four-year school and students entering college directly from high school. Finally, three focus groups were conducted with students who had already completed one year of college at a four-year institution. These focus groups with returning students were used to explore themes and questions that would later inform my interview guide. Due to access constraints, these focus groups were limited to recipients of a Jack Kent Cooke Scholarship and were conducted on location at Scholars Weekend in Virginia. Focus group participants filled out demographic surveys before participation, and each participant had the option as to whether they would participate in future research or not.

Each focus group was conducted in a private room and was audio recorded with participant consent. I transcribed each focus group.

Student In-Depth Interviews

Between 2016 and 2019, I completed in-depth interviews with 150 low-income and first-generation students attending college in Massachusetts, Illinois, Texas, and Oregon. Respondents were actively attending an undergraduate institution when interviewed and were all traditional-age (e.g., 18–22) students who began school at a four-year college in the fall quarter after they had graduated from high school. Of the total 150 students, 100 agreed to participate in a single interview. The remaining 50 students agreed to participate in an initial interview their first year of college as well as follow-up interviews each subsequent year of their undergraduate study. I continued follow-up interviews and surveys with these participants through 2021. Follow-up interviews were primarily conducted in person until I shifted to online interviews during 2020 and 2021 due to travel constraints and the onset of a global pandemic caused by COVID-19. In-person interviews were conducted either in public spaces like coffee shops, cafés, the quad, or dining halls, or in private library rooms or classrooms. I did not find any difference in the content and quality of interviews between those conducted in public or private. I believe that this is due largely to the fact that the public interviews were conducted in either relatively busy and loud environments like coffee shops or environments that provided semiprivate space like the quad, and that students were not concerned about being overheard. Each of the interviews was recorded, transcribed by a contracted transcription service, and each student was given a pseudonym for this project.

I began each interview by asking students to walk me through their average academic week. While the specifics varied, in general each interview covered students' experiences in high school, the college application and selection process, their experiences in college, and their experiences and relationships with their families and friends from their home communities. I also asked students to discuss their interactions with and relationship to any scholarship organizations they were affiliated with, as well as with college offices and services that targeted low-income first-generation students, or, when applicable, students of color, immigrant students, and LGBTQ+ students. When conducting follow-up interviews, I drew on students' responses from prior interviews and surveys to inform my questions. In addition to asking for general updates on the different aspects of their lives, I followed up directly on experiences and themes they had previously detailed. When possible, I also drew on answers to follow-up surveys to inform my questions during these interviews.

Administrator Interviews

In December 2017, I completed in-depth formal interviews with 10 members of the Jack Kent Cooke Foundation Higher Education Division staff. These interviews were conducted at the Jack Kent Cooke Foundation offices in Lansdowne, VA, and were completed in private rooms and tape-recorded with participant permission. The focus of these interviews was twofold—(1) to flesh out my understanding of the operations of the JKCF and (2) to get staff perspectives of the work done by the Foundation—both at the direct service with the Scholars level and at the broader programmatic and organizational ethos level. These interviews lasted between one and two hours and were transcribed using a contracted transcription service. Between 2016 and 2019, I completed semiformal interviews with 30 higher education staff and administrators on different campuses included in my study. My focus in these interviews was twofold—(1) to better my understanding of the programming and resources available on these campuses and (2) to get staff perspectives of the work being done to support low-income first-generation students on their campuses. A number of staff requested that their institutional affiliation not be revealed in this study. As a result, I do not associate staff with a given institution or region when quoted in this study. These interviews lasted between 30 and 90 minutes and were transcribed using a contracted transcription service. All staff and administrators were given pseudonyms for the purposes of this study.

Participant Observation

In order to produce a more robust understanding of the lived experience of low-income and first-generation students, I conducted over 650 hours of ethnographic participant observations between 2016 and

2019 on each of the 18 campuses in the study—with the majority of observations happening on 10 core campuses. Most of my time was spent shadowing students throughout their daily lives, accompanying them on and off campus as they went about their regular schedules. I ate meals with students in dining halls, sat with them as they studied in the library, spent time in the grass on the quad, played games and chatted in common rooms of residence halls, spent hours in coffee shops and restaurants with study groups and respondents' friends, watched them work in their campus jobs, and went to club meetings and events on campus. On some campuses I was able to work directly with low-income first-generation student groups and actively helped plan and run events with these participants. I was able to spend time with five students in their family homes during breaks in the school year. And while this only gave me a small glimpse into this aspect of these students' lives, it proved valuable for framing the ways that I thought about students and their connectivity to their families while in college. I did not spend time with students in their residence hall bedrooms or attend their academic classes and cannot speak to those facets of the student experience.

In addition to shadowing student participants, I asked students to take me on a tour of their campus. Over the course of my fieldwork, I took 114 participant-guided tours of campuses. I asked students to show me what they thought I should know about their campus and found that these tours operated as a great way to get students talking about place-specific experiences they had had in college. I also joined official tours on all but five of the campuses in the study (these five were not offering tours during the days/times I was on campus). I used these tours to get a feel for the ways that the colleges were officially presenting themselves to prospective students and their parents. I did not generally interact with prospective students and their parents during these tours and only exchanged regular small-talk conversations that were not research directed. Finally, I conducted participant observations at the Jack Kent Cooke Foundation's annual Scholars Weekend in 2017 and 2018. I stayed on site during this fieldwork and observed programming and social events, participated in panels as an alumna, and attended staff meetings.

Throughout the course of each of these dimensions of my fieldwork, I took field notes documenting my observations and interactions. The majority of field notes were taken on the Notes application on my iPhone. I leveraged the fact that many of my participants were regularly on their phones and kept my phone readily available for taking notes during conversations. When in settings where participants had their laptops out, I used my laptop to take field notes in much the same way that I did with my phone. At the end of each day in the field, I would flesh out my field notes and write a field memo going over important events that had happened during that day's activities and observations. These field notes and memos were compiled together and coded after I began analyzing my interviews using the codes and subcodes developed through the analysis of those interview transcripts.

Surveys and Administrative Data

Student respondents were asked to complete multiple surveys throughout their participation in this project. First, each student respondent completed a background demographic survey that covered basic demographic information about themselves, information about their parents and families, their family incomes, and information about their academic performance. The response rate for this survey was 100%. After each interview, participants were asked to fill out follow-up surveys that asked them to detail their involvement in campus communities, their work and volunteer involvement, and their course load for the year, and invited them to provide any further information they wished to share. The response rate for this survey was 100%. Interview participants were also asked to complete annual follow-up surveys administered in the fall or winter of the academic year. These surveys included primarily open-ended qualitative questions that asked students to discuss their prior summer, their current academic year, difficulties they were facing, news or important events they had experienced, their interactions with friends and family, and their interactions with their colleges and scholarship organizations. These annual follow-up surveys also asked students to report their academic performance and any changes in their involvement on campus, work history, or additional accolades they had been awarded. The response rate for these ongoing surveys has been 92%. These surveys help produce a robust longitudinal perspective of student experience throughout their college trajectory and have proved very useful for maintaining consistent contact with participants when I could not travel to their campuses for interviews.

Data Analysis

With permission from my respondents, I recorded and transcribed each interview. I began data analysis after I had transcribed eight interviews and continued to conduct data analysis as the study progressed. I coded interviews and ethnographic field notes with digital qualitative coding software, using a multilevel coding approach. I first open-coded the data without using a set of a priori codes, to allow for major themes to emerge from the interview data.[165] Once grouped thematically, I employed second- and third-order coding, identifying codes and developing subcodes iteratively. As new codes and subcodes were added, I returned to already-coded transcripts and recoded them. Throughout this process, I wrote analytic memos and brought data fragments from across interviews and focus groups, field notes, and follow-up surveys to synthesize emergent themes.[166] This multilevel coding approach allows for a robust and thorough analysis of the data and pairs well with an ethnographic methodology that draws on both inductive and deductive approaches.[167]

Positionality

My positionality as a first-generation student from a low-income background who attended a highly selective college is a central facet to this project. These aspects of my identity and background helped me recruit and build rapport with participants during interviews and throughout fieldwork. I openly shared my experiences as a low-income first-generation student with my respondents and participated in a number of group activities for students from low-income first-generation backgrounds. As an alumna of the Jack Kent Cooke Foundation, my status as a Cooke Scholar qualified me as a member of many of my respondents' perceived community. This status not only granted me access to field sites, but I believe it also added a level of depth and familiarity to my interviews with fellow Cooke Scholars. So much so that on a number of occasions I had to ask Cooke Scholars I was interviewing to pretend they did not know me when explaining their interactions and experiences with the Cooke Foundation in order to avoid the dreaded "you know what I mean" response in lieu of describing a detail or experience in interviews. However, my position as a researcher also located me as an outsider who was removed from the stakes associated with campus communities. This positional duality allowed me to occupy an in-between status[168] that I felt minimized bias and produced robust and open dialogue during interviews and fieldwork.

Notes

1. Although it may seem counterintuitive, the universities with the highest tuition price tags are often the most affordable option for low-income students that are admitted. For example, Stanford, the University of Chicago, and Harvard offer full tuition waivers to students from families earning less than $150,000, $125,000, and $85,000, respectively. Many of these schools also provide cost-free room and board for students whose families are below a specified income threshold (e.g., below $60,000 per year at the University of Chicago). In addition, some of these schools provide financial support for living expenses, winter coats, activity fees, books, travel, and more for low-income students whose families are below specified income thresholds (e.g., below $75,000 per year at Harvard). These initiatives target improving affordability in an effort to increase diversity and create a world in which students with family incomes within these ranges would pay less to attend their first year of college at Harvard (with an annual cost of attendance of $79,450 for tuition, fees, room, and board) than the nearby public state university UMass Boston (with an annual in-state cost of attendance of $33,860 for tuition, fees, room, and board). Using the online cost calculators on each of these schools' websites quickly shows that comparing cost of attendance does not show the full story of the cost of college for high-achieving low-income students. If admitted, a hypothetical student with a 4.0 and an ACT of 30 from a family of four whose parents made a total of $75,000 a year would pay $0 to attend Harvard in the 2023-2024 academic year. This same hypothetical student would pay $22,680 (after receiving a merit award) to attend UMass Boston for one year. If this student's family had an annual income of only $30,000 (much like the majority of students in my study), they would pay $0 to attend Harvard. In contrast, they would receive a bill for $6,985 to attend UMass Boston for their first year of college after merit awards and Pell grants were applied.

2. National Center for Education Statistics 2017; National Student Clearinghouse 2014.
3. See Bowen et al. 2005; Stevens et al. 2007.
4. Stevens et al. 2008.
5. See Lee 2016; Jack 2019; Silver 2020.
6. Aries and Seider 2005; Nunn 2021.
7. Ostrove 2003; Armstrong and Hamilton 2013; Benson and Lee 2020.
8. Aries 2008, Redford et al. 2017.
9. Lee and Kramer 2013; Aries 2008; Stuber 2011.
10. Hurst 2020; Mullen 2010; Stuber 2011.
11. Goldrick-Rab 2006.
12. Hurst 2012; Stephens et al. 2012; Morton 2019.
13. Granfield 1991; Stuber 2006.
14. Aries and Berman 2012; Armstrong and Hamilton 2013; Silver 2020.
15. Lehmann 2014; Lee and Kramer 2013.
16. Hurst 2012; Lehmann 2014.
17. Stevens et al. 2008; Stuber 2009; NASPA 2018.
18. See Bowen and Bok 2000; Massey et al. 2003; Redford et al. 2017; DOE 2016.
19. Goldrick-Rab 2016.
20. Museus and Neville 2012.
21. Ovink and Veazey 2011; Upcraft et al. 2005.
22. Rivera 2015; Stuber 2011.
23. Upcraft et al. 2005; Finley and McNair 2013; NCES 2017; NCES 2019.
24. NCES 2019; Bowen et al. 2005; Jack 2019; Lee 2016; Silver 2020.
25. See DiPrete 2007; Birdsall and Graham 2000; Pew 2012.
26. Grusky 2001.
27. Sorokin 2001; Goldthorpe 2000.
28. Featherman and Hauser 1978; Grusky 2001; van Leeuwen and Maas 2010.
29. Erikson and Goldthorpe 2001; Grusky and Hauser 1984.
30. See DeParle 2012; Pew 2012.
31. Stevens et al. 2008; Hout 2012.
32. See Stevens et al. 2008.
33. See Duncan 2015; Ma 2012.
34. Goldrick-Rab 2016; Chetty et al. 2017.
35. See Harris 2017.
36. Massey and Denton 1993; Harding et al. 2008.
37. See Jack 2019; Lee 2016; Lehmann 2014; Hurst 2012.
38. See Morton 2019 for a recent monograph that considers some of these elements from a philosophical perspective.
39. See the NCES 2019 report that compares first-generation student college attendance and persistence to their continuing-generation peers and demonstrates

that the social mobility associated with first-generation status is not as common as the American cultural imaginary asserts it to be.

40. There is no official federal definition of what makes a college or university a highly selective or selective school vs. a less-selective or not-selective school. Many organizations categorize colleges with acceptances rates below 20% as highly selective (with the most highly selective having admission rates closer to 5%) and those with acceptance rates below 50% as selective. For comparison, the majority of four-year colleges and universities in the United States admit more than two-thirds of their applicants. All of these schools included in this study were considered highly selective (14) or selective (4) by these metrics when I began this project.

41. "Nontraditional student" is a term that is most often used to describe college students that are older than the traditional 18–22-year-old college population, but can also be used to describe other characteristics about a student that diverge from the norm (e.g., married students, student parents, students without high school diplomas, etc.).

42. Dwyer and Buckle 2009.

CHAPTER ONE

43. Karabel 2006; Thelin 2004.
44. Thelin 2004; Stevens 2007; Stevens et al. 2008.
45. Stevens 2007.
46. Radford 2013; McDonough 1997.
47. Radford 2013; McDonough 1997.
48. Lucas is referring here to the Common Application. This online application system was established in 1975 and allows students to easily apply to over 800 schools using the same core, or common, application materials. The majority of schools that use the Common Application are private selective and highly selective colleges and universities.
49. Garrett is referring here to an International Baccalaureate (IB) program in his high school. IB programs are offered at select high schools in 150 countries, including the United States. IB programs offer advanced-instruction courses, and students can earn an IB diploma in addition to their general high school diploma. Many colleges and universities accept IB credits for transfer in a way that is similar to Advanced Placement credit.
50. McDonough 1997.
51. QuestBridge is a national scholarship founded in 1987. Applicants apply during their senior year of high school and select from a list of 40 partner schools— ranking their top 12 choices. At the same time, partner schools select or reject these applicants. Students who "match" with a school enter into a binding

agreement to attend that school on a full four-year scholarship. Students who do not match are considered finalists but do not receive a scholarship award.

52. Hamilton 2016; Mitchall and Jaeger 2018; Lee 2016; Roksa and Deutschlander 2018.
53. Radford 2013.
54. Zaloom 2019.
55. Goldrick-Rab 2006.
56. Roksa and Deutschlander 2018.
57. Kao and Tienda 1995; Langenkamp 2019.
58. Carter 2005; Lee and Kramer 2013.
59. Hochschild 2016.
60. Jack 2019; Aries 2008; Goodwin 2002.
61. Wilkins 2014.
62. Radford 2013.
63. Schmid and Jones 1991.
64. Carter 2005.

CHAPTER TWO

65. Benson and Lee 2020; Hurst 2012; Nunn 2021.
66. Nunn 2021; Stuber 2011; Aries and Seider 2005; Armstrong and Hamilton 2013.
67. Jack 2019; Benson and Lee 2020.
68. Aries 2008; Goldrick-Rab 2006; McCabe and Jackson 2016.
69. Nunn 2021.
70. Jack 2019.
71. See Nunn 2021; McCabe and Jackson 2016.
72. Tinto 1993.
73. Rivera 2015.
74. Tinto 1993.
75. Lehmann 2007.
76. Nunn 2021; Benson and Lee 2020.
77. Jack 2019.
78. DiMaggio and Powell 1983.
79. Khan 2011.
80. Stevens 2007; NCES 2019.
81. Massey et al. 2003.
82. Shedd 2015; Lewis and Diamond 2015.
83. Arum and Roksa 2011; Pascarella and Terenzini 2005.
84. Jack 2019.
85. Jack 2019.
86. Hurst 2020; Aries and Seider 2005; Nunn 2021.
87. Nichols 2020; Jack 2019; Lee 2016.

88. Arum and Roksa 2011; Childress 2019.
89. Data for this argument come from the author's ongoing pedagogical research about the impact of a beginning-of-term exercise where students are asked to write the title of a work of fiction on the board that they believe everyone in the room has read. The professor goes through the list with the class erasing any titles that one or more people have not read. In general, either no titles or a select few childhood titles (e.g., *Green Eggs and Ham*) remain at the end of the exercise. The professor then leads the class in a discussion of why there are no/few shared titles, how aspects of identity and background are present in the classroom, the meaning and symbolic weight of the notion of canon, and what it means to build and share a canon as a class. Post-activity and post-quarter surveys of first-generation, low-income, and racially marginalized students indicate that this activity has positive impacts on their self-confidence in coursework, comfort with participating actively in class discussion, and their sense of self as legitimately belonging at their college. This activity is modified from an activity that Dr. Gail Sherman ran in her classes at Reed College.
90. Jack 2019; Khan 2011.
91. Khan 2011.
92. Khan 2011.
93. Goffman 1963; Turner 2001.
94. Hamilton and Armstrong 2013.
95. Tinto 1993.
96. Jack 2019; Benson and Lee 2021.
97. Jack 2019.
98. Angel is referencing a coat brand that was popular on the college campuses I spent time on. These coats are known for being expensive, with the average price of a winter jacket from this brand being $1,000.

CHAPTER THREE

99. Museus and Neville 2012.
100. See Hurst 2012; Stephens et al. 2012; Aries and Berman 2012; Bowen and Bok 2000; Massey et al. 2003.
101. See Clydesdale 2007; Lee and Kramer 2013; Aries 2008; Stuber 2011; Mullen 2010.
102. Thelin 2004; Davis et al. 2011; Fuller 2014; College Board 2017.
103. Fuller 2014; Charles et al. 2009.
104. See Mullen 2010; Hurst 2012; Goldrick-Rab 2016; Seligman 2013.
105. NASPA 2018; Jack 2019; Lee 2016.
106. NCES 2017; NSCH 2014.
107. See Aries and Seider 2005; Stuber 2011; Lehmann 2014.
108. Ovink and Veazey 2011; Museus and Neville 2012.

109. Tinto 1993; Lehmann 2007.
110. Upcraft et al. 2005; Finley and McNair 2013; NCES 2017.
111. See Bowen and Bok 2000; Massey et al. 2003.
112. See Arendale and Lee 2018; Schwartz et al. 2017.
113. See Smit 2012.
114. Vitner 1963; Sandfort 2003.
115. Tinto 1993; Aries and Seider 2005; Lehmann 2007.
116. See, for example, Goffman 1963; Garfinkel 1967.
117. Carla is directly referencing the notion of "ease" that Khan (2011) developed in his study about an elite boarding school, a book (*Privilege*) that she brought up multiple times during our conversations.
118. See Jack 2019 and Nichols 2020 for recent examples.
119. In the film *Pretty Woman* (1990), Julia Roberts plays a character (Vivian) who finds herself required to attend a dinner in a fine-dining restaurant without the expected cultural capital. A series of scenes detail her discomfort with a restaurant of this caliber and her lack of experience and knowledge around rules and expectations. It is clear to the viewer that Vivian is out of place in this social situation.
120. Torres and Charles 2004; Aries 2008.
121. Stuber 2011.
122. See Torres and Charles 2004; Byrd 2017.
123. Bourdieu 1979, 2004.
124. Bourdieu 1979, 2004.

CHAPTER FOUR

125. Andie is referencing a science fiction television show titled *Stranger Things* that was popular while I was in the field.
126. Thelin 2004; Chambliss and Takacs 2014.
127. Bourdieu 2004.
128. Carter 2005.
129. Nichols 2020.
130. Goffman 1974.
131. Chambliss and Takacs 2014; Thelin 2004.
132. See Morgan et al. 2010; Branje 2018.
133. See Hochschild 2016 and Morris 2008 for further sociological research on working-class families and communities and the ways they frame their identities in opposition to upper-class America.
134. Harris 2017.
135. See Branje 2018.
136. Abbott 1981.
137. See Morton 2019.

138. Hurst 2012.
139. Du Bois 1903.

CHAPTER FIVE

140. Ovink and Veazey 2011; Upcraft et al. 2005.
141. Lipson et al. 2018.
142. Clance and Imes 1978.
143. See NASPA 2018.
144. Mills 1959.
145. Carter 2005.
146. Haugen 1954.
147. For recent applications in higher education, see Silver 2020; Morton 2019; Benson and Lee 2020.
148. Collier 2015.
149. See Benson and Lee 2020.
150. This finding supports Hamilton's (2016) research on college student experiences and the role that family and siblings can play in aiding in student experiences while also challenging Roksa et al.'s (2020) research that points to a lack of accessing college-attending older siblings' experiences as resources. This tension points to the need for further research.
151. Lee 2002.
152. Tinto 1993; Lehmann 2014; Benson and Lee 2020.
153. Carter 2005; Aries 2008; Hurst 2012.
154. Holland 2016.
155. Lipson et al. 2018.
156. The LEDA (Leadership Enterprise for a Diverse America) Scholarship supports its recipients beginning in the third year of high school. This scholarship program focuses on support for low-income students around recruitment and admissions, leadership summer institutes, college guidance, and college success.
157. Clydesdale 2007.
158. Chris is referring to the social media platform Snapchat, where users can post images and videos for their contacts to view publicly on their "story" or send media directly to individual contacts to view privately. At the time of my research, Snapchat was popular among college students as a common way to highlight their lives and activities.

CONCLUSION

159. See Vitner 1963.
160. Osborne 2019.
161. Holland 2016; Lipson et al. 2018.

METHODOLOGICAL APPENDIX

162. JKCF 2015, 2016a.
163. Weiss 1994.
164. See Garfinkel 1967; Schilt 2010.
165. Saldaña 2012.
166. Emerson et al. 2011.
167. Saldaña 2012; Van Maanen 2011.
168. Dwyer and Buckle 2009.

References

Abbott, Andrew. 1981. "Status and Status Strain in the Professions." *American Journal of Sociology* 88(4): 819–835.

Arendale, David R., and Nue Lor Lee. 2018. "Academic Bridge Programs." In *Handbook of College Reading and Study Strategy Research*, edited by R. F. Flippo and T. W. Bean, 227–237. New York: Routledge.

Aries, Elizabeth. 2008. *Race and Class Matters at an Elite College*. Philadelphia: Temple University Press.

Aries, Elizabeth, and Richard Berman. 2012. *Speaking of Race and Class: The Student Experience at an Elite College*. Philadelphia: Temple University Press.

Aries, Elizabeth, and Maynard Seider. 2005. "The Interactive Relationship Between Class Identity and the College Experience: The Case of Lower Income Students." *Qualitative Sociology* 28(4): 419–443.

Armstrong, Elizabeth, and Laura T. Hamilton. 2013. *Paying for the Party: How College Maintains Inequality*. Boston: Harvard University Press.

Arum, Richard, and Joseph Roksa. 2011. *Academically Adrift: Limited Learning on College Campuses*. Chicago: University of Chicago Press.

Benson, Janel E., and Elizabeth M. Lee. 2020. *Geographies of Campus Inequality: Mapping the Diverse Experiences of First-Generation Students*. New York: Oxford University Press.

Birdsall, Nancy, and Carol Graham. 2000. *New Markets, New Opportunities? Economic and Social Mobility in a Changing World*. Washington, DC: Brookings Institution Press.

Bourdieu, Pierre. 1979. *Distinction: A Social Critique of the Judgement of Taste*. London: Routledge & Kegan Paul.

———. 2004. "The Peasant and His Body." *Ethnography* 5(4): 579–599.

Bowen, William G., and Derek Bok. 2000. *The Shape of the River: Long-Term Consequences of Considering Race in College and University Admissions*. Princeton, NJ: Princeton University Press.

Bowen, William G., Martin Kurzweil, and Eugene M. Tobin. 2005. *Equity and Excellence in American Higher Education*. Charlottesville: University of Virginia Press.

Branje, Susan. 2018. "Development of Parent-Adolescent Relationships: Conflict Interactions as Mechanism of Change." *Child Development Perspectives* 12(3): 171–176.

Byrd, Carson. 2017. *Poison in the Ivy: Race Relations and the Reproduction of Inequality on Elite College Campuses*. New Brunswick, NJ: Rutgers University Press.

Carter, Prudence. 2005. *Keepin' It Real: School Success beyond Black and White*. New York: Oxford University Press.

Chambliss, Daniel F., and Christopher Takacs. 2014. *How College Works*. Boston: Harvard University Press.

Charles, Camille Z., Mary J. Fischer, Margarita A. Mooney, and Douglas S. Massey. 2009. *Taming the River: Negotiating the Academic, Financial, and Social Currents in Selective Colleges and Universities*. Princeton, NJ: Princeton University Press.

Chetty, Raj, et al. 2017. "Mobility Report Cards: The Role of Colleges in Intergenerational Mobility." National Bureau of Economic Research. NBER Working Paper No. 23618.

Childress, Herb. 2019. *The Adjunct Underclass: How America's Colleges Betrayed Their Faculty, Their Students, and Their Mission*. Chicago: University of Chicago Press.

Clance, Pauline, and Suzanne Imes. 1978. "The Imposter Phenomenon in High Achieving Women: Dynamics and Therapeutic Intervention." *Psychotherapy: Theory, Research & Practice* 15(3): 241–247.

Clydesdale, Tim. 2007. *The First Year Out: Understanding American Teens after High School*. Chicago: University of Chicago Press.

College Board. 2017. "Institutional Grant Aid by Tuition Level and Family Income at Private Nonprofit Four-Year Institutions, 2011–12—Trends in Higher Education."

Collier, Peter. 2015. *Developing Effective Student Peer Mentoring Programs: A Practitioner's Guide to Program Design, Delivery, Evaluation, and Training*. Sterling, VA: Stylus Publishing.

Davis, Danielle, et al. 2011. "The Impact of Federal Financial Aid Policy Upon Higher Education Access." *Journal of Educational Administration and History* 45(1): 49–57.

DeParle, Jason. 2012. "For Poor, Leap to College Often Ends in a Hard Fall." *New York Times*, Dec. 23. https://www.nytimes.com/2012/12/23/education/poor -students-struggle-as-class-plays-a-greater-role-in-success.html.

Department of Education. 2016. "Advancing Diversity and Inclusion in Higher Education." Key Data Highlights Focusing on Race and Ethnicity and Promising Practices.

DiMaggio, Paul, and Walter Powell. 1983. "The Iron Cage Revisited: Institutional Isomorphism and Collective Rationality in Organizational Fields." *American Sociological Review* 48(2): 147–160.

DiPrete, Thomas A. 2007. "Is This a Great Country? Upward Mobility and the Chance for Riches in Contemporary America." *Research in Social Stratification and Mobility* 2 5:89–95.

Du Bois, W. E. B. 1903. *The Souls of Black Folk*. Chicago: A. C. McClurg & Co.

Duncan, Arne. 2015. "Toward a New Focus on Outcomes in Higher Education." Remarks by Secretary Arne Duncan at the University of Maryland-Baltimore County (UMBC), July 27.

Dwyer, Sonya, and Jennifer Buckle. 2009. "The Space Between: On Being an Insider-Outsider in Qualitative Research." *International Journal of Qualitative Methods* 8(1): 54–63.

Emerson, Robert M., Rachel I. Fretz, and Linda L. Shaw. 2011. *Writing Ethnographic Fieldnotes*. Chicago: University of Chicago Press.

Erikson, Robert, and John H. Goldthorpe. 2001. "Trends in Class Mobility: The Post-War European Experience." In *Social Stratification: Class, Race, and Gender in Sociological Perspective*, 2nd ed., edited by David B. Grusky, 344–372. Boulder: Westview Press.

Featherman, David L., and Robert M. Hauser. 1978. *Opportunity and Change*. New York: Academic Press.

Finley, Ashley, and Tia McNair. 2013. *Assessing Underserved Students' Engagement in High-Impact Practices*. Washington, DC: Association of American Colleges and Universities.

Fuller, Matthew B. 2014. "A History of Financial Aid to Students." *Journal of Student Financial Aid* 44(1): 4.

Garfinkel, Harold. 1967. "Passing and the Managed Achievement of Sex Status in an Intersexed Person, Part 1." In *Studies in Ethnomethodology*, 116–185. Malden, MA: Prentice-Hall.

Goffman, Erving. 1963. *Stigma: Notes on the Management of Spoiled Identity*. Englewood Cliffs, NJ: Prentice-Hall.

———. 1974. *Frame Analysis: An Essay on the Organization of Experience*. New York: Harper and Row.

Goldrick-Rab, Sarah. 2006. "Following Their Every Move: An Investigation of Social Class Differences in College Pathways." *Sociology of Education* 79:61–79.

———. 2016. *Paying the Price: College Costs, Financial Aid, and the Betrayal of the American Dream*. Chicago: University of Chicago Press.

Goldthorpe, John. 2000. "Outline of a Theory of Social Mobility." In *On Sociology*, 230–58. Oxford: Oxford University Press.

Goodwin, Latty Lee. 2002. *Resilient Spirits: Disadvantaged Students Making It at an Elite University*. New York: RoutledgeFalmer.

Granfield, Robert. 1991. "Making It by Faking It: Working-Class Students in an Elite Academic Environment." *Journal of Contemporary Ethnography* 20:331–351.

Grusky, David B. 2001. "The Past, Present, and Future of Social Inequality." In *Social Stratification: Class, Race, and Gender in Sociological Perspective*, 2nd ed., edited by David B. Grusky, 3–51. Boulder: Westview Press.

Grusky, David B., and Robert Hauser. 1984. "Comparative Social Mobility Revisited: Models of Convergence and Divergence in 16 Countries." *American Sociological Review* 4 9:19–38.

Hamilton, Laura. 2016. *Parenting to a Degree: How Family Matters for College and Beyond*. Chicago: University of Chicago Press.

Harding, David, Christopher Jencks, Leonard M. Lopoo, and Susan E. Mayer. 2008. "Family Background and Income in Adulthood, 1961–1999." In *Social Stratification: Class, Race and Gender in Sociological Perspective*, 3rd ed., edited by David B. Grusky, 505–515. Boulder: Westview Press.

Harris, Elizabeth A. 2017. " 'I Won't Give Up': How First-Generation Students See College." *New York Times*, May 30. https://www.nytimes.com/interactive/2017/05/30/us/07firstgen-listy.html.

Haugen, Einar. 1954. *The Norwegian Language in America: A Study in Bilingual Behavior*. Philadelphia: University of Pennsylvania Press.

Hochschild, Arlie. 2016. *Strangers in Their Own Land: Anger and Mourning on the American Right*. New York: New Press.

Holland, Donna. 2016. "College Student Stress and Mental Health: Examination of Stigmatic Views on Mental Health Counseling." *Michigan Sociological Review* 30:16–43.

Hout, Michael. 2012. "Social and Economic Returns to College Education in the United States." *Annual Review of Sociology* 38:379–400.

Hurst, Allison L. 2012. *College and the Working Class: What It Takes to Make It*. Rotterdam: Sense Publishers.

———. 2020. *Amplified Advantage: Going to a "Good" College in an Era of Inequality*. Lanham, MD: Rowman & Littlefield/Lexington Books.

Jack, Anthony. 2019. *The Privileged Poor: How Elite Colleges Are Failing Disadvantaged Students*. Cambridge, MA: Harvard University Press.

Jack Kent Cooke Foundation. 2015. 2015 College Scholar Profile. Lansdowne, VA.

———. 2016a. "Scholarship Programs, Jack Kent Cooke Foundation." http://www.jkcf.org/scholarship-programs/.

———. 2016b. College Scholar Applicants and Recipients. Unpublished internal document.

———. 2016c. Undergraduate Transfer Scholar Applicants and Recipients. Unpublished internal document.

Kao, Grace, and Marta Tienda. 1995. "Optimism and Achievement: The Educational Performance of Immigrant Youth." *Social Science Quarterly* 76:1–19.

Karabel, James. 2006. *The Chosen: The Hidden History of Admission and Exclusion at Harvard, Yale, and Princeton*. New York: Houghton Mifflin Harcourt.

Khan, Shamus. 2011. *Privilege: The Making of an Adolescent Elite and St. Paul's School*. Princeton, NJ: Princeton University Press.

Langenkamp, Amy G. 2019. "Latino/a Immigrant Parents' Educational Aspirations for Their Children." *Race Ethnicity and Education* 22(2): 231–249.

Lee, Elizabeth M. 2016. *Class and Campus Life: Managing and Experiencing Inequality at an Elite College*. Ithaca, NY: Cornell University Press.

Lee, Elizabeth M., and Rory Kramer. 2013. "Out with the Old, in with the New? Habitus and Social Mobility at Selective Colleges." *Sociology of Education* 86(1): 18–35.

Lee, Jenny J. 2002. "Religion and College Attendance: Change among Students." *Review of Higher Education* 24(4): 369–384.

Lehmann, Wolfgang. 2007. "'I Just Didn't Feel Like I Fit In': The Role of Habitus in University Dropout Decisions." *Canadian Journal of Higher Education* 37(2): 89–110.

———. 2014. "Habitus Transformation and Hidden Injuries Successful Working-Class University Students." *Sociology of Education* 87(1): 1–15.

Lewis, Amanda E., and John B. Diamond. 2015. *Despite the Best Intentions: How Racial Inequality Thrives in Good Schools*. New York: Oxford University Press.

Lipson, Sarah, et al. 2018. "Mental Health Disparities Among College Students of Color." *Journal of Adolescent Health* 63(3): 348–356.

Ma, Jason. 2012. "Why to Start Preparing for College in Sixth Grade." Forbes Education Online, Apr. 1. https://www.forbes.com/sites/jasonma/2012/04/01/why-to-start-preparing-for-college-in-sixth-grade/?sh=45e1a1b54e29.

Massey, Douglas, and Nancy Denton. 1993. *American Apartheid: Segregation and the Making of the Underclass*. Cambridge, MA: Harvard University Press.

Massey, Douglas, et al. 2003. *The Source of the River: The Social Origins of Freshmen at America's Selective Colleges and Universities*. Princeton, NJ: Princeton University Press.

McCabe, Janice, and Brandon A. Jackson. 2016. "Pathways to Financing College: Race and Class in Students' Narratives of Paying for School." *Social Currents* 3(4): 367–385.

McDonough, Patricia. 1997. *Choosing Colleges: How Social Class and Schools Structure Opportunity*. Albany: State University of New York Press.

Mills, C. Wright. 1959. *The Sociological Imagination*. New York: Oxford University Press.

Mitchall, Allison, and Audrey Jaeger. 2018. "Parental Influences on Low-Income, First-Generation Students' Motivation on the Path to College." *Journal of Higher Education* 89(4): 582–609.

Morgan, Elizabeth, et al. 2010. "A Longitudinal Study of Conversations with Parents about Sex and Dating during College." *Developmental Psychology* 46(1): 139–150.

Morris, Edward. 2008. "'Rednecks,' 'Rutters,' and 'Rithmetic: Social Class, Masculinity, and Schooling in a Rural Context." *Gender and Society* 22(6): 728–751.

Morton, Jennifer. 2019. *Moving Up Without Losing Your Way: The Ethical Costs of Social Mobility*. Princeton, NJ: Princeton University Press.

Mullen, Ann L. 2010. *Degrees of Inequality: Culture, Class, and Gender in American Higher Education*. Baltimore: Johns Hopkins Press.

Museus, Samuel D., and Kathleen M. Neville. 2012. "Delineating the Ways That Key Institutional Agents Provide Racial Minority Students with Access to Social Capital in College." *Journal of College Student Development* 53(3): 436–452.

National Association of Student Personnel Administrators. 2018. "First Generation Student Success: A Landscape Analysis of Programs and Services at Four Year Institutions." Center for First Generation Success.

National Center for Education Statistics. 2017. "The Condition of Education 2017." US Department of Education.

———. 2019. "Persistence, Retention, and Attainment of 2011-12 First-Time Postsecondary Students as of Spring 2017." US Department of Education.

National Student Clearinghouse. 2014. Snapshot Report on Persistence and Retention. Herndon, VA: National Student Clearinghouse Research Center.

Nichols, Laura. 2020. *The Journey before Us: First-Generation Pathways from Middle School to College.* New Brunswick, NJ: Rutgers University Press.

Nunn, Lisa M. 2021. *College Belonging: How First-Year and First-Generation Students Navigate Campus Life.* New Brunswick, NJ: Rutgers University Press.

Osborne, Melissa. 2019. "Who Gets 'Housing First'? Determining Eligibility in an Era of Housing First Homelessness." *Journal of Contemporary Ethnography* 48(3): 402-428.

Ostrove, Joan. 2003. "Belonging and Wanting: Meanings of Social Class Background for Women's Constructions of Their College Experiences." *Journal of Social Issues* 59:771-784.

Ovink, Sarah M., and Brian D. Veazey. 2011. "More Than 'Getting Us Through': A Case Study in Cultural Capital Enrichment of Underrepresented Minority Undergraduates." *Research in Higher Education* 52(4): 370-394.

Pascarella, Ernest T., and Patrick Terenzini. 2005. *How College Affects Students: A Third Decade of Research.* San Francisco: Jossey-Bass.

Pew Charitable Trusts. 2012. "Pursuing the American Dream: Economic Mobility Across Generations." Economic Mobility Project.

Radford, Alexandra Walton. 2013. *Top Student, Top School: How Social Class Shapes Where Valedictorians Go to College.* Chicago: University of Chicago Press.

Redford, Jeremy, et al. 2017. "First-Generation and Continuing-Generation College Students: A Comparison of High School and Postsecondary Experiences." Stats in Brief: US Department of Education.

Rivera, Lauren. 2015. *Pedigree: How Elite Students Get Elite Jobs.* Princeton, NJ: Princeton University Press.

Roksa, Josipa, and Denise Deutschlander. 2018. "Applying to College: The Role of Family Resources in Academic Undermatch." *Teachers College Record* 120(6): 1-30.

Roksa, Josipa, et al. 2020. "Navigating First Year of College: Siblings, Parents, and First-Generation Students' Experiences." *Sociological Forum* 35(3): 565-586.

Saldaña, Johnny. 2012. *The Coding Manual for Qualitative Researchers.* Thousand Oaks, CA: Sage.

Sandfort, Jodi. 2003. "Exploring the Structuration of Technology Within Human Service Organizations." *Administration and Society* 34(6): 605-631.

Schilt, Kristen. 2010. *Just One of the Guys? Transgender Men and the Persistence of Inequality.* Chicago: University of Chicago Press.

Schmid, Thomas J., and Richard J. Jones. 1991. "Suspended Identity: Identity Transformation in a Maximum Security Prison." *Symbolic Interaction* 14(4): 415-431.

Schwartz, Sarah E. O., et al. 2017. "'I'm Having a Little Struggle with This, Can You Help Me Out?' Examining Impacts and Processes of a Social Capital Intervention for First-Generation College Students." *American Journal of Community Psychology* 61(1–2): 166–178.

Seligman, Katherine. 2013. "Hidden Hunger: Some Students Are Scrimping, Skipping Meals to Afford a Cal Degree." *California Magazine* (Cal Alumni Association), Nov. 13. https://alumni.berkeley.edu/california-magazine/online/hidden-hunger -some-students-are-scrimping-skipping-meals/

Shedd, Carla. 2015. *Unequal City: Race, Schools, and Perceptions of Injustice*. New York: Russell Sage Foundation.

Silver, Blake. 2020. *The Cost of Inclusion: How Student Conformity Leads to Inequality on College Campuses*. Chicago: University of Chicago Press.

Smit, Reneé. 2012. "Towards a Clearer Understanding of Student Disadvantage in Higher Education: Problematising Deficit Thinking." *Higher Education Research & Development* 31(3): 369–380.

Sorokin, Pitirim A. 2001. "Social and Cultural Mobility." In *Social Stratification: Class, Race, and Gender in Sociological Perspective*, 2nd ed., edited by David B. Grusky, 303–308. Boulder: Westview Press.

Stephens, Nicole M., et al. 2012. "Unseen Disadvantage: How American Universities' Focus on Independence Undermines the Academic Performance of First-Generation College Students." *Journal of Personality and Social Psychology* 102(6): 1178–1197.

Stevens, Mitchell. 2007. *Creating a Class: College Admissions and the Education of Elites*. Cambridge, MA: Harvard University Press.

Stevens, Mitchell, Elizabeth A. Armstrong, and Richard Arum. 2008. "Sieve, Incubator, Temple, Hub: Empirical and Theoretical Advances in the Sociology of Higher Education." *Annual Review of Sociology* 34:127–151.

Stuber, Jenny. 2006. "Talk of Class and Discursive Repertoires of White Working and Upper-Middle-Class College Students." *Journal of Contemporary Ethnography* 35:285–318.

———. 2009. "Class, Culture, and Participation in the Collegiate Extra-Curriculum." *Sociological Forum* 24(4): 877–900.

———. 2011. *Inside the College Gates: How Class and Culture Matter in Higher Education*. Lanham, MD: Rowman & Littlefield.

Thelin, John R. 2004. *A History of American Higher Education*. Baltimore: Johns Hopkins University Press.

Tinto, Vincent. 1993. *Leaving College: Rethinking the Causes and Cures of Student Attrition*. Chicago: University of Chicago Press.

Torres, Kimberly, and Camille Z. Charles. 2004. "Metastereotypes and the Black-White Divide: A Qualitative View of Race on an Elite College Campus." *Du Bois Review* 1:115–149.

Turner, Ralph H. 2001. "Role Theory." In *Handbook of Sociological Theory*, edited by J. H. Turner. Handbooks of Sociology and Social Research. Boston: Springer.

Upcraft, M. Le, et al., eds. 2005. *Challenging and Supporting the First-Year Student: A Handbook for Improving the First Year of College*. San Francisco: Jossey-Bass.

Van Leeuwen, Marco H. D., and Ineke Maas. 2010. "Historical Studies of Social Mobility and Stratification." *Annual Review of Sociology* 36:429–451.

Van Maanen, John. 2011. *Tales of the Field: On Writing Ethnography*. Chicago: University of Chicago Press.

Vitner, Robert. 1963. "Analysis of Treatment Organizations." *Social Work* 8(3): 3–15.

Weiss, Robert. 1994. *Learning from Strangers*. New York: Free Press.

Wilkins, Amy. 2014. "Race, Age, and Identity Transformations in the Transition from High School to College for Black and First-Generation White Men." *Sociology of Education* 87(3): 171–187.

Zaloom, Caitlin. 2019. *Indebted: How Families Make College Work at Any Cost*. Princeton, NJ: Princeton University Press.

Index

www.ingramcontent.com/pod-product-compliance
Lightning Source LLC
Chambersburg PA
CBHW060036030426
42334CB00019B/2350